WHY THE WHISTLE WENT

En l'honneur de ma charmante épouse Ginette
and
In memory of my parents: James Acheson (1907-1965)
and Wilma Armstrong Acheson, née Chambers, (1915-2008);
and of my brother James (Jim) Chambers Acheson (1938-2007)

Alan R. Acheson

Why the Whistle Went

A MEMOIR

the columba press

First published in 2009 by
the columba press
55A Spruce Avenue, Stillorgan Industrial Park,
Blackrock, Co Dublin

Cover by Bill Bolger
Origination by The Columba Press
Printed by Athenaeum Press, Gateshead

ISBN 978-1-85607-636-4

Table of Contents

Preface

Why write my memoirs: I, a very ordinary bloke, albeit with some extraordinary experiences? Is it worth going public with these? A friend saw that it would be good therapy; but that now agreeable result cannot be construed as motive. C. V. Wedgwood's wise words (in *The King's Peace*) tended to deter: that we 'make the past merely the subject of our own analytical ingenuity or our own illusions'. By contrast, Frank McCourt tended to encourage by commenting that a memoir, being an impression of one's life, gives a certain amount of leeway: 'If an autobiography is like a photograph, then a memoir is more like a painting' (quoted by Brendan O'Neill in *spiked-culture*, 21 June 2001). I decided to paint.

I had a wide canvas to work with. As the eldest of six brothers, a healthy, if straitened, upbringing in Ulster's post-War austerity, one remove from prevalent Protestant poverty; Queen's University, a commission in the Regular Army, teaching in Campbell College and other Ulster grammar schools; headships in two famous Schools, Portora Royal and King's, Parramatta, NSW; flirtations with politics. In personal life, marriage, parenting, long years as a caregiver; grandchildren, divorce and re-marriage. I have lived in four continents, worked in Germany and Guyana, experienced inordinate problems in immigrating to both Australia and Canada. My canvas has extended to cover two very different spheres: rugby union football and the Church of Ireland. I tell of refereeing experiences over five decades, unaware of such a tale by any other 'ordinary' referee. My Church involvement is now in its eighth decade, half a century since I completed four years as an ordinand. I have preached, as an unlicensed layman, in Anglican cathedrals, including Canterbury Cathedral, served on the Anglican Consultative Council and on Church Synods in Ireland (since 1970) and Australia. The

Columba Press, publisher of my *History of the Church of Ireland, 1691-2001*, has published also episcopal and clerical memoirs; I have the honour to be the author of Columba's first lay memoir.

Uniquely, among such memoirs, I provide an index. In the text, members of my immediate family in each generation appear by first name only, as do the late Gertrude Matthews (my former mother-in-law) and my friend Fanta. Abbreviations in the text are given in full when first used. I owe it to my sister-in-law, Janice, that that use is not overdone, that is, abbreviations alternate with names in full to avoid monotony. For The King's School (TKS), I rely on written records: formal correspondence, and Headmaster's Reports. Where I quote from my addresses to the School, the text is that of the words actually spoken, typed afterwards from the pocket recorder that I carried.

I acknowledge gratefully many who helped in a variety of ways along the road. Among friends who read particular sections and commented appositely are Major Richard Kilroy, Dr Kaye Marshall, Caroline Smith and Peter Watkinson; also my daughter Karen and my brother Paul. Other friends supplied facts that had eluded me: the Revd Gerry Murphy and Mike Sweet from the Army; Martin Todd and David Robertson at Portora; Albert Austin and Jill McCullagh of Ulster Branch, Irish Rugby Football Union (IRFU). Brian Johnstone forwarded my Headmaster's Reports after I had left TKS. My brother Jim had jogged my memory about childhood experiences, and my nephew, Dr Peter Acheson, made over to me my letters to Jim from overseas (and from which I quote).

While the perspective on my two headships is my own, two friends of singular wisdom and integrity influenced my fuller reflection on these: the Rt Revd Dr Michael Jackson and The Hon Justice Lloyd Waddy RFD, the latter despite his severe physical weakness in 2008. Two committed friends read virtually all of my text and affirmed or challenged as they found appropriate: Bishop Peter Barrett and David Hewitt CBE. Duane Schermerhorn and Greg Stephens, my generous neighbours in Cobourg, provided technical support and hardware. Linda Hamilton, with much grace, masterminds the index. My wife Ginette, who has for too long had to cope with my lapses into brown study, has been my steady encourager and shrewd sounding board.

I thank especially two other people. First, my editor, Seán O Boyle, for his probing criticisms, his patience as my several drafts evolved into a text fit to publish, and his forbearance under my provocative questioning of his always sound judgement. Dr Marion (Dodie) Pirie, for her part, has given me the benefit of her professional editorial experience – and much more besides. Exasperated at my pedestrian and unimaginative recounting of emotionally charged experiences, she pointed up, with elegance and grace, the inspiration that she clearly saw at work upon me. By adopting verbatim, in the paragraph that follows, Dodie's expression of that insight, I pay her the highest tribute.

Someone once said, 'writing is easy: you just sit down and open a vein'. As I sit here contemplating, I am struck, not by the ease of writing – that flowing vein – but by the beauty and vibrancy of my surroundings. I am sitting in a tiny breakfast room, suffused in light streaming in from two large windows. Large exotic plants meandering up the walls only enhance the vivid blues and yellows that anoint our tablecloth – the colours of Provence; the colours of my wife's French Canadian heritage. This room is like a tiny rainforest where the sun always shines. I have come to love its warmth and welcoming spirit, and I feel blessed to be here. I look up and catch a glimpse of the woman I love. She is petite with beautiful gamine-like features; eyes that challenge and a smile that wraps around everyone she meets. As I watch her at work in our kitchen, I am struck by the incongruity of our union. I am a church historian. My faith is very much part of my personal life. Ginette is a former opera singer (an opera singer no less, I say to myself!) and until this year a faculty member of a University music department. Her faith is summed up in three words: 'I hate religion.' I ask myself, what in my journey has brought me here? It was, ultimately, to solve that conundrum that I decided to write about my life and the people who have touched me, for good or ill, along its engaging path.

Alan R. Acheson
Feast of the Epiphany 2009

CHAPTER ONE

In the Beginning

Memory is the primary and fundamental power, without
which there could be no other intellectual operation.
(Dr Samuel Johnson)

A scout smiles and whistles under all difficulties.
(Law 8: Traditional Scout Law)

I. THE HOLYWOOD YEARS

1. 'Five nines are forty five'

My earliest memory is of being under the stairs in pitch dark-
ness. Six of us: my parents, mother's aunt, Jim, John – just ten
days old – and myself. The Easter blitz of 1941 on Belfast killed
some 500 citizens – more than a single raid by the Luftwaffe on
any British city other than London. Our Dad, watching from ele-
vated Demesne Park, thought that the entire city was on fire.
Next day Jim and I peed beside uncle Robert's car on the way to
Tougherdale, our grandparents' farm outside Gilford. From our
six months' stay there I recall only John's baptism in St
Matthew's Scarva, the parish church of the 'country' Achesons.
Memories on return to Holywood include our railings being removed to assist the War effort, singing 'coming home on a wing
and a prayer' in the school shelter during an air-raid warning,
and the BBC's reporting – impeccably – after night missions by
the RAF over Germany, 'none of our bombers is missing'. I recall
too a GI giving me a packet of chewing gum in Hughes's hair-
dresser shop on Church Road and – on a later visit to
Tougherdale – American soldiers encamped before D-Day in the
woods above Gilford. The dramatic indication of the War, apart
from the crater made by a stray bomb on Holywood golf course,
was the German POW camp off Demesne Road, with its barbed
wire, siren and searchlights.

I have vivid memories of VE-Day, when I was seven. Because
of Belfast's street celebrations, our taxi had to take a circuitous

route to the Clark Children's Clinic. Dr Magowan had urgently referred me because of a sinus-related lump on my forehead. Mr Wheeler operated without delay and for 48 hours I was in intensive care – I can still see my Dad's anxious face at the corridor window. On recovery, I had a penicillin injection every four hours as one of the first civilian recipients of the drug. My forehead scar evinces both the dangerous nature of the surgery and the skill of an eminent surgeon. Mervyn, born in November 1944, had an illness at birth that required his and our mother's admission to hospital. The combined expense, before the inception of the National Health Service, bore heavily on father. As a Northern Bank official he was miserably paid. I recall the long, hot summer when he was on strike. This unsalaried hardship compounded the austerity of the postwar years when everything from meat to sweets was rationed. We were fortunate that eggs and butter reached us from Tougherdale on those weekends when Dad went 'home'.

The glorious winter of 1947 was one of the coldest of the century. It snowed and kept on snowing. With its *raison d'etre* buried deep, Holywood Golf Club opened its slopes to allcomers and many townspeople turned out night after night with their sleighs. In the days before central heating, activity in sub-zero temperatures outdoors was warmer than huddling around a coal fire in a small grate. The sleigh-run started just below the woods and ended at the Demesne Road hedge. The ascent, negotiated by our Mum, Jim and me – both of us under ten – was heavy going, but well worth the effort, for the swift descent, whether sitting or prone, was exhilarating. The curate of our parish Michael Roycroft and his fiancée were keen tobogganers.

Holywood Parochial School was one of the town's two Protestant primary schools. (Lower Sullivan was the other.) Located beside the parish church, it later became the parish centre of St Philip and St James. The formidable Miss McBride taught P1. On my first day she bade another pupil teach me 'how to make 4s', while she and mother attended to enrolment formalities. At the end of every day the 'big girls' came to help us put on our coats. One of them, Thelma Armstrong, became a close friend of our family. In Miss Fry's P2 class, in a small room with a large open fire and with benches but no desks, we learned to chant our pounds, shillings and pence:

Five nines are forty-five, pence three-and-nine ...

Five twelves are sixty, pence five shillings.

However unfashionable later, the method was effective and enjoyable. Many pupils came from the Holywood slums. There was stark evidence of the poverty of the urban Protestant working class with its typically large families before the welfare state brought family allowances and other benefits. One image remains with me. From the school steps I watched an older boy trudge towards the gate on a snowy winter day. He had no coat. His sleeveless jumper was full of holes. His boots were tied with cord and he wore no socks. He carried his battered schoolbag under his arm. But he held his head high, his dignity making light of his poverty. He later became a much-loved clergyman. By 1950, most slum families had been rehoused in what we inevitably called 'the white city', a project of the Northern Ireland Housing Trust on the site of the wartime POW camp.

I had expected to remain at the parochial school, as my brothers were to do, until I was eleven. But in 1947 the churchwardens were Messrs R. J. Grant and James Acheson. Mr Grant, the Headmaster of Sullivan Upper School (SUS), persuaded father to enrol me as a fee-paying preparatory pupil. Mr J. A. Williamson, the parochial school principal, was reluctant to accept that I was leaving and I was sorry to leave, though glad to miss the class taught by the fearsome Mr Reilly, a former Roman Catholic. I returned to the school in 1949 to sit 'the Qualifying', as the 11-plus examination, in only its second year, was popularly known. The familiar environment ensured my success and my secondary education was therefore without cost to my parents.

Mother's aunt, Isabella (Bella) Chambers – whom we boys called 'Deetie' – had left our home after the blitz to live with the Fullertons at Rockmacraney townland near Richhill. Leonard Fullerton's wife Mary was Bella's sister. He and his sister Maggie, who lived with them, were related to the Revd Francis Fullerton Empey, the rector of Fenagh and Myshall. Aunt Bella and I were invited to Fenagh rectory for a week's stay in July 1947. We took the train from Portadown and the bus from Dublin to Carlow, where our host met us. My friend Adrian

Empey has never understood that my holiday at Bagenalstown was with his family – he assumes that I stayed instead in Dunleckney Glebe. But then Adrian, who is younger, does not recall that summer. I remember it well, not least Adrian's asking enviously from his bed, 'Mummy, what time is A-a-a-lan going to bed?' Walton, the eldest of four brothers, was still in term at Portora. Michael, the youngest, was an infant. The second brother Paul (now deceased) was my age and impatient with my ineptitude, whether on bicycle or tennis-court or even playing draughts. Mrs Empey, whom I called aunt Millie, was considerate and kind to a wide-eyed boy of nine from the North and enhanced my enjoyment of this early experience.

Jim, John and I spent other happy summers on the Fullerton farm. We wakened to the cackling of geese, milked the goat, and drank cold water winched from the deep well. Alas! apples and damsons in three orchards never ripened before the holidays ended. We loved the Rockmacraney Pipe Band, led by neighbours Jack and Isaac Albin resplendent in their kilts. The Williamson Albins lived across the fields from us and many ragged, often barefooted children evinced the poverty of rural Protestant families in the 1940s. Kindly May Fullerton used to pack extras into their basket when they came for milk and eggs. On the day it became apparent that they had upped and gone, enquiry as to their destination elicited the response 'Ameri-kay'. It was reported later that they prospered in their new life across the Atlantic.

Although the bread cart came weekly to the top of the lane, groceries had to be carried from Richhill, a round walk of six miles over Manooth. Jimmy McCann's general store fascinated us: It stocked literally everything. We listened on its radio in 1948 to Test match commentary (it was an Ashes summer) and the opening ceremony of the London Olympics – 'The Austerity Games'. We often visited the Smiths in the RUC barracks; Sergeant David Smith was the village policeman. Sundays meant more walking. We boys attended morning service in what auntie May, a precise Presbyterian, called 'the episcopalian church', and evening Gospel meetings hosted by Sam Hewitt in Richhill Castle. Sometimes, if 'word' could be got to the village, a taxi came to the farm. Auntie May knew when it entered the lane, a mile away, by putting her ear to the ground.

In our later teens, Jim and I set off early for Fruitfield to be scratched by gooseberries and stained by blackcurrants. We learned to hold up our buckets for inspection and ask, 'Hey Jimmie! Is them full enough?' (Here 'full' rhymed with lull.) Most of those who pulled fruit alongside us in this strongly Protestant locality were young Catholics from Armagh City.

2. Sullivan Upper School (SUS)

My life centred on SUS for eight years (1947-55). A more affluent ambience and spacious grounds and sports facilities apart, my two preparatory years conferred no advantage: French, Latin and rugby were started all over again in 1949. Most of the newly 'qualified' came from ambitious primary schools in the City suburbs of Belmont, Knock, Gilnahirk, Strandtown and Sydenham. Many were of working class background. Few aspired to higher education and instead took up careers in the civil service, public utilities, banking, nursing and commerce. Some did not stay until Senior, the leaving examination two years after the Junior Certificate. In our family, Jim left SUS early to join the Northern Bank and John the Merchant Navy. Many of my peers cycled to school and on spring mornings I rode to meet them. With these friends from east Belfast I went to support Glentoran at the Oval. I saw Danny Blanchflower, Billy Bingham and Jimmy McIlroy playing for the 'Glens' before they left for English clubs. The Oval taught me a new language: 'Away back to Seaview, McAuley, you baldy fucker' – from a female fan – was an original way of discovering that the player had deserted Glentoran for Crusaders.

The year ahead of us was more academic. Several who had finished below me in the 1951 summer examination skipped a year and joined this academic elite, with the challenge of sitting Junior after one year. The criterion was age: younger than those promoted, I was kept back. My parents did not question the decision. That was simply not done – the school knew best. I was thus denied a competitive academic environment – many in the year above returned for a post-Senior year and won scholarships. Our year meanwhile was made to work for Junior by an able and dedicated staff. Max Gillespie, all intensity and no-nonsense, drilled arithmetic, algebra and geometry into us – as

Ronnie Grime, of like attributes, had done before him. His older brother Charlie Grime fired the imagination as he taught Shakespeare and the Romantic poets with consummate skill, passion and deep love of his subject. He taught me the value of precision and alliteration in English language. Charlie Burrowes, erudite and urbane, was an intelligent and lively teacher of French and, in my case, of German also, taken up instead of Science. Don Tudor-Dicker, with his inspiration and sophistication, gave me a lifelong love of history. (He failed, however, to warn me against plagiarism, a defect that was to land me in trouble at university.) John Frost, enthusiastic and effective, knew how to make up time lost in geography class – his duties as vice-principal often detained him.

The Headmaster achieved results in Latin, though essentially through the fear that he inculcated by intimidation and humiliation, with frequent resort to biting scorn and physical violence. His overrun of his classes showed contempt for waiting colleagues. Previously on the staff of Kilkenny College and married into one of the old Holywood families, the Dunns of Tudor Park, R. J. Grant was a kindlier man than his image allowed. Being close to retirement did not improve his temper. It was the misfortune of his many students who were not competent in Latin that he both epitomised and perpetuated the methods of an older generation of schoolmasters.

My achieving distinction in all subjects in Junior was illusory, the outcome of rigorous teaching and a photographic memory – my mind had not been stretched. Starting autumn term late in 1953, I had no guidance in my choice of A-level subjects. History and English Literature were automatic choices and Latin – my best result – a strong third, but choosing two modern languages was unwise. I began calculus, understood what was going on, but then impulsively dropped it. John Frost was to say that with geography I would have won a State Exhibition – under his teaching Perry Escott came first in Northern Ireland in 1955. But he had not questioned my dropping his subject. As for French and German, with no literature component – Latin was the same – I could not play to my strength. Charlie Burrowes was an exceptional teacher, but I had a poor 'ear' for languages – my Québécoise wife Ginette despairs today of my becoming fluent in French. Two factors made a bad situation worse. Mary Neill and John Wilson were excellent teachers of English and Latin respectively. But as earnest and conscientious rookies in 1955, they were given a torrid time by our irreverent lot. Our general irresponsibility in Fifth Form was duly punished in Sixth Form when, for the first time, the offices of head boy, head girl and senior prefect went to the scholarship year. Attitudes and atmosphere, then, were not conducive to pre-university study.

I achieved second place in Northern Ireland in A-level history and distinction in English Literature also. But all three languages disappointed. I was awarded a county scholarship but fell below State Exhibition and university scholarship standard. The school had in any case not provided (nor had I sought) advice on these scholarships. The able candidates around me – Robin Herron, the head boy, and others – might as well have been on the moon. It was tacitly accepted at Sullivan that, in our family circumstances, an additional year at school was out of the question for me. I assume the point; it was never discussed with me. So it was that I left SUS in 1955. But, as I explain later, entry to Queen's University was by no means a foregone conclusion.

Sullivan Upper gave me a lifelong love of rugby football. In the prep, I had played several matches for Charlie Grime's under-12s. At under-15 level, I was caught by the Ulster Branch regulation that Medallion Shield players must be under fifteen on 31 October. I was ten days on the wrong side and so had to play with (and against) boys up to a year older than I. Richard Jordan whom I propped was 355 days older. Charlie Burrowes kept me in reserve to a strong XV – until the day that Stuart Adair missed the train to Ballymena. I had stayed overnight there with relatives but not brought my togs. Charlie was angry but adamant that I play. My fellow 'subs' supplied jersey, shorts, socks and boots. I packed as loose head in our quarter-final match with Ballymena Academy, the holders of the Medallion Shield. In a tense, tough game we beat them 3-0 with a drop goal. Like other leading rugby schools, Academy had never heard of Sullivan Upper. Some could not take defeat: I was hit viciously in the face off the ball late in the match. Reacting to my distress, Richard Jordan went to the home dressing room, a noble but fruitless gesture. Charlie kept me for the semi-final against Methodist College, writing later that I had ousted Adair with 'a sterling performance against Ballymena and kept it up against Methody'. The semi-final was played at Sullivan; we lost 8-3. Our reputation was riding high and a match was arranged with Campbell College, who did not enter the Shield. Played at Sullivan it was drawn 5-5. Against three top rugby schools, we had conceded only 13 points. Under 10-stone in summer 1955, I weighed appreciably less early in 1952. But I had enjoyed the thrill of having pulled my weight at loose head.

In 1954-55, I played wing forward for Sullivan 1st XV. Of my best friends Billy Starritt captained from the second row and Allan Cooley and John Adams were the halves. The team had an all-round competence and beat Regent House in the Schools' Cup on a sea of mud at Newtownards. That victory earned us a home match against Royal School Dungannon (RSD), a renowned rugby school. They had a Goliath who stood well over six feet. As Robin Herron was sick, my fellow flanker took his place in the centre. A sunny Saturday afternoon attracted a large crowd. Adams broke his collarbone during the first half, and in the reshuffle – substitutes were not allowed – I too moved to centre. We played like tigers in defence and denied RSD any score, even though they had the advantage of the notorious Sullivan slope in the second half. I was in my element. Disinclined to handle the ball, my great joy was tackling – I was overjoyed that afternoon. RSD turned out in strength for the midweek replay at Dungannon and saw us make a disastrous error. When an attempted penalty kick missed our posts, we failed to touch down or make the ball dead, so allowing a charging Goliath in for a try. In all my years of refereeing I never saw such a blunder. It killed our spirit and we lost the match.

The showers at Sullivan were among the best in Ulster. But there was no door to the shower alcove and steam filled the corridor at the boys' wing of the main building. Occasionally through the steam we glimpsed the begowned figure of 'Ma' – Miss W. M. Maconachie, the senior mistress – striding by the gaping alcove. She was of absent-minded rather than voyeuristic tendency and often forgot her proper route in the girls' wing. I doubt that she overheard the banter that her waywardness provoked. It was school policy that showering must finish with a cold shower. This healthy practice was self-enforcing and scrupulously observed. It inculcated in me the habit of a lifetime.

3. Life outside school

Leisure time involved golf, casual employment, church and scouts. Jim and I enjoyed junior membership of Holywood Golf Club. In 1946, we had watched in awe as flames lit up the night sky devouring the old, wooden clubhouse on the Nuns' Walk. There was a more personal disaster on one of Jim's first outings. I had positioned him badly and opened up his face with an iron. He needed many stitches and carried his scar graciously all his life. In my early teens I caddied at the Royal Belfast Golf Club. A school friend who lived near Craigavad introduced me to the club professional, Pat Sawyer. Whenever a party came from Stormont he assigned me to the Rt Hon. Maynard Sinclair, the Minister of Finance, during the months prior to his tragic drowning in the *Princess Victoria* disaster in 1953. On one occasion, the Prime Minister of Northern Ireland, Sir Basil Brooke, was of the party. I do not recall if the golf improved, but the language did.

At Christmas 1953, the Holywood postmaster – Mr Fails, a southern Irishman – employed me to sort the outgoing mail. I used a special frame introduced the previous year. It was more complex than the normal frame and disliked by the regulars. During a 12-hour day, I sorted some 90 per cent of the mail dispatched at the Christmas peak. In addition to the counties and towns of the province, the frame covered Eire, the regions and cities of England-Wales and Scotland, and grouped London postal districts. I learned the county of every town in England. Much mail came from Palace Barracks, where soldiers wrote 'HOLLAND' on the back of the envelope. As the Ministry of Defence (MOD) did not know where the barracks was (I discovered later), their confusion was understandable. I worked with some fine men, my supervisor Frank Reilly, Tom Collins and Milford Herron among the older postmen. As a perk on Christmas mornings, I did a round – mail was delivered on 25 December in the 1950s. I retained my job for six years, two at school and four at university. It was a life in the day of a student.

The parish of St Philip and St James, with a vicar and two curates, had almost a thousand families. Godfrey Brown, the conductor of the Ulster Orchestra, was parish organist. Archdeacon Manning, who had been an Army chaplain in the First World War, retired and was succeeded in 1945 by Eric Barber, the rector of St James's, Belfast, a parish that had suffered severely during the blitz. A High Victorian architectural gem, our church (on Church road) boasted a belfry with a peal of eight bells: they were heard to best effect high in the Holywood hills. The parish sponsored most of the parochial organisations typical of the 1950s: Scout group, Mothers' Union branch, badminton club and Youth Guild. Canon Barber was a devoted pastor, with a strong record of home and hospital visiting. Before Morning Prayer each Sunday, he stood at the top of the steps in his cassock and shook hands with hundreds of his parishioners. He was an elegant preacher: his sermon series ranged from the Book of Job to *Pilgrim's Progress*. He expounded the Bible each winter at the well-attended midweek Parish Fellowship. One sad night he announced its cessation. In depriving scores of his best people of this spiritual sustenance, Canon Barber aligned his populous parish with others that offered no fellowship to their people midweek, a situation that lasted until the charismatic movement of the 1970s challenged this lethargy. As I perceived later, closure of the Parish Fellowship was a sad illustration of how the Church of Ireland lost its way – and many of its people – during the 1950s and 60s.

Bishop W. S. Kerr, a noted scholar and author, confirmed me in 1954. When I had started Sunday school, a big curate who had digs on Demesne Road near our home held my hand on the way there; he was George Quin. Tony Lucy, the diocesan architect, taught the senior class. He had a penchant for the prophetic: we often strayed into the Book of Revelation. The lovely Paula Lucy was, like her parents, in the choir – until the day that a dashing young curate (and effective preacher) Herb O'Driscoll married her and took her off to Canada. Our Dad was treasurer of the parish's Freewill Offering Scheme, with some 700 subscribers. It was our family's weekly task to 'do the envelopes'. Charlie Grime produced the Youth Guild's annual play. In one production he cast me as an American who came to Belfast to research his ancestor, a US Army General. Guild members took Communion one Sunday a month with breakfast afterwards. My first girlfriend, Jean Gordon, and I were Guild members. Jean's father Sam Gordon was the butler at Stormont Castle. We went there when the Prime Minister and Lady Brooke were away – but stayed 'downstairs', of course.

4. 3rd Holywood

Our Skipper was the remarkable Stewart McCadden. Previously scouter-in-charge of 2nd Holywood, the parish troop, Stewart was 21 when he founded the Thirds as an Open group in 1943. Its cub pack began in 1946, with the admirable Birdie Heasley as the founding Akela. In the early years the troop had no fixed abode; when I joined in 1949, it was meeting in Lower Sullivan School. As Group Scout Leader (GSL), however, Stewart was as-siduous in attracting adult support – it was hard to say 'no' to him. Committed men and women, mostly parents, organised fundraising activities through the Group Committee, bought a site in Ean Hill, and in October 1950 – the 7th anniversary of the Group – opened its first hall, a wartime Laing-type hut. The an-nual Group Show was always enjoyable, its success due both to the meticulous preparation of fine leaders and to dedicated vol-unteer support. Troop nights on Friday took place outdoors in the spring. Memories remain vivid: making plaster casts of bad-ger tracks, roaming county Down under the harvest moon in the annual midnight cycle-run, singing Taps around the dying em-bers of campfire, and the habit, unique to the Thirds, of 'sleeping out' – that is, without tents. It was so ingrained that Ronnie Kells and I even slept out one December night during our First Class journey. And Ivan Nelson and I tried, in a tent in the garden of the vacant Methodist manse, to better Skipper's record of 100 nights sleeping outside: we fell short of our target.

The troop's *raison d'être* was camping. We had accessible loc-ations: the deserted but unspoiled Redburn estate, former home of the Dunville family, and the spacious grounds of the Kennedy family's idyllic Cultra Manor, now the site of the Ulster Folk Museum. At Redburn, we camped, not on the lawns beside the derelict mansion, but at the top of the hill that rose steeply behind both it and the nearby Nuns' Walk, with the

Antrim hills in full view. That vista was available only after we had scaled – with tents, poles, patrol boxes and rucsacks – what Ken Christy designated 'that unforgiving slope'. And the Cultra haven could be enjoyed only after the troop trek-cart, laden with the same paraphernalia, had been pulled and pushed along the Bangor Road, the pushers praying that the heavy traffic would give us a wide berth. Weekends prepared us for summer camp. A stickler for doing things 'the 3rd Holywood way', Skipper demanded the highest standards in campcraft, conduct and dress code – particularly with the perverse brim of our scout hats. If it required five minutes on a cold morning for boys in shorts and 'gutties' to stop shivering, so be it. And if kindling wood was sodden and the fire impossible to light, it must still be lit without paper.

For my first summer camp, in 1949, we entrained to Larne and cycled to Lord Antrim's estate at Glenarm. It rained incessantly – it was July after all – and on one atrocious day the GSL of 1st Bangor, Rennie Graham, moved both troops to a farmer's byre for the night. Skipper was away visiting the 2nd Holywood camp and was livid on return to find us not in our tents. The rain pursued us in 1950 to Mourne Park, Lord Kilmorey's demesne near Kilkeel. There was no rain in 1951 at Phasel's Wood in Hertfordshire. Skipper's planning of this 17-day adventure was meticulous. We alternated days in camp with outings to London from Apsley station. In this Festival of Britain year the superb South Bank Exhibition was a special attraction. On our meal allowance of 2s.6d (five bob a day) we could eat our fill at the self-service in Lyons Corner Houses and still get change! We stayed one weekend on the City of London Sea Scout Guardship berthed close to Tower Bridge. Sleeping on deck, I enjoyed the intriguing sounds and smells of the Thames. Alas! I lost my scarf, so earning Skipper's exasperated 'Alan, you are impossible!' But a wily Fox – Richard Jordan (who else?) – had a spare scarf, and wrath abated. Richard was to endure some ragging when we attended *Carousel*, with its unfortunate lyric 'you're a queer one, Julie Jordan'.

Easter camp was for patrol leaders and seconds. The best was the 1952 cycle tour of Tyrone and Fermanagh, from Baronscourt to Ely Lodge, in our quest to find a summer campsite. My first visit to these western counties was memorable for the friendliness of their people and the dry weather – vital when we slept out. We took bicycles that summer to Lord Erne's Crom Castle, our chosen site, and went to church on an island in Upper Lough Erne where the rector was Dean Grant, brother of the headmaster of Sullivan Upper. Tynan Abbey was our 1953 venue. Sir Norman and Lady Stronge invited us into their beautiful home and posed with us for photographs. Another pleasing memory of Tynan is the Girl Guide Company from Lisburn in which we took a keen interest! In 1954, our 'Operation Cymru' took in five campsites in Wales. The first was on a hillside above Llangollen. Though we attended its International Eisteddfod, we were in camp when we heard in the evening stillness the Oberkirchen boys' choir from across the valley – an indelibly lovely memory. We climbed Snowdon from our final campsite in the National Park. Castlerock in 1955 was a rare experience of a July heatwave. It was my final camp as patrol leader of the Foxes and a third success in four years in winning the coveted Camp Trophy. For Enniskerry in 1956, on Lord Powerscourt's estate, I had graduated to scouter and acted as quartermaster. With activities in my student life taking over, however, it was the last of my eight enriching summer camps with the Thirds.

Skipper placed little emphasis on proficiency badges, much on the essentials of scouting. After camping in Canada with Queen's Scouts unskilled in campcraft, I understood the strengths of the McCadden philosophy. So too did Ronnie Kells, whom I had recruited. Ronnie left Sullivan Upper before taking Senior and retired as chief executive of the Ulster Bank. In his speech at the 2005 annual dinner of the 3rd Holywood Association, Ronnie reflected on the troop's influence. Because it demanded the highest standards and taught the value of teamwork, he had (he said) learned valuable lessons for both life and business. Scouting had given him opportunity 'to learn by doing, and how to look after others and myself. It taught me to think and plan ahead.' Simply put, profoundly appropriate.

Scouting had meanwhile brought other experiences. In 1953, Allan Cooley and I joined the Essex Senior Scout expedition to Europe. A Rotarian, H. R. (Brubs) Bridge of Leigh-on-Sea, had befriended Allan when in 1952 he attended the mini-jamboree at

Belfairs. We visited Eunice and Brubs in their home overlooking the mudflats and musselbeds of the Thames estuary. They insisted that we strike our tent at Belfairs and stay with them. On expedition, we trekked from Eindhoven to Maastricht, relieved by a ride on a barge plying the busy Maas (Meuse), with stark evidence of war devastation all about. From 1954 Brubs and Eunice welcomed me in their home as their Irish 'nephew'.

In 1955, I had the privilege of attending the 8th World Jamboree at Niagara-on-the-Lake, Ontario. Commander Cotton skippered the Ulster troop of four patrols, with Colin Angliker as troop leader. Together with the Staffordshire troop, we flew the Atlantic in a chartered Skymaster, a wartime transport aircraft. Our pilot told us that 'a little lady called Connie' – it was the hurricane season – had forced him to divert to Reykjavik; we flew thence to Gander and Toronto. I carried the troop flag at the 3-hour march past in 100-degree heat. I also joined the choir for Sunday service in St Mark's Anglican church: 'They think here that I have a good voice', I wrote home. We visited Toronto's National Exhibition Centre, having been ferried across Lake Ontario on the *SS Cayuga*. With private hospitality as part of our 'package', David Dowey and I were the guests of the Robinson family at Port Credit. He and his family immigrated to Canada soon afterwards. By contrast, I would not see Canada again until 2001.

II. FAMILY MATTERS

1. 12 Demesne Park

Family life was never dull. Two more brothers arrived, Paul in June 1948 and Chris in 1952. But we still lived in a rented house where eight of us shared two bedrooms and a boxroom. In autumn 1956, however, father bought a three-storey house – 20 Demesne Road. Ironically, Jim had already left home and John soon afterwards. Demesne Park had been a superb location overlooking Belfast Lough. We watched the cross-channel ferries sailing to Liverpool, Glasgow and Heysham – they were always on time. Growing up in sight of water has made me unsettled during those rare periods when I am landlocked. With our friends in the Park, we roamed freely over the golf links – to the quarry, the nutwood-tree copse, the bluebell woods.

As the eldest, I had much responsibility. With no car, shopping had to be carried up two hills; I dreaded seeing '½ stone potatoes' on the list. As baby-sitter when my parents played badminton on winter nights, I was often frightened, imagining faces at the window and turning out lights so as not to be seen. Mother said later that I should have confided my fears, but from misplaced loyalty I said nothing. We older boys had our particular household chores, in my case drying dishes and vacuuming. My outdoor task was cutting hedges, the sole manual skill that I acquired other than wielding an axe. My parents banned me from engagement with electrics and (from 1957) bade my brothers not to let me near the television. Helpfully, they would explain, 'to be so clever, Alan is very dense'. Deemed absent-minded at home, I was comforted by Mr Frost's perception that I was merely unrelated.

Our parents worked hard. Father devoted most of his limited leisure time – the bank worked on Saturday mornings – to our family needs: he mended shoes, grew fruit and vegetables in both the garden and a rented plot in Lemonfield Avenue, and even tried cutting our hair until John's howls ended that experiment. Mother was indefatigable. On a limited budget she reared us on plain, nourishing food – porridge, champ, stew, broth, French toast. Every Saturday we observed the ritual of passing a pot of broth through the hedge to the Ballaghs in exchange for a bowl of pudding. With no washing machine, mother did everything by hand. The dirtiest rugby togs and the detritus from scout camp never daunted her. And she did 'wheel the mangle round the yard', close to a wall contraption known euphemistically as a meat-safe. She still found time to bake for parish functions – she was an excellent home-baker – and to support 3rd Holywood events. In another context, mother's spelling and grammar were impeccable. She taught me that a preposition governed the accusative. I was to have colleagues, both Oxbridge graduates, one an Army officer who said 'between you and I', the other a housemaster who would invite me for a drink 'with Ronale and I'. Mother knew better. She also possessed an indomitable will and strength and enjoyed perfect health.

Before starting at university in 1955, I kept house while our parents holidayed in Scotland. I had four brothers to look after –

Chris, as so often, went to David and Sheila Lindop; Sheila was Thelma Armstrong's sister. My day was made when Paul, an angelic seven, arrived home from school and asked 'Ally, what's for tea?' When I told him he would say 'Oh good! – I'll go up-round-the-corner and play first.' Paul had a beautiful voice and I much enjoyed his reading to me while I cut the hedges that autumn. It was early duty for this future Young Actor of the Year, television sports presenter and popular after-dinner speaker.

Out of her disturbing childhood experience (detailed later), mother suffered from a possessive insecurity and craved affection that father, with his reserved country upbringing, was incapable of providing. To escape tension and to find space and peace from the intrusions of five brothers, I absented myself often. I did A-level revision at Redburn: from my tent I roamed the hills declaiming French verbs and Shakespeare. I often walked the roads of county Down at weekends. In 1954 John Adams and I hitch hiked our way south. By kind permission of Canon Russell, we camped in the grounds of St Luke's rectory in Cork. When we had taken a bus out of Dublin, the conductor, hearing our northern accents, said meaningfully, 'We will be up to see you one of these days.' As a bus conductor was among those captured soon afterwards when the IRA raided the Army barracks in Omagh, I wondered if it were the same man.

On some autumn nights in 1952 I had attended the city mission led by John Wesley White, a Canadian evangelist, in a marquee on a blitz site in High Street. One night a young minister with a strong voice appealed for men to distribute tracts outside pubs at closing time. When only a handful volunteered, Ian Paisley responded, 'God help the city of Belfast!' Well, yes.

We holidayed at Seapark, between Portrush and Portstewart. Mother's sister Etta owned Rockcrest, one of the insanitary shacks that disfigured the north coast in the postwar years. Uncle Vincie, aunt Martha and our four cousins came from Glasgow every August. Margaret, the eldest, was my first teenage crush! We shared everything, from Barry's amusements and the Causeway electric tram to swimming in the rock pools and gathering dulse. Summer 1952, however, was our last Seapark holiday and Warrenpoint next year our last family holiday. Jim and I hated visiting Glengormley, home to mother's eldest sister Marie and her husband Jimmie Tainsh, and our cousins Brian, Maureen, Anne and Deirdre. There was nothing personal in this: our dread related to the journey, often on a winter night. We took the bus to Belfast, walked from Oxford Street to Castle Junction, and boarded the Glengormley tram. Dread deepened whenever we saw 'via Duncairn Gardens', fifteen minutes longer than the Carlisle Circus route. As it was, the monstrosity clanked its way for miles and seemingly hours, the late night return being even more interminable and usually very cold. The trams were later replaced by those 'silent harbingers of death', the Belfast trolley buses.

2. *The Chambers family*

Our maternal grandparents lived in Ballymena. Robert Chambers (Pop) had joined the Black Watch in 1914 and was absent when mother was born on 6 January 1915. Her maternal uncle William Armstrong had been posted missing – his body was never found – and she was christened Wilma Armstrong. After the War, Pop resumed his milk-delivery business in Kinhilt Street, before moving to the Dans Road near Galgorm. As a boy I was terrified of him: he was surly, bad-tempered, and addicted to his pipe – I dreaded having to hand him his spittoon. Our grandmother Lizzie (Mum) was his second wife; his first wife had died in childbirth. She was of lighter disposition, good-humoured and kindly. My happiest memories of my grandparents are from Seapark. Mum died in 1946 at only 61, Pop soon afterwards. I was often sent to stay with my aunts: Etta and Florrie (Chambers) and Doreen, who was married to Arthur McNinch, an old 8th Army soldier. I spent the daytime in the town between Etta's wallpaper shop and Doreen's hairdressing business and evenings at either the Towers or State cinema. Card playing and smoking usually continued in the house until after midnight and as I slept on a pullout settee, I had to wait up in the smoke-filled atmosphere. My aunts were kind to me, but as my brothers never accompanied me I was intensely lonely. Even watching Ballymena United play Belfast Celtic at the Showgrounds on Christmas Day did not compensate. As with the two farms of my childhood, the house had no books and I acquired a literary deficit that lifelong reading has not been able to cancel.

Kinhilt Street was a welcome diversion. I loved the byre and the pigs which uncle Jimmie now owned, aunt Madge was warm-hearted and welcoming and my four cousins good company. Barbara, who became a nursing sister, married George Dennison. Until 2007, they lived in Athgoe Castle near Naas. Both Barbara and our cousin Margaret, who married Jerry Fuller and lives in New Zealand, are among my closest friends. Mother's twin aunts lived next door in Kinhilt Street and welcomed lonely boys. Dressed alike, with aprons over their long, sombre dresses, dignified and serene, aunts Sarah and Maggie had twinkling eyes and a fund of stories. Elsie and Jessie, daughters of two sisters who had died young, lived with them. Their household in the 1940s reflected the suffering of their generation: potential husbands had died in battle and postwar epidemics had taken away the young – three Chambers sisters had died of tuberculosis in as many years. But it was nonetheless a household wondrously at peace, full of love and simple goodness.

Lizzie Chambers's affectionate nature was denied to her daughter Wilma: at age two, she gave her away to the childless Jack and Bella Chambers. With her husband at war, my grandmother was on her own with many mouths to feed, and it is pertinent to say only that her decision has borne harshly on my mother all her life. As a child, she wanted for nothing materially and received a good education. She was an accomplished pianist, took pupils, and until she married at 21 was assistant organist in Wellington Street Presbyterian Church. Unlike her parents' home, her adoptive home was strictly religious and she attended school and church twice on Sundays. Her childhood was lonely: she saw her brothers and sisters daily, but lived apart from them. Worse still, her aunt and uncle lacked the emotional and imaginative capacities needed for nurturing a sensitive child, and she was also subjected to beatings and cruel and capricious treatment, on one occasion being released from dark confinement by her angry grandmother. Agatha Christie's account of her mother's similar upbringing is apposite. Among its consequences (Christie wrote in her *Autobiography*) were the insecurity and oversensitivity to rejection, real or merely imagined, which persisted throughout her mother's life. During my tribute at mother's funeral, Christie's account was read by grandson Luke Acheson.

Jack Chambers was some 25 years older than his wife Bella. He sold his house and business in Bridge Street, Ballymena and moved to Bangor for his health's sake. After he died, Bella Chambers returned to Ballymena, and for company took in 'respectable' lodgers such as bank officials. My father was one of these. Seven years older than mother, he fell in love with her when she was sixteen. They married on 9 September 1936, with the reception at Granville, Bella's home on the Cushendall Road. Bella had been left property in Belfast with substantial rental income. Mother recalls being sent out of the room whenever her aunt's very religious brother came to advise her on managing her properties. He made such a good job of it that Bella Chambers, with or without her knowing consent, was left with nothing. Soon after their marriage, she moved to Holywood to live with my parents, initially in a bungalow at 2 Demesne Park. She brought with her all that remained to her – the furniture from Granville.

3. The Acheson family

In 1903, Robert Acheson married Sarah Margaret Brown in St Paul's, Gilford. He was a tenant farmer, she a village girl. Their thatched, whitewashed cottage in hilly Drummiller townland looked out over the Belfast-Dublin railway line and to county Armagh beyond. Here they reared their family of seven sons and two daughters. My father, the third child, was born on 28 June 1907. Grandfather moved house later to Tougherdale in Kernon townland, and bought his land – in both farms – under the provisions of the Land Purchase Acts. Though now in Tullylish parish, he still attended Scarva church. Father cycled to Banbridge Academy after early morning stints on the farm. On joining the Northern Bank, he was posted to Dublin where his lodgings initially cost more than he earned. He joined St Kevin's church and its thriving Christian Endeavour. After transfer to Ballymena, he became a bell-ringer in St Patrick's parish church.

Tougherdale was a two-storey farmhouse, with byre, stables, barns, and what Australians call a dunny – an outdoors dry closet. Of the farm's 100 acres, half was steep hillside that could not be ploughed. A branch railway line bisected it: linking Banbridge with Scarva, it was plied by a diesel that served the villages of

Lenaderg and Laurencetown, and the Kernon and Drummiller townlands. The arable land grew hay to be stacked, corn stooked, and flax pulled. Two strong carthorses, Bob and Dick, were the pride of the farm in the 1940s, harnessed in season to plough, harrow, roller, binder and hayrick. I was elated as a young boy to be hoisted on to the back of one of these magnificent horses at the end of his day's work, and grasped his mane as he made his own way home by road. As I was seldom left unsupervised, I found it exhilarating. One sad day, however, the horses were led away, and all their tackle thrown on the dunghill – saddles, reins, harness, bits and bridles. This sacrilege was induced by the arrival of a tractor. The hens, scavenging freely in two large gardens, were grannie's speciality. I was not allowed to milk but often fed the hens. The farmyard cats were doled out warm milk from the byre but were otherwise not fed – they were meant to hunt, even though one had a leg missing. We boys used to smuggle meat to them. One of my regular duties (as 'the College boy') was to bring the men their tea in the field. With the kettle and heavy mugs I carried a basketful of barnbrack, soda and wheaten bread, thick with homemade butter and jam. I had my reward when I heard the call, 'Here comes Ulln with the tay.'

The glory of the farmhouse was the kitchen. A large fireplace dominated, the fire constantly kept going by floor-mounted bellows that provided air by an underfloor duct. I was often bidden to 'stir the bellows' and read while turning the wheel. Elaborate wall-mounted apparatus allowed capacious, soot-covered utensils to be hooked above the fire – kettle, griddle and potato urn. A long handled prong ensured that toast was made without the toaster being burned alive. An elegant paraffin lamp lit the kitchen. Raising the wick too quickly blackened the globe; the secret was to sprinkle salt down on it. The kitchen so heated and illuminated was a social attraction for extended family and neighbours, especially on a winter night. Handheld paraffin lamps lighted the way to the other rooms, except the parlour – 'the room': it was seldom used. I always found it thrilling, if incongruous, when my lamp illuminated in the bathroom a buxom Miranda, the ocean raging at her back, as she declaimed 'If by your art, my dearest father.' Upstairs, I told grannie the nightly fib that my lamp was out, before turning it up to read into the early hours as soon as she closed her door.

We loved our visits to Tougherdale. We read the *Northern Whig*, a change from our *Belfast News Letter* and *Daily Mail*. Grannie was rather rigid in personality but kindly, grandpa more relaxed – though given to ordering 'hold your tongue!' if our chatter provoked him. John once obeyed him literally and got into big trouble. We drank buttermilk and cabbage water. We tried to hide our mirth when, at our porridge, grannie instructed 'put milk on them'. Broth too had a plural appellation. Grannie had a shop in the 'middle room', supplied from Dunbarton Stores, uncle Robert's shop in Gilford. A weekly highlight was the visit of his 'man', the grimy Tommy Dawson, his lorry piled high with bags of coal and other necessities. The milk cans were collected daily from the yard gate. On the weekly churning day relays of men pounded the chest-high churn with a pole inserted through a hole in the lid until the milk became butter. Catholic neighbours came to the yard to buy paraffin or to pump water from the well. Two sisters, Mona and Jean McKiverigan, carried all the water for their household in two pails apiece. We played with their brothers Brian and Tom, before the latter went off to join the Irish Free State army. This interaction with Catholics was unusual for us. With schooling in the province divided by religion, and with sport in the segregated schools divided on cultural lines, there was no opportunity for us to mix with Catholic children in Holywood. That lasted until I went to Queen's.

All the Protestant children in three townlands attended the Sunday school taught by the Miss Lockharts in a simple schoolroom provided by Gilford Presbyterians. A hedge separated it from our farmyard hens. Church in Scarva was part of the Sunday scene. Before an Austin 8 was acquired, I walked the six miles there and back with grannie to evening service. Though over 60, as a hardworking farmer's wife she took it in her stride. The men sometimes tracked the railway to Scarva – the diesel did not run on Sunday. It was always waiting, however, when the train from Belfast pulled into Banbridge station past the long strips of linen bleaching in the fields. On one return journey to the city, I was invited to ride in the engine and watched the driver manipulate his controls and the fireman ply his shovel, a fascinating if rather grimy experience. Another memory is of going by bus with uncle Eric to Banbridge, where he had a haircut after his long week on the farm. The cosy, vibrant atmosphere of a bustling Ulster country town on a winter Saturday evening in the late 1940s was pure Thomas Hardy.

The local dialect was something else. Grandpa, who had no French, encouraged his cows homeward with calls of *chez*. Grannie, before she swept the kitchen floor, covered it with tealeaves to prevent a *stour*. She always *wet* the tea. The fields had *sheughs* and the Drummiller farm was approached on uncle Charlie's *loanen*. We woke to shouts from the yard of *'whoa! back-ar-that'*. We learned to *whist* when adults talked, not to *founder* on a winter day, and not to *cowp* the milk pails. We often espied *thon* farmhouse across the fields.

Robert Acheson was a leader in his community. He served for decades on the select vestry of Scarva parish, and on Banbridge Rural District Council. (I read its minutes in the dunny, supplied there for another use!) When he was 22, he became Worshipful Master of Drummiller Orange Lodge (LOL 2012), and held this office continuously for 31 years – until 31 December 1930. He 'lived in love and charity with his neighbours' and always attended their funerals in Roman Catholic churches. Every 12th July, after the traditional raising of the banner at the Master's house, he led his lodge down the hill to join Gilford District. They stopped at the nearest house, Barney McKiverigan and Robert Acheson shook hands, and the lodge resumed its walk. The simple civility thus observed by the Orange Master and his Catholic neighbour epitomised the goodwill in this mixed community. Its men worked together at threshing time, at its concomitant cull of rats by men and dogs, and during other phases of the farming cycle. Catholic and Protestant enjoyed equal voting rights, the same national welfare benefits and health service; they shared too the rural deprivation of electricity and mains water. They came together at wakes in one another's houses. When Robert Acheson died early in 1968, Catholic neighbours attended his wake. Months later such traditional courtesy became impossible: the civil rights campaign and the tensions to which it gave rise polarised this peaceable county Down community.

Grandpa was not faultless. He once pushed Paul off a moving tractor; and, in a temper, took a strap to a severely brain-damaged cousin of ours. But essentially he was a man of wisdom and humour. Whenever grannie scolded him, he said nothing but gave me a surreptitious wink. He was, too, complete in himself and contented in his environment. During the 30 years that I knew him, he was never away from Tougherdale (except for one brief spell in hospital). Conscious that his brother Jack had destroyed himself through alcohol, he was a teetotaller. Short in stature, he was healthy, fit and strong. He rode a bicycle until he was over 80. When the house was being re-roofed, he insisted that he rather than I carry a tarpaulin up the ladder 'for fear Alan might hurt himself' – I was twenty then, 60 years his junior. We once spent two raw April days in a shed beside the railway halt preparing potatoes for seeding. It was tedious work with numb fingers, but conversation never flagged.

Robert Acheson was conscious of the weight of the past. If anyone lauded my progress, he would approve, then add quietly 'but Alan has had the opportunity'. In its early phases, he was sensible of the family's transition from landless labourers to university-educated professionals, and of the realities that sustained it. Like my father, he influenced that transition by his hardworking example. James Acheson inherited also his father's deep faith, integrity and catholic spirit. In their different environments, each was a gentleman. I never heard either man swear: the closest father came was 'bad cess to it!' Nor did I ever hear from them a word derogatory of Catholics or critical of friends or neighbours. They were Ulstermen indeed in whom there was no guile. I have always been thankful that both my father and grandfather died before it was given out to the world that Ulster Protestants were intolerant bigots.

III. QUEEN'S AND AFTER

1. Undergraduate and ordinand

I nearly became a landless labourer; Queen's University refused me a place. The problem was O-level Maths: with only 123/400 marks, I was close to 30 per cent perdition level. As I was then in Canada, father went to the university for me. It was new territory for him and he charted his way adroitly. He asked how Queen's could reject an applicant with three distinctions in Junior Maths. At that, attitudes changed. Nine months later I won the sole Foundation Scholarship awarded to an Arts undergraduate in 1956. That achievement had seemed improbable after my admissions tutor had suggested I read philosophy with my history and Latin. Though I never understood a word, I dithered for weeks before confiding in my tutor, Prof Michael Roberts, who had me transferred to the German department. I spent the Christmas holiday copying up notes and two terms enjoying German literature – there was no oral. Most of the small German class passed but two-thirds of the large Latin class failed. I was accepted for the Honours course in Modern History, with no degree examinations until finals three years later. An alert Old Portoran, Gerald Carew, told me about the Scholarship. I entered just in time and became a scholar of Queen's.

Undergraduate life was richly varied. The annual history students' conference involved long winter minibus outings – we were in Galway when news broke of Manchester United's tragic losses in the Munich air disaster. I joined Queen's Officers Training Corps (OTC). During the IRA's campaign of violence from 1956 we guarded our drill hall nightly, a too-dependable source of extra income. I was not a committed cadet and did not take 'Cert B' because I had no intention of joining the Army. Among my new friends, Clive West taught me to drive after I obtained a full driving licence, 1950s-style, simply by paying 2s.6d. My second home was 42 Adelaide Park, the Belfast home of my friends Austin and David Hewitt. Their father Thomas Hewitt was inspirational in his friendship, sharing with me not only his books – I slept in the library – but also his erudition. Mrs Lily Hewitt received me with warm affection and Dorothy, Norman and Christine, the other siblings in this lively and talented family, were equally welcoming.

I often stayed in the Londonderry home of my Queen's girlfriend, June Cooke. June accompanied me on two summer visits to Brubs and Eunice. One of the sounds of the Fifties was Brub's singing 'Will your anchor hold?' aboard his boat in the Thames estuary. I did not seek paid employment during the summer. With income from two scholarships and OTC and post office earnings, I was able to pay my way at home and engage in student missions in Belfast supported by most local churches. After the first (York Street), I was elected to the organising committee for the second (Sydenham), and as chair for the third (Mount Merrion). In 1959, T. S. Mooney invited me to be chaplain at the annual Crusader camp at Guysmere in Castlerock – Crusaders Union is an interdenominational federation of Boys' Bible classes in Britain and Ireland.

The Church of Ireland had then no centralised selection procedures for men seeking holy orders. Queen's graduates normally went on to the Divinity School in TCD and took the two-year course prescribed for the divinity testimonium. During four years, I attended ordinands' conferences in the Ballyholme Hotel or Murlough House and parish visits organised by Eric Elliott, the clerical Northern Education officer. Although Holywood parish had three ordinands, Canon Barber – certainly in my case – took no interest in our vocation. I was encouraged, however, by Canon George Quin, the vicar of Ballymacarrett, and offered warm-hearted friendship by him and Dr Norah Quin. Whenever I cycled to St Patrick's for Sunday evening service, I was invited to the vicarage for dinner. When the senior curate of the parish, Dr M. W. Dewar, was appointed rector of Scarva in 1956, Canon Quin took me with him when he went to 'preach in' the new rector. The Dewars invited me to lunch when I was at Tougherdale and Michael Dewar plied me with books and expositions on church history. Today's scholarly consensus that early Anglicanism was a halfway house between Luther and Calvin was first taught me in Scarva rectory 50 years ago.

From my involvement in the Church of Ireland Centre in Elmwood Avenue, the visit of the former Bishop of London, Dr J. W. C. Wand, stands out in memory: I have a signed copy of his *The Four Great Heresies* (1956). The Centre had no chapel. Services were held in the Catholic Apostolic church in Cromwell Road. The Dean of Residence, Edgar Turner, trained me in tasks appropriate for an ordinand and I robed for special occasions. Ours was an uneasy relationship: I interpreted my Evangelical churchmanship too rigidly and was often a trial to the dean. That we are friends today is tribute to Edgar's gracious and catholic spirit. As an ordinand, I identified with the Divinity Hostel. I was there, having driven to Dublin with Clive West, when the new professor of ecclesiastical history, Dr G. C. B. Davies, turned the Saturday evening devotions into a Bible-reading with his exposition of the ninth chapter of Hebrews. I joined also in the visit of the Dublin ordinands to the Assembly's College in Belfast. Professor F. E. Vokes of TCD unwisely chose the occasion to speak provocatively on church government and was wiped all over the floor in Professor J. M. Barkley's response.

The Assembly's College was familiar ground: I had tea with the resident body weekly. In these years, too, I had the privilege of preaching in three Presbyterian churches – Sinclair Seaman's and Ulsterville in Belfast, Harryville in Ballymena. Although a fringe member of the Student Christian Movement (SCM), I was committed to the Christian Union (CU). An early meeting allowed me to make a pot of porridge, leave most of it for the family, cycle to Queen's, pray and be in time for a 9 o'clock lecture. I was first elected to the executive committee, then as CU president for 1957-58. The CU had until recently been reclusive, with even university sports suspect. My predecessor Bill Campbell, a fine hockey player, challenged this mindset, while a new breed of members involved in men's and women's hockey and Senior rugby – Austin and David Hewitt and Denis McDevitt played for Queen's 1st XV – helped me to maintain the momentum. Rag Day had previously been taboo also and I urged CU members to turn out. Their response was such that Des Abernethy, the President of the Student Representative Council, applauded my initiative in a generous letter of thanks.

Queen's CU was affiliated to the Inter Varsity Fellowship (IVF) and many of us attended its spring conferences at Swanwick in Derbyshire. Two staff became personal friends. Oliver Barclay, the Universities' Secretary, walked the strand at Greystones with me in May 1957 when we were guests at the house party of Dublin University Christian Union (DUCU). In September 1959, Dr Barclay and I represented Inter-Varsity Fellowship at the Paris conference of the International Fellowship of Evangelical Students. Its President, Dr Martyn Lloyd-Jones, spoke encouragingly to me about my public speaking. Donald English came to Queen's as Travelling Secretary: his gentle personality and pastoral gifts influenced me greatly. I was a guest at their wedding when Don married Bertha Ludlow of Bangor in 1962. I served on IVF's national student executive as secretary for overseas students, the more gladly as many of my friends at Queen's were from Commonwealth countries. Milton Hsu, an engineering student from Mauritius, became a particular friend. I had met him when engaged in London on reception of overseas students. We travelled to Belfast after I had introduced Milton to Brubs and Eunice – he became their Chinese 'nephew'.

2. Career choices

I had 'loved Paris in the fall', but now lived on overdraft. On graduating with an Upper Second, I had decided to defer divinity and teach. In the summer SUS had recruited Tom Hooks from Ballyclare High to succeed Don Tudor-Dicker. While I was in Paris, John Frost spoke to his counterpart, R. E. Russell. He appointed me to teach history and (ironically) geography. My starting salary on scale 5, for 'good honours' graduates – no professional qualification was required – was £725 per annum, increased from £610 on the very day I started: 1 October 1959. My salary was two-thirds of that earned by my father after 30 years' service. Except that I did not receive it: County Antrim Education Committee had 'overlooked' my arrival, and could not pay my first month's salary until mid-November. It was an early lesson in educational management. In March 1960, Roy Alcorn resigned to tour with the play *Over the Bridge* and Mr Russell offered me his post of second history teacher in Joe Williams's department. This welcome promotion did not reduce my exposure to two hideous school buildings: the Ropeworks – a former mortuary without windows – and the inelegant North End Hut. After travelling by public transport from Holywood for a year, I found digs, initially with Roy and Vi Kennedy on their farm at Whitepark – I had known Vi (Beatty) in Rockmacraney. I made sure that I marked homework in the school on the evenings that the Ballyclare Male Voice Choir practiced there.

I led expeditions during school holidays to the youth hostels at Knockbarragh in the Mournes and Gortin Glen. Sally Grant was a supportive colleague: Billie and she came on three

Mournes outings and became good friends – as Sally remains after Billie's death in 1980. At Easter 1961, I took a school party to London assisted by Joe and Mary Williams. I had not prepared as thoroughly as Skipper in 1951, and we arrived at Easter Saturday without a booking for a show. I began telephoning. The operator I spoke to was from county Tyrone. She pledged to stay with me until my quest succeeded, as it did after some ten enquiries – all made without charge. It is always good to have connections.

Each summer I was an officer at Inter Schools Camps: Carrickfin in the Rosses, Inch Island on Lough Swilly, and Castle Archdale in Fermanagh. At Carrickfin in 1960, Rupert Darling gave me the senior tent, fine young men including John Matthews and Terence Brown from families known to me. During the 1961 camp, I learned that my father had been appointed manager of the Banbridge branch of the Northern Bank. While it was a homegoing for him, he suffered from angina and would take on a branch with a notoriously tragic history. Any misgivings were, however, overborne by father's relief at being promoted (he was 54). The family left Holywood at Hallowe'en 1961 for the magnificent four-storey bank house in Bridge Street, Banbridge. My link with my hometown continued through the Crusader class which David Hewitt and I, the formally appointed leaders, had started in 1960. It grew so strongly that we won the Crusaders Union national trophy for outstanding progress. John Frost wrote approvingly to me about its influence within SUS. My finest achievement in these years was to attract David Hewitt to Holywood. He married Margaret Meharg and they set up home in the town. David became an elder in Bangor Road Presbyterian congregation and a governor and parent of Sullivan Upper.

Although I had shelved divinity, I was still attracted to Dublin – to research the Church Evangelicals in Ireland. An appropriate bursary was available in TCD and Prof Michael Roberts at Queen's supported my application. Prof G. C. B. Davies saw me in TCD early in 1962. To my dismay, he dismissed my plan on the express grounds both that my exploratory research was inadequate and that he himself, as he candidly disclosed, knew nothing of Church of Ireland history. Dr Davies advised me to apply to the Revd Dr Barkley, his counterpart at Queen's.

My rebuff at TCD meant continuing in salaried employment. Joe Williams pressed me to remain at Ballyclare High, but although I had enjoyed my three years in this excellent school I sensed that if I were to stay I might never leave. I therefore applied for the post of civilian instructor at the North Irish Brigade Depot. Before my interview in Lisburn, I overheard reference to 'the candidate'. There were no other takers, it seemed, for a post offering allowances for a longer teaching year and evening duty. This was MOD fiction: the teaching year was in effect shorter and work overall less onerous than in a grammar school, with no homework to mark or reports to write, and a lunch break of 90 minutes instead of the ten minutes available after school lunch duty. The new post offered therefore both a substantial increase in salary and reduction in workload. I left Ballyclare High in June 1962; Robert Fitzpatrick was promoted in my place.

3. Pan-evangelical and Church of Ireland

At the annual Queen's CU conference in 1958, a group led by Dennis Kennedy and composed mainly of hockey types lightened the atmosphere by rendering, to the tune of John Brown's Body:

> Down with all this holy Joe stuff [thrice]
> Or we'll all join SCM.

I recalled this irreverent wisdom when reflecting on experiences, at Queen's and after, in both pan-evangelical and Church of Ireland contexts. The dichotomy implied here cannot be pressed too far. Godfrey Brown, president of Queen's CU in 1955-56, became Moderator of the Presbyterian Church in Ireland. Cecil Kerr, president of DUCU in 1957-58, became internationally the best-known priest of the Church of Ireland. Founding members of Holywood Crusader class have served their churches with distinction; one – Ken Clarke – is Bishop of Kilmore. Again, the most arresting preaching that I heard at Queen's was not at the CU but at the mission sponsored by the deans of residence. Canon Bryan Green's lunchtime lectures on young adult love and sexual relations packed the Whitla Hall; most returned for his evangelistic evening lectures. In point alike of his intellectual vigour and emotional power, and his skills as orator and apologist, Green was an outstanding missioner. And yet, as its president, I had had to advance the IVF 'party' line that the Christian Union could not formally support his mission, although individual members might do so. The three deans were incredulous; I was uncomfortable with the semantics.

IVF's doctrinal basis, which staff and office-bearers must subscribe, was critically viewed by one of its vice-presidents, David Torrens, professor of physiology at TCD. He saw the assertion that the scriptures 'as originally given' were infallible, as disingenuous. He binned IVF's annual invitation to affirm his assent – primarily because his Brethren background indisposed him to subscribe such confessions. His thinking influenced mine. In 1961, the Inter-Varsity Fellowship offered me the full-time salaried post of Travelling Secretary for three years. I was unhappy with IVF's *modus operandi*: I had not been consulted, references had been sought surreptitiously, and I was asked, not to apply for, but to accept, the position. I took up 'as originally given' with Dr Barclay, who pronounced it a not insuperable difficulty. But perturbed by my tongue-in-cheek comment that I was 'a man of extreme extremes', he withdrew IVF's formal offer of employment. Professor Torrens, for his part, was 'reported' by a zealot among TCD students. Having never subscribed IVF's doctrinal basis, he was now required to do so. Eminent in his profession and close to retirement, he was a founder and lifelong supporter of DUCU and friend of Dr Douglas Johnson, the General Secretary of IVF. His background apart, he was temperamentally averse to subscription. All of that counted for nothing. He was struck off as a vice-president. Cecil Kerr, who was close to him, contested this action in vain. However defended, the Inter Varsity Fellowship's treatment of David Torrens had been heartless and squalid.

Clive West had introduced me to Professor Torrens, and I was always welcome in his rooms at No. 36. I first stayed there when I spoke at DUCU at Hallowe'en 1959. When I succumbed to 'flu, my host nursed me for two days then walked me to Amiens Street station. He carried my bag just as he always cleaned my shoes – it was pointless to protest. He arose around 5.00am; his open Greek Testament indicated his morning habit. He made superb breakfasts of Haffner's sausages, bacon and egg, and his homemade tarragon mustard. While he was busy, I read his *Church Times*. I accompanied him one Sunday morning to the 'teaching' ministry in the Brethren's Merrion Hall – he never attended the earlier Breaking of Bread (I did not presume to ask why). When I was his guest at Hunter's Hotel, we walked to church at Nun's Cross. The rector came to our pew and said, 'I believe you are someone important.' The professor replied, 'No! I am Torrens of Trinity College'. In humility, that said it all.

A native of county Derry who had lost neither his accent nor his rustic simplicity, David Torrens held his chair for decades and was sometime Dean of the School of Medicine. Every year he discarded his notes and re-wrote his lectures. The many visitors to his rooms sat around the turf fire. Students came to borrow milk, ask how to sew on a button, or simply enjoy his company. In the evenings and at weekends he acted as *de facto* doctor and chaplain; no request for his help was ever refused. He ordered lunch for me one Sunday at the University Club, then left to visit the infirm widow of a former colleague who lived in a Dublin garret. From June 1962, I was glad to drive him in my new minivan, whether through his beloved county Wicklow or from Dublin to Belfast, where he stayed in the Ulster Club.

IVF intransigence was matched by Church of Ireland intolerance. When Lady Wakehurst, wife of the Governor of Northern Ireland, honoured BCMS (the Bible Churchmen's Missionary Society) with her presence in Belfast's Clarence Place Hall, Dr Sydney McCann presided – no bishop would touch BCMS. George Quin staffed his parish of Ballymacarrett with Evangelical curates but his catholic spirit was exceptional. Bishop F. J. Mitchell of Down was inhospitable to Evangelicals and Archdeacon Mayes of Armagh implacably hostile. One incident spoke volumes. When Harold Magowan, curate of Antrim parish, seceded and joined the Free Presbyterian Church, two ordinands of Evangelical tradition had their bursaries withdrawn. The brutal, sectarian injustice of that action shook me to the core. When the *Church of England Newspaper* (CEN) invited me to write an article for its St Patrick's edition of 1961 – an archbishop and divinity professor also contributed – I dwelt on the invidious situation of Irish Church Evangelicals. Although both the *Belfast News Letter* and *Belfast Telegraph* took up my article, no one in authority discussed it with me. Nor did anyone query my not applying to the Divinity School. I had, it seemed, fallen off the Church of Ireland's map. My *CEN* article, however, taught me an important lesson: I could not have engaged in trenchant criticism as a cleric; as a layman I was accountable to no one.

One retired cleric did comment on my article. He was a quintessential Catholic Anglican. He commended me on the spirit and style of my writing. He approved, if rather guardedly, my observation that, although spared the excesses of the Anglican Catholic revival, the Church of Ireland had been denied its devotional depths as well. At any rate, I now stood taller in the estimation of this singular priest. He was the Revd W. G. Acheson, my grandfather's younger brother. Self-educated, he had often been found asleep at Drummiller with his books around him and his lamp still burning. He matriculated at TCD, took degree and divinity testimonium, and was ordained in Ossory diocese (deacon 1921, priest 1922). He worked for some time with the Bush Brotherhood in Australia. In the national bicentenary year of 1988, I told Sydney diocesan synod with pride that William Gordon Acheson's was the second name in the list of clergy (an appendix in *Sydney Anglicans*) who had served the diocese over 200 years.

W. G. Acheson returned to England and was for 40 years vicar of St Stephen's, Lewisham in the diocese of Southwark. He came to our home each September when on leave; he was fond of both my parents. In 1954 he invited me to stay. He had a devoted housekeeper, Miss Lawrence, and a silent waiter delivering meals from her basement kitchen to the dining room. When, on the first morning, I appeared there in shirtsleeves, my host asked politely if I had a jacket. Then sixteen, I learned much from my great uncle in conversation and first read *The Times* in his vicarage. I attended my first West End play when he took me to Christopher Fry's play *The Light is Dark Enough* in the Aldwych Theatre. Father Willie was a devoted priest: he said daily Mass in St Stephen's before breakfast, heard confessions weekly, and centred his spirituality on the Stations of the Cross. He was sensitive to the differences between us – my bedroom alone was without a crucifix. On Sundays, with his blessing, I went up to St Martin-in-the-Fields.

Uncle Willie retired to Rostrevor. He engaged his niece Amy and her husband Sam Briggs to look after him. Devout Baptists, they were devoted to him. His Anglican Catholicism had, I believe, no expression in Ireland of which he was aware. I suspect that he heard Mass among local Roman Catholics. He died in January 1966, and was buried in Scarva churchyard. I was with my grandfather at his brother's funeral. They had always agreed to differ. The old Orangeman lived to erect a headstone for the faithful Catholic priest, recording with pride his long incumbency at St Stephen's, Lewisham. The simple memorial says much about both men.

* * *

Reflecting on the Acheson family over the six generations that extend from my great-grandparents to my grandchildren, I have no recollection of ever hearing my grandfather Robert Acheson talk about his parents. He was but fifteen when his father died and his brother William Gordon Acheson a child of two. My great-grandparents, John and Rachel Acheson, are buried in Ballenaleck old graveyard situated between Scarva and Tandragee. The headstone erected over their graves, replete with much family detail, lies broken in two. My hope is that, with the consent and co-operation of our cousins, the headstone will be repaired and restored to its place over our great-grandparents' grave. The dearth of information about them was such that when my second daughter was given the name Rachel, I was unaware that my great-grandmother's name was Rachel. I have long had a sense, deriving in part from physiognomy, location, and circumstances – why an Acheson family of no property, living in penury, in this area? – that our forbears came from 'the wrong side of the blanket' in the noble family of Acheson, Earls of Gosford, previously resident at Markethill. I have, however, yet to research the matter and until then can but speculate. I am gratified that Rachel has recently taken up Acheson family history via the internet, and look forward to the fruits of the quest that she is pursuing with strong interest and application.

CHAPTER TWO

The Army and Northern Ireland

Any fool may write a most valuable book by chance, if he
will only tell us what he heard and saw with veracity
(*Thomas Gray, 1768*)

News is becoming our greatest fiction.
(*Darryl Duke, Canadian film director, 1966*)

I. HER MAJESTY'S LAND FORCES

1. Towards a commission

The North Irish Brigade had been formed from three elite regiments: the Royal Inniskilling Fusiliers, the Royal Irish Fusiliers
(the Faughs), and the Royal Ulster Rifles. On 27 August 1962, I
reported to the Brigade Depot at Eglinton, the Fleet Air Arm's
wartime base in county Londonderry. The Commanding Officer
(CO), Lt-Col John Nixon, an Old Portoran, encouraged me to
identify fully with the unit's life, and I played for the XV and
lived in the Officers' Mess. I imbibed Army tradition: the mug of
strong, sweet morning tea brought by a batman, extended Mess
lunches for distinguished visitors, and Regimental Guest Nights,
complete with kilted piper encircling the table while the port
was passed. During my year there, Lt-Col Harry Baxter succeeded
as CO, and Capt Mike Sweet, previously in Kenya with 2nd Bn
Coldstream Guards, replaced Capt John Ellams as Senior
Education Officer. The winter of 1963 was severe. On glorious
February days two subalterns and I pounded the snow-covered
hills overlooking the Foyle. As so often after a severe winter, the
summer was superb. As a country member of Portstewart Golf
Club, I played there regularly with Jim who was working in
Coleraine. I stayed overnight often at Wyncroft, the hospitable
home on Strand Road of my friends Roddy and John Matthews.

I had meanwhile applied to join the all-officer Royal Army

Educational Corps (RAEC). After a screening at Lisburn, I was assessed over three days by the Regular Commissions Board (RCB) at Westbury in Wiltshire, and recommended for a commission. The Chief Education Officer at HQNI, Lt-Col J. T. (Jim) Sleator, a shrewd and affable Irishman, had obtained prior permission for me to defer joining in order to lay the foundation for my PhD. Accordingly I left Eglinton in August 1963. I had three prior commitments, the first the Crusaders' expedition to Montenegro led by John Briggs. By a neat timing we assembled in London the day my RCB ended. With (exceptionally) a room to myself, I had spent evenings there completing my chaplain's talks for epilogues. My memories from three weeks' hard trekking are the wild beauty of the Montenegrin landscape, the friendly curiosity of the mountain people, and the loveliness of serene Sarajevo; and later the enchantment of the islands and ancient towns of the Adriatic with four magical hours in Venice, before sleeping on the luggage rack – we drew lots for places – of the overnight express. I recall too the calibre of my co-leaders and their bonding with the boys. One was Stuart Presley, whom I would know later as Stuart Ó Seanóir of the Manuscripts staff in TCD.

My second diversion that autumn was touring Ireland with John Matthews and sleeping in the back of my minivan on an inflated lilo. We located Peter Roe's memorial in Kilkenny and Yeats's grave at Drumcliffe. We enjoyed Sunday lunch with the Jeffers family in Bandon and an impromptu Bible study with Robert England and Clive West in Galway. We had surreptitious baths in Acton's Hotel in Kinsale after booking dinner, and almost choked when dinner at Shannon Airport cost us 17s.6d. Finally, Sullivan Upper employed me for two months while Tom Hooks was in the USA. I had the pleasure of observing John Frost's inimitable style as Headmaster, being warmly welcomed by my former teachers, and (on departure) dating the Head Girl, Kathleen Bailie. Settling to research at last, I spent January 1964 at Tyndale House in Cambridge, where Dr Leon Morris was warden. His Australian compatriot Colin Tunbridge, also an Anglican priest, was on sabbatical and we became friends. While I was in Cambridge, Brubs died suddenly at 52. I had stayed with Eunice and him the previous August after an interval of four years and now attended his funeral in the packed Methodist church in Leigh-on-Sea. The Revd Tom Sutcliffe ended his moving eulogy with 'Goodnight, my friend; on some better shore, bid me "good morning!"' Eunice later placed a stained glass window of nautical theme in Brub's beloved New Road chapel, with the simple affirmation 'his anchor held'.

Cambridge had returned me to studious mode but my primary sources were in Dublin. Noel Towe, late of Sullivan Upper and Holywood Crusaders, invited me to share his rooms in TCD, and with the Junior Dean's permission I lived in No. 4 in February and the Rubrics in the spring. I worked at the RCB Library (RCBL) in St Stephen's Green and at either the National Library or TCD Library in the evening. Noel and I sometimes played squash in the early hours. I owed much to Noel's genial tolerance, the courteous efficiency of Geraldine Willis at RCBL, and not least Stanley and Margaret McElhinney – their beautiful home in Dalkey was my weekend retreat. Finally in stifling heat in London I accessed the archives of the Church Missionary Society, located in Salisbury Square off Fleet Street.

2. The Army School of Education (ASE)

On 1 September 1964 I reported to the ASE at Wilton Park, Beaconsfield. The School's Language Wing trained the Army's Russian specialists and employed White Russians. Major J. F. (Jock) Moffatt commanded Officer Wing. One of his training Captains was Jim McClean whom I had known in Queen's OTC. We seventeen trainees were probationary Second Lieutenants in Her Majesty's Land Forces, with daily pay of 34s.6d. As RAEC was the only combatant Corps to train its own officers, our course divided into military and specialist halves divided by Christmas. We were drilled by a Guards RSM and given weapons training by Gurkhas. John Birkbeck and I shared a room in a hut beside the stately White House that was the Officers' Mess. When most others left at weekends, I roamed the luxuriant Buckinghamshire countryside in that sun-drenched autumn – and began to write. In midweek, I either refereed or played for the ASE XV, which – on posting from Eglinton – John Ellams captained.

There were two interruptions to routine: a week's encampment beside the old Menai Bridge, with adventure training in the Welsh mountains, and three weeks' attachment to units in Germany, in my case 1st Royal Tank Regiment (1RTR) at Hohne. Its Officers' Mess was Goering's magnificent former hunting lodge at Bredebeck. It was not the only reminder of the Third Reich: the site of Belsen concentration camp was nearby. I contemplated its horrors in solitude on a depressing November day. As it was a bad time of year to join a unit in BAOR, the 2ic asked apologetically if I could keep myself occupied. When I suggested writing my thesis his relief was palpable. For three weeks I did little else. The regiment compensated me: I spent an evening with their 7 Armoured Brigade neighbours, 1st Bn The Royal Irish Fusiliers, at Trenchard Barracks, Celle, and enjoyed the Faughs' boxing tournament; and then went to RTR's independent squadron in Berlin. I had the fascinating experience of travelling in *The Berliner*, the British military train from Brunswick to West Berlin, with blinds compulsorily down throughout its daylight passage of East Germany. Equally fascinated, I joined three corporals of the Royal Military Police on a routine patrol of East Berlin, where they gathered intelligence of Soviet troop movements from tank tracks in the snow.

Sadly, the motif of these months was death. When Sir Winston Churchill died in January 1965, a party of us from Beaconsfield queued all evening to salute his lying-in-state in Westminster Hall. During each of three leaves I attended a funeral in county Down. My grandmother Acheson died at the Hallowe'en break and Kathleen Bailie's grandmother McCracken during Christmas leave. Funerals, like so much else, come in threes: but father's death during the February break was as sudden as it was poignant. James Acheson had gone to Dublin – his first visit since the 1920s – for the England match at Lansdowne Road. He declined to travel by car with my brothers and me because he did not want to disappoint his friend, former RUC Head Constable Hayes – they went together in Banbridge RFC's coach. After the match, father was taken ill but rejected the advice of a doctor at Sutton to go into hospital in Dublin. Club members brought him home by car. We knew nothing of his ordeal until the sad party arrived at the bank house after midnight.

The doctor diagnosed a heart attack and Dad was admitted to Craigavon Hospital. He died early on Sunday 14 February 1965.

At daylight I had the sombre duty of breaking the news to my grandfather. As he had lost his wife of more than 60 years fifteen weeks before, the shock might have killed him. His resilience proved strong and his innate courage and dignity were prominent both on that bleak morning and at the funeral two days later. Father's funeral was hugely attended. At the service in Holy Trinity, Banbridge we sang Psalm 15 – the Christian gentleman's psalm – and two of his favourite hymns. Canon Eric Barber preached with comforting sensitivity. We chose a route to Scarva that brought our Dad for the last time through the townlands of Kernon and Drummiller. James Acheson was buried in Scarva churchyard in the same plot as his mother. She was 84 when she died; he was 57.

Major Moffatt was at once supportive. He offered me a week's compassionate leave, soon extended to two. Mother needed support. Only six weeks past her 50th birthday, she had no time to grieve. By a thoughtless Ulster tradition, we had dozens of visitors to cater for – some came every day and stayed all day. And scores of letters to reply to: I drafted three model letters and mother completed the task in her own hand within the fortnight. I stood also *in loco parentis* for Paul, sixteen, and Chris, thirteen, both at Banbridge Academy. The annual play was staged just after father's funeral, with Paul as Christy Mahon in Synge's *Playboy of the Western World*. To his considerable acting skills, Paul now added courage. He had to close out Act I with the lines:

'I'm thinking this night wasn't I a foolish fellow
Not to kill my father in the years gone by.'

The family must of course vacate the bank house. The directors of the Northern Bank generously allowed mother to stay on for up to six months and gave her an *ex gratia* payment equivalent to a year's salary, so enabling her to buy a house mortgage-free. On return to Wilton Park I learned of my posting to Palace Barracks, contrived by Colonel Jim Sleator. Given MOD's penchant for getting detail wrong, my posting order gave 'Calva Barracks, Holywood', a site not yet excavated in that ancient town. I had joined the Corps with five years seniority, 30 months each for my honours degree and teaching experience – the maximum possible. It was now activated. I would be gazetted Captain at 1 September 1965. And with immediate effect – that usually ominous Army phrase – my daily rate of pay was increased to 46 shillings, backdated to 1 September 1964. It was sweet compensation for the penniless months before I was commissioned.

3. *The poor bloody infantry (pbi)*

From Easter 1965 until late 1967 I was based at Palace Barracks, including seven months on tour in British Guiana (BG). I was attached first to 1st Bn The Devonshire and Dorset Regiment (1D&D) until its departure to Germany, and then to 1st Bn The Middlesex Regiment (1MX) on its arrival from Gibraltar. For courses in the Army Certificate of Education (ACE), I taught at Palace in the spring and at Thiepval Barracks in the autumn, when I was driven daily to and from Lisburn by staff car. With overseas deployment in 1966, however, education went out of fashion. I had only one four-week course in BG, for corporals seeking promotion to sergeant. Two were best friends Cpl Robinson from the Shankill Road and Cpl McLean from Dublin. Away from the Education Centres, I visited Irish soldiers on pre-release attachment to Belfast firms, many located off the Falls Road, where I drove unarmed in uniform, unthinkable several years later.

I attended as many courses as I taught. Colonel Sleator took up places allocated to his RAEC officers and regularly sent me to Wilton Park, first for the Teaching of Science course at Eton, run by College staff. Colonel Jim thought it would be good for my soul! The more comprehensible Teaching of English course included a scintillating presentation on *Ulysses* in the Mess one evening after dinner. The CO of 1MX, Lt-Col John Shipster DSO, vied with Colonel Sleator and nominated me for the two-week Regimental Accounts course at Worthy Down, where I tramped the Hampshire grainfields in perfect spring conditions in 1967. Not to be upstaged, Colonel Jim had me travel for other reasons also: I refereed the inter-Corps rugby match RAMC v REME at Aldershot and represented the Command on Army rugby business in London. Early in 1967, indeed, I was away from Palace Barracks more often than not. I sometimes flew. Although cheaper, flying on duty to Great Britain was not then reimbursed. The usual practice was to fly and then claim motor mileage allowance, with the connivance of unit paymasters. It saved time in the face of official intransigence.

Sport was an integral part of Army life. In the deceptively quiet mid-1960s, Colonel Sleator organised rugby and golf for the GOC Northern Ireland, General Sir Ian Harris. He encouraged me both as golfer and referee. For the Command's two-day autumn golf meeting in 1965 at the new Malone Golf Club, Colonel Jim stood me down from teaching at Thiepval – sport took precedence – and he and I represented RAEC in the inter-regimental foursomes. My golf and rugby were in vogue with both units. Enjoying Mess membership at nominal rate, fellow officers and I played at Royal Belfast Golf Club – promotion indeed for its former caddie. And I both refereed and played rugby in Guyana. Sport reinforced the lesson that my acceptance was through engagement other than teaching. I had first learned it on the parade ground. My being employed 'at regimental duty' involved orderly officer duty while I was a subaltern. When I mounted the Palace and Kinnegar guards, I observed faces at the windows of the Officers' Mess. The ceremony went over flawlessly, however, and never again drew an audience. I was less assured during early morning sword drill, with the RSM's sharp tongue directed at us subalterns. One was 'H' Jones, who was to be awarded a posthumous VC in the Falklands War. I was intrigued by the discrepancy between officers and men. After watching the men choose from six choices at both the roast and grill bars in the cookhouse, I found corned-beef fritters on offer in the Mess – period.

Being based in Ulster made personal life smoother. Mother and I jointly owned the family car, more feasibly after she moved in August to the Cavehill area of North Belfast beside her sister Marie. With my furniture delivered to Palace Barracks, my room became the envy of the Mess. I resumed my research. Mr Hutton of the Public Record Office transferred the Roden Papers to QUB library so that I might access them after work. In 1966, I spent my pre-embarkation leave researching in Dublin. I was there in March when Nelson's Pillar was blown up. On the advice of John McVeigh with whom I stayed, I did not wear my Regular Army tie when inspecting O'Connell Street! As to my extern student status in the Faculty of Theology, Professor Barkley decided not to divulge my absence overseas: he saw Queen's with its 'red tape' as more pedantic than TCD – he always wore his Trinity tie. As the Army paid my PhD fees, Professor John's stance was justified. I would arrive in British Guiana with much material to assimilate and seven months in which to work on it. David Hewitt received, read and forwarded all to my typist in Belfast (the widow of a Presbyterian minister). Kath Bailie had meanwhile begun a relationship with Malcolm Montgomery, a 1MX subaltern whom she was later to marry, and I with Priscilla Matthews – we had first met when Cilla was home from Clarendon School and I was staying at Wyncroft. Her father, Dr Sydney Matthews, had died ten weeks after my father's death. With Cilla at TCD, we could be together in Dublin before I flew overseas.

1MX deployed to Guyana just four months after arriving in Palace Barracks. The first hint of that move had come, typically, in a letter that I received from Captain Mike Martin RAEC, who was in BG with 1st Bn The King's Regiment (1Kings). Colonel Shipster read the letter avidly – he was notified of his unit's move only later. Caledonian Airways flew the battalion to Georgetown during the two weeks before Easter. In the 1960s, infantry units based in Northern Ireland regularly undertook short tours of BG. 1 King's, based at Ballykinler, replaced 1D&D there on that battalion's return to Palace Barracks. But it was crass stupidity, close to the 50th anniversary of the Easter Rising with its anticipated tensions, to reduce Regular infantry strength to one battalion – 1 King's, on their return to Ballykinler (with leave due for all ranks).

British Guiana/Guyana

Ironically, BG was free of civil strife during our tour there. When the colony became independent Guyana on 26 May 1966, the battalion – it was part of British Force Guiana, a full Colonel's command – became formally the guest of Forbes Burnham's government. With no internal security duties to perform, it engaged in training the Guyana Defence Force, battle and adventure training, rest and recreation, sport and social life. Battalion HQ was in Georgetown, the capital. HQ Company, under Major Mike Hayward, was stationed at Atkinson Field, an hour away, beside the airport (now Cheddi Jagan International Airport). My letters home dwelt on the monotony of our life there: the same food and company, the incessant rain (it was the rainiest season for 80 years), the tedium of long tropical nights. I made two rum-and-gingers last all evening – the clear Caribbean rum was potent stuff. The Boeing that came and went every Sunday carried most of my letters, delivered two days later. Letters posted in Ulster up to 5.00pm on Fridays – addressed to BFPO 9 – arrived on the Boeing.

On most days we had shed boots, putties and hose-tops by midday – we seldom wore shirts. My work was of the light duty variety: member of Boards of Inquiry, officer in charge of the Sergeants' Mess, paying the base's civilians, assisted by a Pay Corps corporal, and auditing the accounts of the Field Post Office staffed by a warrant officer in the Royal Engineers (Postal Services). I escaped often to the rugby pitch near Georgetown, both as player and referee, and kept fit by running – in my Army boots – around the perimeter of the airfield. I achieved a high place in the Company's annual fitness tests: scaling a wall, leaping a ditch, and firing a sub-machine gun, after a long road bash in full combat kit.

The Army Air Corps pilots often got me airborne. (We had the RAF there also: Flight 2012, the same number as Drummiller LOL.) The most memorable flight was inland to Mackenzie, centre of bauxite mining, where I refereed at a Sevens tournament. The CO and Major Nick Carter collected me on their way from Georgetown – a full complement for the Alouette. Colonel John appointed me Baggage Officer for the return to Palace Barracks, so ensuring that I would be on the last flight out of Guyana, in late October 1967. As I had flown out with the Advance Party – I am not sure why – it meant that I was among the select group who were first out and last home. Our departure marked the end of the Army's long engagement with Britain's only colony in South America. But not before the Beating of Retreat in Georgetown: 'a magnificent and memorable affair [I wrote

home] – our Band and Drums, plus mounted Police, and thous-
ands of spectators. That was followed by the Force Farewell
Cocktail Party.'

Late in the tour, I had taken part in one of our regular expeditions to the remote Kaiteur Falls. On 3 September 1966 I wrote to
Jim about the experience:

> Of the week past, a day each way was spent on a large
> ferry, along the coast and far, far up the mighty Essequibo
> river; then a day in a 3-ton lorry, travelling 100 miles
> along sandy, rutted jungle tracks; and the third on a row-
> ing boat with outboard engine going up the Potaro river –
> we had to change boats twice because of rapids, carting
> all our gear (including cartons of beer cans!) at most ½
> mile and at shortest 200 yards. Two nights were spent at
> Wineperu, where we have an Adventure Training Camp
> (about 12 men go there each week, also on the ferry); two
> at a Government-run Rest House; and two in a primitive
> hut near Kaiteur ….
>
> The Falls are 741 feet high. They are much higher than
> Niagara but not nearly as wide. The big difference for me
> was that they are set in complete isolation, surrounded by
> jungle vegetation, mountains etc as far as the eye can see –
> virgin, unspoiled, almost untouched country. At Niagara
> it is all commercialisation – souvenirs … honeymoon hotels,
> the Honeymoon Bridge, sightseeing boats etc, litter, noise,
> people. At Kaiteur it is complete peace and the entire
> view is majestic – one of power and purity.

Vesting Day for the Queen's Regiment was 1 January 1967.
Celebrations at Palace Barracks were muted. As 1MX became
4th Bn The Queen's Regiment (4 Queen's), the change was seen
as a death sentence, a foreboding soon justified. In this context I
reflected on my experience with the infantry. As orderly officer,
I had had close-up experience of 1D&D. Several officers with
whom I served became generals and brigadiers; others were
decorated for gallantry on later tours in Northern Ireland. But I
had found the unit oddly dysfunctional and its morale poor. As
for 1King's, the only trouble that 1MX had had in BG was when
the former battalion was passing through our lines before de-

parting the colony. By contrast, 1MX/4Queen's was a self-respecting, well-integrated unit, superbly led, with motivation and morale of the highest calibre. Yet of the three battalions, 4Queen's was disbanded, while the others survived.

Marriage

On my return from Guyana, Cilla and I became engaged in Dublin on Remembrance Sunday. We attended St Patrick's Cathedral, where the Royal British Legion furled after service the standards that it dare not parade publicly. Professor Torrens took us to lunch. Cilla had earlier abandoned her TCD course in Fine Arts. Her father had, inappropriately, influenced her to try for medicine and then science. Her heart was in Fine Arts but a carefree spirit and a series of romances had distracted her. We were married on 6 May 1967 in Victoria Memorial Hall in Belfast. As was Brethren custom, a layman officiated – Ross Pinkerton, a close friend of Cilla's family. Janet Cartwright, a Clarendonian friend, was chief bridesmaid and David Hewitt best man. I focused on my bride's radiant beauty and her word-perfect memory – we made our vows without pause or prompt. A Guard of Honour (one of the last in public in Belfast city centre) was found from 4 Queen's: Captains Jimmy Wild and Ron Morris, particular friends from Atkinson Field, and four sub-alterns. Colonel Shipster, who often baulked at regulations, had ironically enforced the order proscribing 'Blues'. I wore morning dress with Army personnel in Service Dress. To the consternation of our Army guests the reception at Abbeylands was 'dry', even though none of the bride's family (or mine) was teetotal. Colonel John presented us with the painting *Steady the Drums and Fifes*, which featured 'The Diehards' at Albuhera during the Peninsular War. We honeymooned in the Manor House Hotel at Killadeas and a Connemara cottage rented from an Oxford don. Our first home was a flat in Victoria Road in Holywood.

In July 1967 I was warned for posting to BAOR in September, initially to rural Detmold but changed to Dortmund in the not so rural Ruhr. Having failed to finish my thesis in time for summer graduation, I resolved to complete it before leaving Ireland. I needed four weeks, of which pre-embarkation leave provided two. The balance was supplied gratuitously by the MOD. Cilla received details of her flight. I received nothing – only wives were important, it seemed. Days before Cilla's departure date, I enquired about my flight. I had been overlooked, and could not be found a flight for a fortnight! I completed the thesis, dedicated it to my many friends in 4 Queen's, and left the final chapters for Robert Fitzpatrick to proof read. Queen's University awarded me a doctorate in theology. It was conferred *in absentia* at the winter graduation of 1967. I had earmarked the third copy of my thesis for the RCB Library: it was 'lost' by my co-supervisor, Prof J. C. Beckett, who had not once spoken with me in four years.

4. British Army of the Rhine

On arrival in Dortmund I was not Major Phil Creedy's favourite officer – he had had to teach my courses in my absence. I consoled him by buying his car, a Ford Taunus that I later sold on to John. As to accommodation, I had few qualifying points for a married quarter (MQ). But we were unexpectedly offered a city centre penthouse that officers with families had rejected. Living on the Westenhellweg we literally looked down on Germany at work, with both boardrooms and typing pools busy before we got up. I had no traffic problem at any hour – Germany was still at work when I got home. It was not so easy to evade the emissions of the five Dortmund breweries – whatever the wind direction. We were less cossetted than other Service families, living away from our self-sufficient garrison with its post office, schools, churches, NAAFI, and anglophone civilian workforce. We were more exposed, too, to reminders of the War. My Dresdner Bank in the city centre still displayed photographs of the devastation caused by Allied bombing raids. It was a strange sensation to drive in uniform through the city en route to the garrison's Remembrance Service. One evening we visited a crowded inner city pub. It froze into sullen silence at our entry. We gulped our drinks and fled, pursued by a patron who spat after us.

The Commander of Army Education Services (CAES) in 4 Division, Lt-Col John Farmiloe, paid me an early visit. I feared the worst but Major Creedy's agitation suggested otherwise. I was then summoned to Rhine Army HQ at Rheindahlen for interview with the Commander Education BAOR, Brigadier 'Ginger' Evans. Referring to my profile's stated interest in International Studies, the brigadier explained that the Junior Officers Education (JOE) scheme in 4 Division, hitherto staffed partly by lecturers from Southampton University, would henceforth be taught entirely by his RAEC officers. He offered me appointment as assistant tutor in 4 Division and I accepted. It was a plum job: courses ran from October until Easter; the tutors then spent a term at Cambridge. In the two other BAOR divisions, the tutors were peripatetic; in 4 Division the students came to tutors based in the Higher Education Centre (HEC) Germany. That its Commandant was the genial Colonel David McNeill, a Dubliner and TCD graduate, enhanced its attraction for me. The HEC might have been located anywhere in BAOR – it later moved to Mülheim; but in 1967 it was in Dortmund. I was glad not to be in Detmold. Our penthouse was safe. All I required was a new parking space in West Riding Barracks. I occupied it for almost three years.

Major 'Smudge' Clarke-Smith was the senior tutor. He asked the Christian names of our young officers at interview on arrival. One cavalry officer responded, 'Actually, sir, I am Prince Alexander of Yugoslavia'. Bad staff work had caused Smudge acute embarrassment. He and I formed a good team. Early in 1968, we were invited to lead a study day for the officers of a Canadian regiment near Soest, and were heard attentively and treated hospitably by these fine soldiers. It was the last we saw of them: Pierre Trudeau soon moved Canada's 10,000-strong NATO contingent south to the American zone. Domestically, Cilla was expecting our first child and inclined to return to Ulster for the birth, due in early March. But on 10 December 1967 I wrote to my mother that Cilla had changed her mind: 'It has not been an easy decision for her to make, but I think she has been finally influenced by her desire not to be away from me.' In the event, however, Cilla flew home in February – at eight months she did not look pregnant. Our change of plan meant that, as my JOE commitment lasted until April, I would miss our baby's birth and first weeks.

That unhappy prospect was averted when Southampton insisted belatedly on its contract being honoured and sent a lecturer to teach the final month alongside Smudge. I was therefore asked, not so much to stand aside, as to disappear! There was a second stroke of good fortune when Colonel Briggs, who managed the garrison's housing, intimated gratuitously that, as we had never complained about our penthouse, he was moving us to the 'police flats' – so-called because HQ Polizei Dortmund-Öst occupied the ground floor of the block. I therefore took possession of a newly furnished flat – and left it vacant for three months.

I drove to Rotterdam in spring sunshine, arrived in Hull on a Friday morning and set out for Stranraer. The Taunus lost its exhaust as I rounded Scotch Corner; I had it replaced in Boroughbridge. After this delay, I had to drive the 75 miles from Dumfries in as many minutes, no mean feat on the A75 of 1968, where I met the inevitable flock of sheep. At Stranraer I learned that my grandfather had died the previous day and that his funeral would be on Sunday 10 March. In its early hours Cilla began labour. Gertrude and I brought her to the Robinson Memorial Hospital in Ballymoney. Neither Roddy nor John, both medical students, heard sounds in the night. I spent time with Cilla on my way to the funeral. As the rural custom was, I paid my final respects to my grandfather in his open coffin at Tougherdale. Later I was introduced to our beautiful Karen Jane. I had not been present at her birth, but the miracle was that I was in the province at all. Stanley McElhinney and I reflected on a momentous day in the ancient words, 'The Lord gave, and the Lord has taken away; blessed be the name of the Lord.' Weeks earlier, Stanley had written me that Professor Torrens had died and that at a memorial in TCD chapel, the Archbishop of Dublin had given the blessing. It was overdue public recognition of David Torrens's life of service to Trinity College.

I reported in April to Dr Leslie Wayper, Fellow and later President of Fitzwilliam College, who advised the Ministry of Defence on officer education. (His *Mars and Minerva: A History of Army Education* would be published in 2004.) I attended Dr Wayper's tutorials and lectures that he arranged. At a lecture in the Guildhall chaired by Sir Eric Ashby, the Prime Minister of Singapore, Lee Kuan Yew, spoke against the din created by a mini-mob outside and had to stop when a missile showered glass at his feet. He pronounced all such demonstrations in spring 1968 'a synthetic revolution'. The applause he drew silenced the abuse outside and he concluded his lecture in peace. In May I met Cilla and Karen off the Liverpool ferry in our new car, a Ford Corsair 2000E, and we made for Tai Marian – my first visit to Marjorie and Gwen Williams's hospitable home in the beautiful setting of Marian Cwm in the Clwyd hills. On 8 June 1968 Karen was baptised by Derek Kidner in the Round Church, Cambridge. Before returning to Dortmund, we attended the conference of the Officers Christian Union (OCU) at Swanwick. I had joined the Cambridge OCU group, drawn mostly from officers on Services-sponsored degree courses. At the passport office in Peterborough we had Karen added to a passport – a requirement that we had overlooked until the last minute.

Dortmund at last

Our settled situation was a welcome novelty. Except in the months before our marriage, Cilla had missed continuous home life from the age of ten; I had been a peripatetic bachelor for seven years. Again, Cilla's relief at shedding her Brethren background was profound. She became, if not an uncritical, certainly a natural Anglican. We had space to think about our marriage. Cilla had a problem with my temper, whether quick or sullen. She encouraged me to overcome it (as she had seen her father do). She had difficulty too with my studious inclination. I had acknowledged – in the preface to my PhD thesis – how the first months of our marriage had been taken up (in Cilla's phrase) with 'that wretched thesis'. Further, I saw Cilla's possessive love for Karen (born when Cilla was 22) as compensation for her sense of teenage rejection, sometimes bitterly expressed. Cilla, for her part, thought me wanting in affection. I thought that transference and lack of capacity on her part to accept affection. We did not, however, discuss these attitudes or address the issues from which they derived.

I was not without some use as a father. When Karen had gastroenteritis and was not eating, Cilla fell asleep exhausted, fearing the worst. Drawing on my memory of infant illnesses, I made tomato soup and tentatively offered Karen some. She refused it. I tried again, with the same result. After many refusals, she at last took a sip, then another. I held my breath until Karen cleared the plate. She survived!

Our new police flat was a delight. Among my students who came to dinner were members of the King's Troop, Royal Horse Artillery. Father Gerry Willacy, the Garrison's Catholic chaplain, joined us for Karen's first Christmas, and at another time Barry McKnight, a young gunner who taught in the garrison Sunday school. We welcomed too the magnificent wolfhound – a regimental mascot – brought by his Irish Guards master. Capt Peter Heaney RAMC lived with Cilla when I was in Cambridge in 1969, before a MQ became available for his family. Of overseas visitors, John Wesley White, associate evangelist with Billy Graham, invited me to the platform during Crusade Europe that was relayed from Dortmund to other cities. Friends from Tyndale House stayed with us. Jan Cartwright came to help when our serene and gentle Alice Rachel was born in the British Military Hospital, Iserlohn on 26 February 1970. I was present at Rachel's birth, but only just: wearing Service Dress under the theatre gown, I was ushered out lest I faint! After Dortmund Garrison published Rachel's birth as an 'accidental occurrence', she was wisely issued with two birth certificates, one by the Consul General in Düsseldorf, the other by BAOR.

We returned to Ireland for family weddings. Both Mums came to us, as did Paul. We towed our caravan at long weekends to the charming Mosel valley and on annual leave to Mondsee in Austria. Like the rest of BAOR, we were away when the alert Red Army invaded Czechoslovakia during a long weekend. For our tax-exempt car, petrol was purchased on coupon at net cost, and holiday travel was reimbursed within West Germany and up to 50 miles into any bordering country. This was appreciable whenever we drove 500 miles to Austria and enhanced when we re-crossed the border to buy petrol. Nor did a fluctuating exchange rate affect us. The pound, worth DM11.15 when we had first arrived, fell to DM8.50 with James Callaghan's devaluation of November 1967. But pay and allowances continued to be credited at the old rate.

Major Ted Gibbons was senior tutor in my final year; we lectured sometimes to Staff College aspirants. One course I attended was at Chatham House – Cilla and I stayed in the Nuffield Club in Eaton Square. In Dortmund Garrison, I served often on Courts-Martial, normally with a Judge Advocate from UK as president of the three-member court, and for a year as secretary-treasurer of the Garrison Officers Mess. During a NATO exercise in North Germany, acting as facilitator for visiting senior officers from UK, I booked hotels, met flights and laid on transport. I had meanwhile come under RAEC encouragement, as a graduate, to transfer from short service to a Regular Commission, and discussed with staff officers at Rheindahlen a possible career path. Lt-Col D. E. Ryan, CAES 4 Division, wrote in my confidential report of March 1969 of my personal and intellectual qualities and of the favourable report by HMIs on my work. He wrote that (at 31) I was capable of a major's appointment and concluded: 'a capable officer with much potential who would be an asset to the permanent cadre of the Corps'. That potential was not to be realised. My political activity later that year ruined it. My final months of service divided equally between JOE duties and leave. We visited the Dutch tulip fields, toured the Black Forest, and bought wine on the Mosel. We left Dortmund for Portstewart in early July, parking our caravan at idyllic Marian Cwm *en route*. At 31 August 1970, I gave up my ID card, received my gratuity, and transferred to the Regular Army Reserve of Officers.

II. NORTHERN IRELAND

1. *Towards North Down*

In 1968 the province exhibited both positive and negative images. It exported twice as much as the Irish Republic, in *per capita* terms four times as much. It was a law-abiding community: no murder was recorded that year, serious crime was negligible, and the Royal Ulster Constabulary (RUC) numbered only 3000 regular officers. Ulster's two communities celebrated their tribal festivals with bands, banners and marching, while observing – as Sir Fred Catherwood wrote – the 'quiet understanding that Orange and Green should avoid provocation, should not march down each other's streets'. Negatively, the province's politics were stagnant. The Unionists were permanently in power at Stormont, the Nationalists without power or patronage. One-party rule was not democracy. Many MPs were returned unopposed – a travesty overturned by John Hume and Ian Paisley in 1969. Monopoly of power produced arrogant domination on one side, dangerous frustration on the other. In the Westminster election of 1955, Sinn Féin polled some 150,000 votes. Much of the Catholic-Nationalist community, without overt provocation, thereby gave notice that it would consider violence to overturn the *status quo*. Despite later misinformation, it would be a long time, even with voting age lowered to 18, before Sinn Féin improved on its 1955 vote. The state of the province, then, well illustrated why, in Todd Gitlin's analysis of the sixties, 'years of hope' give way to 'days of rage'.

The Protestant Churches acquiesced in stagnation. Among the few prophetic voices, the Revd Alan Flavelle lambasted fellow Presbyterian T. S. Mooney for turning a blind eye to injustice in Londonderry – the entire province paid a heavy price for that Unionist cesspool. Derry had its prophet, however, in Victor Griffin, rector of Christ Church, fearlessly outspoken in opposing corruption. Amid the violence, the rector of Agherton parish, Jim Kennedy, said in a sermon that the Ulster torment had arisen because Protestants 'did not know the heart and mind of Jesus Christ'. As a judgement on evangelical Protestantism it was apposite, in the period before David Hewitt and others challenged its mindset through ECONI – the Evangelical Contribution on Northern Ireland.

Initially, few outsiders understood how Ulster functioned. The politically correct 'sectarian' was seldom applied where it was warranted. In the 1950s, Canon Eric Barber advised a parishioner that he would secure a school principalship – he had missed out on several – only if he became a Presbyterian. Mr Hetherington took this advice and soon became a principal. Sectarianism could not obtain here as between Catholic and Protestant because the Northern Ireland government financed Catholic 'maintained schools' outside its 'state' system. For her part, Mrs Hetherington served on a local authority in North Down that used a points system when allocating houses. She was understandably angered by allegations that 'public housing policy' discriminated against Catholics. Lord Cameron's Commission – it reported in 1969 – was asked to review only six councils out of more than sixty. It found that Unionist Councils housed Catholics in substantial and proportionate numbers and that most discrimination was not between, but within, the two communities. The Woodvale Defence Association, for its part, pointed out that, for Protestants, discrimination was between those 'in the know' and those not. Again, the local government franchise, confined to ratepayers and business property holders, allegedly discriminated against Catholics. Until July 1966, four of my brothers and I could vote only in parliamentary elections. The local government franchise in fact discriminated against Protestant professionals, with marriage and home ownership delayed until our late twenties.

The Northern Ireland process of 1968-69, defying convention and devoid of commonsense, comprised the Civil Rights campaign, the People's Democracy march and Burntollet, and the coupon election that effectively ended Terence O'Neill's premiership and gave credibility to Ian Paisley. It evoked tensions that erupted in violence. In August 1969, the Army took to the streets in aid of the civil power. I found these events distressing and their interpretation in the media disturbing. My alarm deepened when I went (from Cambridge) in April 1969 to hear Bernadette Devlin's insidious maiden speech at Westminster. I wrote to Labour MPs who engaged with Ulster affairs; every one responded. I offered my analysis to *The Times*. It was declined on the incredible ground that an article on Northern Ireland 'datelined Germany' would lack credibility. And I sought Unionist nomination for the Westminster seat of North Down. I was a serving officer and not a party member. My hometown, however, gave encouragement. John Frost epitomised it when, in a postcard of characteristic brevity, he wrote, 'You do well to stand: your name and your person are held in the highest regard among us.'

I faced a daunting task. The perception that George Curry MP was unlikely to be readopted had attracted ten rival candidates, among them former Stormont MP Austin Ardill and Hubert Dunn, scion of an old, respected Holywood family. The front-runner, however, was James Kilfedder, an Old Portoran, who had been nursing North Down since losing his West Belfast seat to Gerry Fitt in 1966. I flew to Belfast to begin canvassing:

for ten days in July, for four weeks in the autumn. Cilla, five months pregnant with Rachel, was often with me. David and Margaret Hewitt were supportive: I stayed in their home and printed their address on my card. At the adoption meeting in Newtownards on 15 October 1969, I spoke from the heart and felt the packed hall respond warmly to the spirit of my speech. My impromptu replies to questions from the floor were well received. But I was up against a streetwise professional who had the good fortune to draw a later speaking slot. It did not help me that on the previous weekend soldiers had shot dead two men on Belfast's Shankill Road. Kilfedder's speech cynically exploited the tensions surrounding that event. Even so, I forced a second ballot. Kilfedder attracted 550 votes. Gratified to attract 345, I was left to wonder what I might have achieved in four months as against my four weeks of pre-release leave.

2. Life in civvy street

With the Army's door closed to me, I had to go elsewhere. In a sequel to my North Down bid, Mr F. C. Tughan CBE, one of its sponsors, invited me to apply for the post of Northern Ireland specialist at the Conservative Party's Research Department. Its Director, Brendon Sewill, interviewed me at Smith Square in January 1970, but wrote to say that the successful applicant Peter McLachlan had 'even higher qualifications'. Professor Bill Wallace at the New University of Ulster had earlier talked informally to me about teaching in his department. But in the event he brought colleagues with him from Durham and otherwise appointed only staff with university experience: one was my friend Dave Sturdy, who had taught in TCD. (Wallace never appointed a woman or an Irishman.) But grammar schools – so I thought – were different. I was delighted when the Headmaster of Belfast Royal Academy (BRA), Louis Lord, after first consulting with John Frost, interviewed me for the Head of History post. He paid my expenses from BAOR – and appointed his acting head, Winston Breen. Rashly confident of success at BRA, I had not applied elsewhere. Impulsively, while still in Belfast, I contacted the well-known girls' school, Victoria College (VCB). The Headmistress saw me next day and appointed me Head of History. More out of relief than conviction, I retreated to Dortmund.

On return to Ulster, we bought a house in Lisburn. After restrictive flat life, we gardened while our daughters amused Tara, our Airedale pup. On 27 April 1972, our handsome son Philip James was born in Laganvalley Hospital. Bishop Quin baptised Philip in Scarva church. That summer Dean John Watson warned us that Northern Ireland cars were at risk in Donegal. We were sad not to return to Carrickfin, where Joe and Bella Boyd and their talented family had first welcomed us on to their land in 1970. We towed our caravan to Ballycastle instead, parking on Danny McAllister's land and visiting Gangie Burns in Strandview Gardens.

Despite having left VCB in 1971 on appointment as Head of History in Friends School Lisburn, I was unsettled professionally. The relentless pressures of teaching, oversize classes, and the lack of 'club' facilities, were irksome to me after agreeable Army life. My teaching salary was 25 per cent below my Military Salary. I had in 1971 applied for the correlated headships of Omagh Academy and Cookstown High School but had learned that, while my Army service and PhD had guaranteed interview, success for an outsider was a different matter. Happily, I remained an insider with the Army. I lectured to junior officers in Belfast, at Thiepval, and at Ebrington Barracks and Ballykelly Airfield in county Londonderry. The Chief Education Officer at HQNI, Lt-Col Campbell Ritchie, an Ulsterman, was welcoming and I enjoyed good relations with successive JOE organisers. One was Major Fraser Morgan. Clari and he, friends from Dortmund, lived with us in 1971 until their MQ was ready. Cilla and I slept in our caravan and our girls shared with the three Morgan children.

After interview in London late in 1972, I accepted the post of Senior Lecturer in Social and Political Studies at the Royal Military Academy (RMA), Sandhurst. Formal confirmation was delayed until March 1973 – the fourth time in a decade that I had been security cleared. This delay allowed me to test the converse of my personal dilemma. Certain to be shortlisted, I applied for two headships. Portadown College considered me to be too young (I was 35), and Portora Royal School too inexperienced. After all the rejections from October 1969 (North Down) to March 1973 (Portora), I was relieved to be reaffirmed by the

Army. I visited Sandhurst and was allocated a house on Matthew Road. I was to start at the RMA on 1 July 1973, with family and furniture to follow. Two countervailing influences, however, were at work: misgivings arising from my visit to Sandhurst, and (here I anticipate) evident regret within the Church of Ireland. But without either house or job in Ulster, I saw no means of retreat – until inspiration came to me from the floor of the Friends' minibus.

3. Campbell College

An outdated *Belfast Telegraph* showed that Campbell College had advertised for a Head of History. When on impulse I telephoned, Miss McAlpine, the formidable Headmaster's secretary, accepted my call only because she thought I was the College doctor, Dr Denis Acheson. She indicated frostily that applications had closed. Thus discouraged, I applied. The Headmaster, Robin Morgan, and John Young, the outgoing departmental head, interviewed me. Both my doctorate and Service record at last worked for me. Morgan, a Scot, had served in Malaya with the Gordon Highlanders; we enjoyed a relaxed rapport. With the Sandhurst post in hand, I was in a strong position. I was able to negotiate favourable terms in point both of salary and allowances and leave of absence. This last perquisite, which Morgan honoured until he returned to Edinburgh in late 1976, did not endear me to colleagues; but I was otherwise welcomed by the Common Room. And Rona McAlpine became a good friend.

In 1973, two-thirds of Campbellians were boarders. The College worked a six-day week, with three sports afternoons including Saturday. The House system was strong with a full complement of resident staff in the boarding houses. We non-residents staffed the Duty Master roster; a Sunday on duty meant thirteen working days without a break. I settled into this engaging scenario with relief. With its superior staff-pupil ratio, Campbell offered smaller classes and more non-teaching periods than most schools. I loved its correspondence with Service life, in point of the routines and atmosphere of a resident community and with the Common Room akin to an officers' mess. Its bar operated on the same honour basis and was open every evening and from lunchtime on sports afternoons; Newcastle Brown was available on tap. Ex-Service colleagues included Peter Evans, the vice-master – he always called me 'Acheson' – Allan Bush, who had won the MC at Arnhem, and David Young, a wartime RAF pilot. Allan Bush involved me in his mock interviews for Oxbridge candidates. The Common Room's two formal dinner nights, with log fire in winter and croquet on long summer evenings, were good occasions for members and their guests.

The History department had character of it own: Robin Morgan taught some classes, Chris Gailey provided continuity and a succession of able young medievalists flair – Trevor Poots and Terry Barry briefly, and Keith Haines, who was to succeed me as departmental head and write the College's centenary history. I had joined the Common Room on the same day as a young chemist, Dr Ivan Pollock. The three PhDs on the staff – the other was Jack Nesbitt – were known popularly as Papa-doc, Captain-doc, and Pollock-doc. Ivan Pollock succeeded Sidney Moore as librarian and myself as director of VIth Form Studies. He was appointed Headmaster of Campbell College in 1986.

Examination work was an absorbing sideline. I was an examiner in A-level history with both the GCE-board of the Northern Ireland Examinations Council (NIEC) and the Oxford and Cambridge Board. Though the latter did not convene meetings of examiners, its monitoring was effective. John Burridge, NIEC's chief examiner in A-level history, became a friend and often stayed with us. Burridge's professional integrity was in marked contrast to one chief examiner who took his own A-level students discreetly through papers he had set. I was appointed chief examiner with the CSE-board of NIEC, and was privileged to identify with the creative and imaginative methods by which history was taught and examined in the secondary schools. This demanding work had its rewards but was poorly remunerated. I once interrupted my A-level marking to pay the window cleaner. On a quick calculation, I made his hourly rate three times mine.

4. 'Fairly quiet in Northern Ireland'
Soon after return to Ulster, I joined LOL 2012 in the Field at Gilford on 12 July and studied the demeanour, hands and faces of the west Down Orangemen. There were no professionals

among them – other than clergy and Capt L. P. S. Orr MP, a son of Gilford. Socially these men were from small farms and factories, shopkeepers and tradesmen. Ethnically they were descended from the planted English rather than the Ulster Scots with whom the media ignorantly lumped them. Tribally they were free of the triumphalism so often attributed to them. Their predominant emotion in the grim killing days of 1972 was fear – of what the carnage might lead to, and locally as to who would next become terrorist victims.

Out of my perceptions, I tried throughout the 1970s to interpret the Northern Ireland situation wherever opportunity presented – in the Church of Ireland, the Unionist Party, and the Army. I was much in the public eye. The *Ulster Star* reported my speech to Lisburn Unionists under the banner headline, 'The days of the Unionist Party are numbered'. In a speech to its Maze branch, I criticized the *Irish Times* for its failure to express sympathy with the family of Stormont minister John Taylor after a near-fatal gun attack. The newspaper's response was to republish its copy, and, stung by my charge of editorial bias, to devote an editorial to me under the heading 'Carry on, Captain' (7 March 1972). I gave a paper that year at a London symposium. *The Church of Ireland Gazette* published it later in two parts. My title – *Fairly Quiet in Northern Ireland* – was BBC-speak for a night when explosions and killings were merely in single figures. With subtitle 'The media and the Northern Ireland crisis', I wrote:

> An interesting, though insidious, process has clearly been at work in the Ulster situation. Its method is simple, its progress certain. The process is this: any point, true, half-true or false which is continually alleged will presently be assumed to be true and thereafter asserted as the truth.

The *Gazette*'s editor, Canon Andy Willis, saw me indebted to Marshall McLuhan. To my chagrin, I had to tell him that I had never read this distinguished Canadian.

A belated opportunity to contribute to a national newspaper came when the distinguished journalist T. E. (Peter) Utley invited me to write an article to mark the 175th anniversary of the Act of Union of 1801. It was to be published in the *Daily Telegraph* on I

January 1976. Peter Utley was unwell at the end of 1975. He had overlooked the fact that, with the print unions then in control, the paper would not be published on New Year's Day. The editor, William Deedes MP, whom I had met in London earlier, wrote to me, apologised for the oversight, and enclosed a cheque for £60.00.

As to the Army, in September 1969 I had visited a transformed Palace Barracks. Five officers now slept in my old room. Military life was no longer golf but deployment on the streets. It was light years away from 39 Brigade's exercise in June 1967, in which we had inanely 'flushed out' terrorists in the Sperrins. In Germany early in 1970, I was invited to lecture at study days in both 3 Queen's and 1KOSB, among the many Rhine Army units warned for posting to Northern Ireland. Official briefings were simplistic and inept. In trying to instil reality, I dwelt on the incipient terrorist threat. In August 1970, I visited 1 KOSB again – on the day that a petrol bomber they had shot in Belfast was buried. I found that, as I had forewarned, trouble on the streets had inculcated a new understanding of Ulster realities. In April 1971, a score of young officers reported for my study day at Girdwood Barracks. Some who had been up all night containing riots went to sleep. I brought them awake by discarding Henri IV and the politiques and initiating a lively discussion on Northern Ireland. I was next engaged to teach a week's course at Ballykinler from 9 August 1971. On that day internment was introduced, with my course an inevitable casualty.

The Ulster emergency was a godsend to Rhine Army. Some units were spared disbandment, including 2nd Bn Scots Guards whose young officers I had taught. Again, with the protracted stalemate in the Cold War, boredom was an enemy. To be diverted to internal security duties, albeit within the United Kingdom, was a relief to most BAOR units. As against that, grasp of the purpose of their mission in Northern Ireland was at best muddled during the critical early stages, the provocation of their presence to the Catholic community misunderstood, and their preparedness minimal. Effectiveness was further undermined by government's destruction of intelligence sources. The MOD film *Keeping the Peace*, much used in our courses in Dortmund, was redundant in Ulster, its principles discarded.

Soldierly reaction to misinformation and operational restriction was not always pretty: the roots of 'Bloody Sunday' are found here. That tragedy needed neither Lord Saville's inquiry nor Martin McGuinness's call for British apology – only honest recognition of inexorable realities. Derry apart, the capricious and cruel abuse of Protestant rioters in East Belfast and the chilling 'shoot to kill' policy in Catholic North Belfast, were early phenomena unreported by the media, which adopted double standards in respect of excesses, actual or alleged, by the RUC and the Army. And behaved unprofessionally with it: Colonel Campbell Ritchie, acting as liaison for HQNI with the press, shared with me his anger that some reporters who filed purported eye-witness copy had never left their hotel.

A dangerous general situation had both personal courage and tragedy as its human concomitants. I talked with two serving members of the Officers' Christian Union. One whom I met in the home of a clergyman had just completed two years as undercover in West Belfast. The other, whom I had known in the Cambridge OCU group in 1968, had come to collect the body of his brother-in-law, an officer who had been killed on the Falls Road. He was very bitter and told me that he had lost his Christian faith. It is a poignant footnote.

III. AMONG THE BISHOPS

1. The General Synod and its committees, 1970-82

Church life in the Army had been different. Garrison chapels were sparsely attended. We gladly worshipped among the committed, whether they genuflected or stood on their heads. Cilla taught Sunday school and I sometimes preached. I met the Deputy Assistant Chaplain General Rhine Area, Gervase Murphy, at a Lay Readers' course at Church House, Wüppertal – I was a guest lecturer. Gerry had played at full back for Ireland when curate of Shankill parish, Lurgan, and been one of my boyhood heroes. By 1969, however, I had been without Irish Church engagement for seven years. I discovered that the Church of Ireland was still there when I was asked to stand for its General Synod: with Scarva as my nominated parish, I was elected for Dromore diocese. In May 1970 I flew from

Düsseldorf to Belfast, borrowed John's Taunus (I had brought him spares) and reached Dublin in time for the pre-Synod service in St Patrick's Cathedral that marked the centenary of disestablishment. Lord Soper was the guest preacher.

At the Irish government's reception in Dublin Castle, Caroline Williamson asked 'What are you doing here?' I returned her question, for Caroline had in character crashed the party with fellow TCD student Colin Smith, to whom she introduced me. Colin and Caroline Smith were to become two of my closest friends. I made my maiden speech the first day of Synod on the Evangelical tradition of inner city Dublin parishes now to be grouped with St Patrick's. Bishop Armstrong took up my concern in his gracious response to the debate. When I rose to speak on the second day, Archbishop George Simms, who had learned my identity only the day before, called 'Captain Acheson' with the instant recall and inimitable courtesy that were characteristic of him. In 1971, with liturgical revision all the rage, I spoke in terms sufficiently erudite to win Bishop H. R. McAdoo's public approbation. When the Liturgical Advisory Committee (LAC) came up for re-election, Jim Getgood's proposed from the floor that my name be added. Synod agreed unanimously. The LAC at its next meeting assigned me to its Holy Communion sub-committee, chaired by Bishop McAdoo.

Friendship with Bishop John Armstrong was a welcome outcome of my first Synod meeting. He twice stayed with us in Lisburn. On one visit he spoke to the new Lisburn Cathedral branch of the Church of Ireland Men's Society of which I was the chair. We had invited Men's Society members from nearby parishes. As a Northerner resident in the Republic, Bishop John shared valuable insights with us – his visit was just after Bloody Sunday – and helped our understanding of the complexities of fraught North-South relationships at a time of tension, confusion and mistrust in Ireland.

In 1972, Synod met against the background of violence and killings in Northern Ireland. I resolved to speak as proactively and as prophetically as I knew how. My speech dwelt on the fear, alienation, and stoic resilience under terrorist assault, of the northern Protestant community. I said that it was the better able, out of long experience, to endure terrorist violence, but that it found propaganda unendurable. I highlighted the contumely directed upon Protestants, quoting Lord Monson's speech in the Lords in October 1969:

> It is not often, my Lords, in recent times, that a group of people has been so aggressively vilified as the Protestant community in Northern Ireland.

I spoke extempore, in plain terms, but with conviction and passion, and observed the evident relief of northern members of Synod. Canon Eric Barber, no mean orator, told my mother that mine was one of the two best speeches he had heard in 20 years at the General Synod. By now I had achieved some notoriety, and in the triennial election of 1972 advanced from bottom place to top in the list of lay representatives from Dromore. If there was any danger of such prominence going to my head, it was shattered by a wise and spirited woman. I had foolishly got involved in Synod debate about the stole, a sad digression from essentials at a critical time. It was scorned in Dr Norah Quin's dismissive words: 'Alan! Belfast is in flames. And all the Church can talk about is a piece of cloth!'

By 1973, I was a member of the Church Unity committee of General Synod. I had appeared on Bunny Carr's RTÉ programme with Dean Victor Griffin and J. L. B. Deane. When I accepted the Sandhurst appointment that year, reaction in the Church gave me to think again. Bishop Armstrong expressed his regret to the General Synod. The Primate and Mrs Mercy Simms invited Cilla and me to a private farewell lunch at the Palace. Barry Deane, arriving late to a Church Unity meeting, pronounced its nominees for Ballymascanlon deficient because my name was omitted, only to learn of my impending departure. It was thus that I missed the historic first meeting in 1973 of the Irish Council of Churches and the Irish Episcopal Conference, held at the Ballymascanlon Hotel in county Louth. But I was there a year later. Bishop McAdoo and I were assigned to the joint working party on the Sacraments. Its work was intensive and its meetings frequent. I hosted one of them at Campbell College. The Bishop of Down and Connor, Dr William Philbin, invited me to be chauffered with him to meetings in Dublin. We discussed the BBC's *Today* programme – we were both avid fans.

Bishop McAdoo and I were not always in accord. It showed when T. S. Mooney and I tabled a minority report. Cardinal Conway summoned me to the rostrum and I won from Archbishop Alan Buchanan this accolade: 'Boy – you can speak on your feet!' It seemed impromptu but I had anticipated being called and was well prepared. Bishop McAdoo did not speak. He said to me that it would have been unedifying to have had two Anglicans quoting Hooker at each other! The working party on the scriptures had Dean Tom Salmon and the Revd Robert England as its Church of Ireland members. Robert was not in the public eye, nor even on General Synod, but our Church wisely recognised his scholarly abilities. And given recent repudiation of its Evangelical tradition, it was significant that he and I, both in our mid-30s, should thus be paired with two eminent churchmen.

My most fascinating experiences were with the Role of the Church committee. Appointed in 1969 to advise the Archbishops on the Northern Ireland crisis, it had Bishop Gordon Perdue as chair and Canon E. P. M. Elliott as secretary. Eric Elliott once said to me that he found its work exhausting in that he was engaging with some of the Church's finest minds. They included when I joined them Bishops Arthur Butler, Robin Eames, Samuel Poyntz and George Quin; Dean Victor Griffin and Archdeacon Gordon McMullan; the Rt Hon David Bleakley, Prof Alan Browne and Senator Trevor West. (After Miss Elizabeth Coulter left to become Headmistress of Sherborne Girls' School there was no woman member.)

Meetings with public representatives in Dublin were an integral part of our work. Off the record and not reported to General Synod, their purpose was to voice Protestant concerns throughout Ireland, especially in the North. A long session with the Dáil All Party Committee concluded with dinner in Leinster House. I was a member of the deputation led by Bishop Quin to meet Mr Patrick Cooney TD, Minister for Justice. The entire committee met with the Taoiseach, Mr Jack Lynch TD, and the opposition leader, Dr Garret Fitzgerald TD.

These discussions were candid and constructive – until the night that we met with Mr Brian Lenihan TD, Minister for External Affairs, at Church of Ireland House. Whether intimidated by the venue and the number present, or by their integrity and intelligence, the minister appeared neither to understand nor to want to understand what we said to him. I tried a confrontational approach. Gordon McMullan, characteristically, was calm, courteous and conciliatory. Robin Eames, seated beside me, simply gave up. Turning his back to the minister, he said to me in audible, angry tones, 'Arthur [Butler] has buried three good men recently, and I have buried five, but this ... man has not the faintest idea what we are talking about.' As we dispersed, a kindly voice enquired where I was going. When I replied, 'Home to Portora', Dr Alan Browne insisted that I was in no fit state to drive, and took me home with him. His wise and gracious intervention in a distressing situation still warms my heart.

In the dangerous 1970s before going to Portora, I normally travelled to Dublin by train. I never wore my British Warm overcoat in Belfast and instead carried it inside out over my arm. But I wore it without fear in Dublin on the long walk from Amiens Street (later Connolly) Station to Rathmines late on winter afternoons.

The sense of being valued by the Church gave me confidence. Other than briefly as diocesan reader in Down – I was never licensed in Clogher – I held no office in parish or diocese. My patch was the General Synod. From 1979 I was Down & Dromore's under-45 lay representative on Standing Committee. I seconded its Report to General Synod in 1982. On the issues both of women's ordination and remarriage of divorced persons in church, I spoke in 1980 in favour of change – both were rejected. (I had briefly been a member of the Select Committee on Remarriage.) I continued to speak on Northern Ireland and contributed to the Church's publication, *Issues in Ireland Today* (1980). I defended the IRFU's tour of South Africa, quoting the splendid Irish forward who refused to condemn the host nation because there were 'enough bloody troubles in me own country'. My speech caused anger on the Synod platform but allowed the floor to erupt with relief. John Crookes, Dean of Armagh and a Hon Secretary of General Synod (and a former Senior player), thanked me privately and commented that, after the Primate had condemned the tour, no cleric dared express dissent.

I had a variety of other commitments also. At Bishop Quin's invitation, I was guest speaker – I was not a member – at the Down diocesan synod. I spoke at the Coleraine, Lurgan, and Clogher 'clericals' on historical and liturgical themes. Whenever I stayed at the Divinity School, Canon John Brown had me assess sermons given by his students. I wrote my first book review – of Brian Inglis's *Casement* – for the CEN, on the recommendation of Archbishop Simms. I had preaching engagements also: at a service for the East Derry deanery, in parish churches as different as Kill o' the Grange and Magherally, and at Sunday chapel at both Campbell and Portora. In one medium I was a failure. I took part in UTV's religious discussion programmes, once as the chair. I relax only in front of a live audience; the larger it is, the more relaxed I become. Faced with cameras, by contrast, I was uncomfortable, self-conscious, and ineffectual. It did not help that I was offered no training at the Church of Ireland's media facility in Dublin.

2. *The Anglican Consultative Council*

In 1980, David Bleakley completed his term as one of the Church of Ireland's two representatives – Bishop Armstrong, soon to be elected Primate, was the other – on the Anglican Consultative Council (ACC). Standing Committee voted on five nominations to succeed him, four clergy and myself. In my proudest moment as a churchman, I was appointed to the ACC for nine years – three Council meetings. The next (ACC-5) was due in September 1981. The Portora Board generously granted me two weeks' leave of absence. I told my School that the Council usually met overseas – ACC-4 had been in Kenya – and enjoyed the laughter when I disclosed that ACC5's location was Newcastle-on-Tyne. The Roman Catholic College, St Mary's, Fenham, was the venue. I was able *en route* to leave Cilla and Karen in Colwyn Bay at the start of our daughter's first term at Rydal School. The opening service was in a packed Durham Cathedral, where I proceeded alongside Archbishop Armstrong who thought he was in heaven. ACC's chair, the Sydney layman John Denton, became a personal friend. Otherwise I got to know best the members of my working party, especially Paul Reeves, the Archbishop of New Zealand, Archdeacon Yong Ping Chung of Sabah, and June Cuffley from Jamaica.

At Council, I was able to take one initiative. The Anglican-Roman Catholic International Commission (ARCIC I), of which Bishop McAdoo was co-chair, had recently completed its work. It had published Agreed Statements on ministry, authority, and the Eucharist. I believed that its successor (ARCIC II) should address the critical Reformation issue of justification, and proposed accordingly at a plenary session. My motion was passed. The Council thereupon requested ARCIC II to take up justification, and the ultimate outcome was the Commission's Agreed Statement, *Salvation and the Church* (1987). The Preface acknowledged that ARCIC II had addressed justification at the request of the ACC. My initiative received national attention. *The Times* reported it on successive days (18 & 19 Sept 1981), *The Irish Times* on 18 September. *The Church Times* quoted my speech extensively on 25 September. Dr John Stott identified the historic significance of what I had achieved: he wrote to me that Archbishop Loane had failed in 1978 to persuade the Lambeth Conference to take up justification. (Because of the historical importance of the outcome, the text of my speech at ACC-5 is given in an appendix.)

The press reported also my comment, made during ACC5's debate on inter-Church relations, that in Ireland it was the Catholic bishops, and not their people, who were 'brutal and bigoted'. As Archbishop Armstrong had spoken in the same debate, Douglas Brown interviewed us jointly for *The Church Times* and reported our comments on education, mixed marriages, and moral law as they affected relationships between the Irish Churches. *The Irish Times* had reported both of my speeches. In its columns on 24 September, Bishop Cahal Daly surmised that I might have been misquoted and called on me to 'take early steps to inform us publicly as to what precisely' I had said at Newcastle. In my response to Bishop Daly published by *The Irish Times* on 1 October 1981, I explained what I had meant by my provocative soundbite. I dwelt on marriage law in the Republic, with its denial of the civil right of divorce, and 'the cynical (as it seems to us) device of annulment, with the human suffering that these entail'. And with reference to Archbishop Armstrong's complaint that our Church was 'bled by how they operate mixed marriages', I in turn enquired:

Would Dr Daly accept that, as experienced by our Church of Ireland people, this operation is 'brutal' in its effects; and would he accept also that those so treated are inclined to see the operators as 'bigoted'?

In 1975, Archbishop Simms had asked me to represent the Church of Ireland at an Irish Forum at the University of Massachusetts. The conference had its chilling side. Armed guards were posted on every floor of the hotel in Amherst. There were no incidents, but of the paramilitaries present, several – both loyalist and republican – were assassinated in Ireland later. I spoke frequently in debate. Of delegates whom I got to know, Glenn Barr accepted my invitation to Campbell College to debate power sharing. One incident stands out in memory. Civic and church leaders in western Massachusetts attended the official reception. I talked with an Anglican bishop and accepted his expression of sympathy over the violence in Ulster. On the local television news the night before, I had witnessed serious rioting in nearby Cambridge where the bishop lived. I in turn expressed my sympathy to him over the violence there. Acutely discomfited, the bishop quickly moved away from a guest using the wrong script.

One episode still affords great joy. When he was a curate, Ken Clarke wrote to tell me that he was resigning his orders to become a Presbyterian minister. He said simply that he was disillusioned with the Church of Ireland. His letter neither posed a dilemma nor sought advice; it presented a *fait accompli*. It also provided a challenge. I loved this man and knew his worth. I had known 'Fanta' from his childhood, taught him in Holywood Crusader Class, spoken at DUCU when he was president. I had stayed with his wife Helen and him during the General Synod meeting of 1972 and been present at Ken's ordination in Magheralin church that summer. My response was clear. I determined that this outstanding priest and potential leader must not be lost to the Church of Ireland. I wrote to Ken setting out the reasons why he should revoke his decision. I learned later that my letter had been (in his words) instrumental under God in his decision to stay. Whenever today I see the Right Revd K. H. Clarke in episcopal procession, I ask myself in awe and pride, 'Is Fanta also among the Bishops?'

3. More personal

The Belfast years were richly varied in family life. In 1973, we bought a house on Castlehill Road at Knock, and after a short course at Cregagh 'Tech' Cilla started her pre-school playgroup, so making excellent use of our spacious house and secluded garden. Rachel and Philip were involved until Rachel joined Karen at Penrhyn preparatory school; Philip enrolled later in Greenwood primary school. We often roamed the attractive grounds of both the College and the nearby Stormont estate. Then in 1976 we bought Kilnacarra from Maurice Shillington. This magnificent property at Glenmachan had deterred conventional suburbia. It had a septic tank. It had no mains water. The cellar flooded and had to be constantly pumped out. Drinking water was pumped from a well, non-drinking water by an ingenious system from a dam. We loved the place. Our Airedales loved it too. Tanya had joined Tara, and they had freedom to roam at will. When we were burgled while away in Donegal, Tara led us on our precipitate return to the spot in our glen where our silver had been buried. We installed an oil-fired central heating system, employing as before in Castlehill Road Freddie and his team from west Belfast – the second time that these hard-working Catholic men had on our account risked their lives by travelling to east Belfast, such was the brutal reality of the 1970s.

Summer 1976, hot and dry, had not been the ideal time to buy Kilnacarra. Eric Dunlop of Abbey National required a guarantee that the well would not run dry. I replied that only God could provide it. Presumably he did, for we heard nothing more. Happily, the attraction of Cilla's playgroup was so strong that most parents drove the extra distance to Glenmachan. With the Airedales I roved C. S. Lewis's beloved Castlereagh hills and their extensive barley fields farmed by Will Galway, a friend from SUS days. During the royal Jubilee Year, we found the perfect spot from which to watch the lift-off for the Queen's first ever helicopter flight – she flew over our heads on her way to Hillsborough Castle from Belfast Lough. We had good neighbours and enjoyed in particular the friendship of Colonel and Mrs Ronald Greeves in nearby Altona. Cilla was sad to leave the warm-hearted Canon Herbert Frizelle in St Elizabeth's,

Dundonald. Brian Courtney welcomed us to Knocknagoney church.

We continued to widen our circle of friends and welcome guests to our home. Some were speakers whom I had invited to address the Middle Sixth. Archbishop Simms honoured the College on two such occasions, lecturing in his inimitable style on the Book of Kells. He stayed with us in Castlehill Road and on the second occasion came to lunch at Kilnacarra. When T. E. Utley lectured, his wife and he spent a weekend with us and later invited me to stay in their London flat, where John Biggs-Davison MP joined us at dinner. From Dublin, we welcomed Senator Trevor West – our children loved the way he could wiggle his ears – and Dr Kenneth Milne, a *rara avis* as a most thoughtful bachelor. Our hospitality was reciprocated. Trevor West was often my host in TCD. Dr Milne invited Cilla and me to lunch in the University Club in company with his rector John Paterson, after we had attended the Eucharist at St Bartholomew's. Guests from England included Sir Norman Anderson, Chair of the House of Laity in the Church of England's General Synod, and Dr Roger Beckwith, warden of Latimer House Oxford. Old friends from Holywood and new friends in Belfast visited as well.

Our home from home, however, was at Southpark in Foxrock. With hospitality offered by Dublin diocese to General Synod members, I was assigned in 1973 to Edward and Liz Orr. They overcame their shock on finding that I was not – had someone been winding them up? – 'a retired GP, teetotaller, and fierce Evangelical'. Their hospitable home was always open to us, and our families became close. The Orrs stayed with us both at Knock and Glenmachan.

We were close also to Bishop George and Dr Norah Quin. During the diocesan mission led by David Watson, we housed two of his team from York – a husband and wife – at the bishop's request. We were glad too to help the Quins escape the tensions of East Belfast when they went to our caravan in the Rosses. From nearby Campbell, I was able to attend the annual ecumenical luncheon hosted by the Quins at the See House each Christmas. Waiving formality and examination, Bishop Quin commissioned me as a diocesan reader in 1977.

Every summer as a family we parked at our glorious county Donegal retreat on the Boyds' land at Carrickfin. It was a joy to see our children contented with the natural and innocent pleasures of Atlantic strand, safe swimming, rock pools and dulse. With the Campbell term ending later than at our children's schools, I left Carrickfin at 5.30am on Mondays and spent fruitful days picking our strawberries and marking A-level history papers. With two willing grandmothers taking it in turns to relieve us, Cilla and I retreated each Hallowe'en to another haven at Ballyedmond Castle Hotel (now alas! a private fiefdom). We enjoyed the serene loveliness of Rostrevor and the hills around Carlingford Lough and visited Cecil and Myrtle Kerr in the Christian Renewal Centre.

Our idyllic situation did not last. When we moved to county Fermanagh in 1978, we tried unsuccessfully to find tenants for Kilnacarra. We sold privately to friends without benefit of estate agent. It was heart breaking to leave this unique and delightful property. That it had appreciated by over 60 per cent in two years did nothing to assuage our emotional loss. As the Headmaster's House was not yet ready for occupation, the Bursar offered us accommodation at either Rossfad House or with Renee Benson (retired Head of Maths at Portora) in Willoughby Place. Declining his offer, we left Kilnacarra to live in our own caravan in the School grounds. It was an inauspicious start to our life at Portora Royal School.

CHAPTER THREE

Portora Royal School

Education is an admirable thing, but it is well to remember from time to time that nothing that is worth knowing can be taught. *(Oscar Wilde)*

In his years here, Dr Acheson made significant impact. He saw the need for change, for reappraisal, for planning. Much of the impetus he gave is now bearing fruit.
(R. L. Bennett, Headmaster's Report, Portora Speech Day, 1983)

I. THE IMPORTANCE OF BEING EARNEST

1. Enniskillen Royal School

A contestant in the BBC's *Mastermind* programme offered as his special subject *The Life and Works of Samuel Beckett*. Asked 'what famous Irish school' Beckett had attended, he answered 'The Royal School, Enniskillen'. In the 17th century, James I had set aside land in the escheated counties of his Ulster Plantation to endow 'Free Schools' for the sons of the planted population. So were founded the Royal Schools in Armagh and Dungannon, Cavan and Raphoe. The fifth Free School, for Fermanagh, was located first at Castle Balfour in Lisnaskea, then in Enniskillen town, and from 1777 on Portora Hill overlooking the town. It would become known as Portora Royal School, though technically still Enniskillen Royal School. To mark the 400th anniversary of their foundation, the five schools published *The 1608 Royal Schools celebrate 400 Years of History 1608-2008*. Messages of congratulation by the Queen and the President of Ireland grace this beautifully produced book. In the Portora section, Richard Bennett has presented Portora's history over four centuries with authority and flair.

Whatever its founding purpose, Portora became during the 18th century Ireland's premier boarding school. Its Anglican ethos and unique character were attractive to families of the

Protestant Ascendancy throughout Ireland. Most of its boys entered Trinity College Dublin – itself richly endowed with Ulster land – many to become clergy of the Church of Ireland. During the 19th and 20th centuries, the Army recruited Portorans and advanced many of them to senior rank, while Guinness's brewery vied with both Church and Army as a major employer of Portorans. While Portora is famous for educating Oscar Wilde and Sam Beckett, and the hymn-writer H. F. Lyte, it boasts Old Portorans (OPs) of distinction in other fields also. Surgeon John White OP arrived in Sydney with the First Fleet in 1788. Of late 20th century Army officers: General Sir Ian Harris, General Sir Charles Jones, President of the Royal British Legion, and his son General Sir Edward Jones, Gentleman Usher of the Black Rod and Colonel Commandant of the RAEC. Sir Charles and Sir Edward Jones were the only father and son members of the Army Board in the 20th century. Sir Charles's brother, the Right Hon Edward Jones, was a judge of the Northern Ireland High Court.

In the Church in the late 20th century, three Archbishops of Dublin engaged with Portora: Alan Buchanan as Chairman of Governors, Donald Caird as chaplain, and Walton Empey as a boarder. Two Old Portorans were successively Bishops of Connor, Dr Samuel Poyntz and James Moore. Portora's symbiotic relationship with the Church of Ireland was epitomised when in 2002 Dr Michael Jackson returned from Oxford – by way of the Deanery of Cork – as Bishop of Clogher.

In the four centuries of the school's existence (to 2008), there have been twenty-four Headmasters, most of them clergy. During the 19th century, the Viceroy in Dublin appointed the Masters, as they were then styled. One grateful Master placed a portrait of the 7th Earl of Carlisle in the entrance hall at Portora – Carlisle was Viceroy under Whig-Liberal governments. When the governance of the school was, by Act of Parliament in 1891, vested in the Fermanagh Protestant Board of Education, the powers of the Portora Board of Governors, as it became customarily known, included the appointment of the Headmaster.

In the boarders' dining hall I sat facing the list of Headmasters. I had particular reason to reflect on two of my twenty-one predecessors. During one Christmas holiday, I answered the door to an American who exclaimed 'Headmaster Dunkin!' Slow in the uptake, I identified myself, only to discover that the visitor was celebrating William Dunkin (1746-63). Disappointed of a bishopric, Dunkin had been offered the Mastership of Portora. A reputable poet, he consoled himself by composing his verse on the banks of the Erne. As I said to the school, it was encouraging to think that about the year 2210 another American might turn up and exclaim 'Headmaster Acheson!'

The other Head to attract my attention was Reginald G. Burgess (1915-17). A retired solicitor in Wales who identified himself as his son asked me if I could provide information about his father. His poignant letter explained that, after his father had drowned during their summer holiday, his mother had returned to England with his sister and himself and had never talked about his father. All I knew was that, in a double tragedy, the family's French governess had also drowned. It seemed that she had got into difficulties when swimming and that the Headmaster had perished in a gallant attempt to save her. To best help Mr Burgess, I put him in touch with the Revd D. L. Graham, who had been Head of School (Head Boy) in the 1920s and Headmaster (1945-54). Douglas Graham met with Mr Burgess and told him all that he knew, including, as he put it, the Common Room gossip of his day – that the drowning had been a suicide pact. Between us, Douglas and I cannot have been much comfort to a man seeking the truth about his father; but canards are not always comforting.

As indicated earlier, the Board had interviewed me for the headship when the Revd P. H. (Val) Rogers retired in 1973, but had appointed T. G. Garrett, eleven years my senior. I was, however, fascinated by Portora and applied again when Tom Garrett was appointed Principal of RBAI in March 1978. In January, I had applied for the headship of Royal School Armagh but interviewed badly – my heart was not in it. Before applying to Portora I sussed out the situation discreetly: I did not want a second rejection. With like discretion, the Dean of Clogher, Thomas Clements, encouraged me – he had been Acting Chairman in 1973. Only two others were interviewed, one being David Robertson, a member of Portora Common Room. Headmasters of Portora were traditionally members of the Headmasters'

Conference (HMC). I was invited to its annual meeting in 1978 pending decision on my application for membership. Meanwhile, Dr Noel Galbraith a distinguished alumnus whom I knew in the Church, inducted us into the Portora scene – Cilla and I were his guests at Killyhelvin for the Regatta.

To mark my appointment to a headship I gave £25.00 to the Silver Fund of the HQ Mess of the RAEC at Eltham Palace. It was recorded in *Torch*, the Corps journal, as given 'on retirement', an error that rather missed the point.

2. *Change and decay*

Lyte's words in *Abide with me* were applicable to Portora, as I perceived it in September 1978: strangely dispirited, lacking self-belief, uncertain of its direction and, under a Labour government, faced with the imminent prospect of ceasing to be a grammar school. Boarding numbers had fallen and academic standards had deteriorated. The Secretary of HMC warned that unless I could show evidence of remedial action, Conference would suspend my membership. The Department of Education for Northern Ireland (DENI), for its part, informed me that the lower enrolment entailed the loss of three 'points', with consequent reduction in salary for three teaching staff. Again, there were obvious anomalies in the ordering of school life. The chaplain, the Revd Desmond Kingston, had Sunday duty but no part in conducting worship at daily Assembly. As for the boarding community, aside from sport and chapel, torpor took over at weekends. With too few resident staff, two excellent housemasters in Robert Hort and David Robertson were under much pressure.

The internal division of the school, moreover, was an anachronism: however viable in the 1960s, the existence of Gloucester House as a junior school on a separate site and with (mostly) its own staff, was indefensible in 1978. Much needed capital was needlessly tied up, and there was wasteful duplication of resources, under-utilisation of classrooms at Portora, and some questionable practice, as with the van that shuttled up and down bringing meals from Portora to Gloucester House. John Mills, the headmaster, and his wife Gretta gave a total commitment but reality defied both economics and commonsense.

The critical issue, however, was that non-resident Gloucester House staff were under great strain in supporting their tiny boarding community and some, including a married couple, were close to breaking point given the frequency of duty.

A new Headmaster had, then, an agenda for action. I acted immediately on urgent issues, more gradually on others. I appealed to DENI not to enforce the intended salary reductions – an easier course than having invidiously to decide whose salaries to cut. My appeal was upheld. I could not of course disclose this negotiation to colleagues. I gave the chaplain his place at Assembly: Desmond Kingston and I conducted worship on alternate mornings. With the duty problem at Gloucester House, I was able to direct some immediate relief from Portora to ease the strain and tension; but the very existence of Gloucester House needed reappraisal. For the boarding community at Portora, I created the new post of Director of Activities. In September 1978, I had walked senior boarders through the county on Sunday afternoons, but I needed a more proactive solution. Opportunity arose when Miles Hulme wrote to me. When my secretary Jean Clarke advised me where to put such 'unsolicited applications', I responded 'Not this one; I am very interested in this man.' Finding income for a new post was not easy, but the Bursar produced funds somehow and Miles became Director of Activities. I could foresee what he had to offer Portora. Miles Hulme served Portora for nearly 30 years as housemaster and Head of Geography and his wife Lisa, previously on the staff of Omagh Academy, as Head of English after my time. In 1997, at a Joyce-Beckett Award evening in Dublin, Lisa hugged me and said, 'But for you, we would have gone back to England.'

To tackle the problem of poor academic standards, I created the post of Senior Tutor and appointed R. W. L. Hort, MA (Cantab). In engaging his long underused abilities, I ensured that Robert Hort's influence would improve the school's academic performance and enhance its reputation. His enlightened policy on patterns of VIth Form study and curricular work and his introduction of a staff Summer School were invaluable initiatives. Robert Hort complemented my unobtrusively reliable deputy, W. R. Moore, an old soldier, for whom I revived the title

of First Master. Bryan Morwood MC was another ex-Service colleague.

My freedom of action generally was circumscribed in that the
Board of Governers had approved a peculiar management for
the school. It had appointed as Bursar Sam Burnside, a retired
businessman and former Mayor of Enniskillen, initially on a
part-time basis. At the time I became Headmaster, Mr
Burnside's commitment, authority and salary were all being ex-
panded. His contract (approved after my arrival) was incompat-
ible with my contract and in violation of the provisions of the
Act of 1891 that defined the Headmaster's authority and powers. Headmaster and Bursar were in effect constituted a joint
authority, reminiscent (unwittingly) of the polity upon which
Campbell College had been founded in 1894, with two headmasters, the one on the academic, the other on the 'business'
side. That dichotomy had soon proved to be flawed in concept
and disastrous in practice, and had been abandoned by
Campbell. My successor at Portora, Richard Bennett, was to dis-
card it early in his headship and resume the legal authority and
powers of the Headmaster. His background and training, however, were different from mine, as were his circumstances in
1983.

For my part, I felt that I had no alternative but to go along
with the Board's joint authority. It suited me in that I had little
interest in day-to-day administration. It worked in so far as Sam
Burnside and I enjoyed a good personal relationship: we played
golf at Murvagh and attended the weekly Rotary Club lunch.
The situation was nonetheless productive of tension. And in that
the operative axis in the school had become Hon Secretary-
Bursar, rather than Chairman-Headmaster, I was effectively on
the margin of decision taking and direction of policy. That in
turn exacerbated the traditional Portora problem – notorious
throughout its wider community – of a difficult relationship between the Board and its Headmaster.

The Fermanagh Protestant Board of Education had originally
comprised appointees of the Churches and co-opted members.
After Portora became a voluntary grammar school financed
largely from public funds, DENI appointed a third of its membership – that is, six of the eighteen governors. The respective

strengths of the Churches in the county were reflected in their representation, the Church of Ireland having most, the Methodist Church rather fewer, and the Presbyterian Church in Ireland, numerically weak in Fermanagh, the least. By tradition, the Board elected as its Chairman the Bishop of Clogher for the time being. (That tradition would be breached early in the 21st century but repaired when Dr Michael Jackson was, after an interval, elected Chairman.)

Bishop R. W. Heavener was Chairman in 1978. Before I arrived, the Board had, at Sam Burnside's prompting, discarded its specialist committees and created an executive committee chaired by its vice chairman. The Bursar, as Clerk to the Board of Governors, presented the business at both the Board's quarterly meetings and monthly meetings of the executive. Other than the clergy, few Board members were professional men. The Earl of Erne was a committed and shrewd Board member, but the Rt Hon Harry West, a former Stormont minister, had withdrawn (temporarily) from the Board in protest at its leaking of confidential information. The death in October 1978 of James Malone, a former Chief Officer of the Western Education and Library Board (WELB) made matters worse. I suggested to Bishop Heavener that he propose from the Chair the co-option of Dr R. E. Brandon, who had recently returned home on his retirement as a consultant psychiatrist in Derby. The Bishop duly proposed Dr Brandon and the Board, although taken aback by its chairman's unwonted initiative, co-opted him. Dick Brandon gave me loyal support until I left Portora. Joan and he made Cilla and me welcome in their home, Castletown Manor at Monea.

3. 'Believing in itself again'

I announced that my primary aim was 'to have this great school believing in itself again'. Communication was vital and Assembly provided a ready platform. On a January morning in 1979, after heavy snow, my reading of G. M. Hopkins's *Snow in the Suburbs* was punctuated by the late entry of boys to the Steele Hall, fresh from snowdrifts throughout Fermanagh. The solution was obvious: to move Assembly from 9.00am to 11.00am, before break. We made the change. It meant a carefree experience, free from distraction, with the entire School present. Staff marvelled that no one had thought of it sooner. I enjoyed the daily rapport with the school: we celebrated and laughed, and sometimes grieved together. I spoke extempore but kept speech and body language under control: pupils complained that I gave them no gesture to imitate and no stock phrase to parrot. I guarded my tongue too. Whereas my predecessor had talked incessantly about Campbell College, I resolved never to mention the place. This produced a tricky moment on only the third Friday of my first term, as the next day's fixtures were against Campbell. I announced at Assembly: 'All our rugby teams will be in action tomorrow against … against … one of those Belfast schools whose name escapes me.' (Tell it not in Belmont!) I learned later that Chris Welch had arrived home and said to his mother, 'The new Headmaster could not even remember what school we are playing tomorrow!' Maureen Welch reflected for a second, laughed and retorted 'Don't be silly, son! I see what the Headmaster is about.' It is always good when parents get the point.

In December, we revived the moribund VIth Form dance. Cilla and I received the boys and their partners with a glass of sherry. During my first term I had gauged the strength of sport and other traditional Portora activity. My own engagement with football was appreciated – the captain of the Portora XV was styled Captain of Football – even if Tom Elliott as master in charge regarded me warily. With soccer I encouraged Trevor Smith and his team. I had myself played soccer for Sullivan Upper – illicitly: we had had neither recognition nor support. Ironically our soccer stars played rugby for the school. I was glad to jettison the absurd grammar schools' prejudice against soccer and watch the Portora XI play midweek.

I had never before been involved with rowing and was captivated by its skills and grace. Portora hosted two events in the Irish Rowing calendar: the Erne Head of the River in March and the Portora Regatta at the end of June. The School – like the Amateur Rowing Association – was fortunate in having David Robertson's organising flair deployed in both. My favourite moments were at the boathouse during the VIII's training sessions on the Erne under Robert Northridge's inspired coaching. In the twilight of a winter evening, I resolved that the Portora VIII would return to the Henley Royal Regatta after a prolonged absence. In July 1980, accordingly, Portora resumed its place in the Princess Elizabeth Plate. To reappear at Henley out of the mists of Fermanagh was achievement in itself; to defeat Emanuel School in the first round was a well-deserved success. Nor was it any disgrace to be beaten in the 2nd round by Buckingham, Browne and Nichols High School, one of the North American schools that were then tending to dominate this prestigious event.

Portora's Cadet Corps presented a problem. It lacked adequate staffing. In July 1980, the Corps was able to attend annual camp in England only because I accompanied it on the Irish Sea crossings myself. Want of strong leadership at camp in BAOR in 1978 had landed me, months later, in a contretemps with the CO of an Irish battalion who assumed naïvety on my part as to Army procedures. Again, the liaison officer at HQNI was a plausible and arrogant individual. These local difficulties aside, I had long been convinced that the Cadet element of the Services was a waste of public funds. I had noted that at first hand at Queen's and observed it again at Campbell. That Denis Grant commanded the Campbell CCF with efficiency and style did not alter my basic thinking. I closed down the Portora Cadet Corps without provoking a riot.

Encouraging individuals to believe in themselves was part of my strategy also. Of my two Heads of School in 1979-80, Trevor Stirling was academically brilliant. A typical dayboy, he intended to go up to Queen's. In attempting to interest him in entering for a Cambridge scholarship, I offered to make him Head of School – an office traditionally reserved for boarders. Trevor was initially reluctant but agreed on one condition: that I secure for him an apprenticeship at Short Bros for the six months before he went up to Cambridge. Colonel Jim Sleator, the CBI's Regional Director, had been Guest of Honour at my first Speech Day in May 1979, and through his good offices the apprenticeship was secured. In September, I met in Cambridge with the Senior Tutor of Sidney Sussex. Trevor had asked me to raise several points with him. Mr Green responded that in order to 'get that boy' he was willing to 'bend every regulation in the book'. Trevor duly won his scholarship and obtained 5th place in the Engineering lists.

Marcus Harvey, who succeeded him, was an outstanding footballer. He had played for Ireland in the Sevens' tournament at Under-16 level and was in the senior Ulster Schools' squad for the 1979-80 season. I drove him back to Portora from Ravenhill after the first interprovincial match and decided then to appoint him Head of School. Marcus's background had been unsettled: his father had died and his mother was unable fully to support him. Generous men in the wider Portora community helped pay his fees. (We were able to raise funds for his younger brother Robert also, and with the support of Alan Reynolds, Principal of Dalriada School, he joined us at Portora.) Before appointing Marcus, I consulted senior colleagues. Some were opposed, others doubtful. Ed Rowlette, wise elder statesman, said that it would take courage to appoint Marcus, but that if I did, he would support me. In the event, Marcus Harvey brought authority and style to his office and his confidence soared. He had been only a reserve before Christmas, but afterwards played at centre for Ulster and was selected for Ireland. He played in all the schools' internationals. When he left the field injured at Twickenham, Ireland was leading. His absence was crucial to the result and England won. The assured development alike of this fine athlete and of the able academic, were among Portora's successes in a year that both had graced.

During the next years, more Portorans followed Stirling to Sidney Sussex. They included Leo McKinstry, another Head of School, and James Morrow, later two of my particular friends. The school had a vital link with the college through one of its Fellows, Old Portoran Geoffrey Switzer. The services, too, attracted many Portorans. I formed a group for potential officers and was assisted sometimes by serving officers, including my old friend John, now Lt-Col Ellams. The brothers Shaun and Chance Wilson were among those who were later commissioned in the Army. From my own experience with the RCB and the Admiralty Interview Board (detailed later), I counselled my boys not to be put off by 'English bullshit' when they went before either Board. I encouraged them to rely on characteristic Portoran traits: self-assurance, initiative, sturdy independence, manliness, pride, and instinctive respect for authority.

Three boys from Munster House were, in the same year, recommended by the Admiralty Interview Board (AIB) for commissions in the Royal Navy. Two were at Portora: Paul McAlpine, who was to carry the Queen's Sword at Dartmouth, and David Storrs, the Head of School. The third, Peter Reilly, was at Cambridge. Lists of successful AIB candidates were published in the national press, with the name of his school given after each boy's name. For security reasons this practice was not adopted for candidates from Northern Ireland. I record this triple success of my Portorans with much pride. I suspect that few schools in the United Kingdom have emulated it. I believe that no other house has matched the achievement of David Robertson's house at Portora.

I have reason to be proud of my staff appointments. For Gloucester House, requiring both an English specialist and a resident, I interviewed one applicant in the home of Douglas and Ann Graham at Lockeridge in Wiltshire, and the successful applicant, Michael Green, in Mike and Pat Sweet's home in Warwick. Michael was an excellent teacher (as Karen can testify) and effective in the boarding community. I interviewed Martin Todd in the home of the Headmaster of Cheadle Hulme, Colin Firth. I knew that Martin was right for Portora as soon as I met him. He has served the School in many capacities: Head of Biology, housemaster, senior tutor with Sixth Form and Head of Careers; and with scouts, canoeing, and a highly successful angling club. Paul Johnson has made his mark both in lead roles in musical productions and in administration. Douglas Hutton, appointed Head of the Art Department during my last year, designed the sets for plays and musicals for 25 years and donated to Portora the bust that he created at the centenary of Oscar Wilde's death. It is pleasing, too, to note the progress of excellent staff that I had inherited. Robert Northridge OP, the epitome of all that is best about Portora, deservedly became the Deputy Headmaster in 1987. Trevor Smith, whose personal professional development and CDT Department I had encouraged, is now, fittingly, Vice-Principal (Curriculum and Staff). Trevor had interviewed me as part of his degree project before I left Portora and presented me with R. S. Peters's *Ethics and Education*.

4. Girls and Masonic Boys

One means of inculcating self-belief was to follow through on enunciated policy. Before my arrival, the Board had resolved to recruit girls to Portora; but virtually no action had been taken. Gloucester House had some girls, both day and boarding, Portora only three girl boarders. With the school's traditional sources of boarding ailing and the security situation a deterrent to recovery, it was vital to recruit girls if boarding at Portora was to survive. I made it my priority. In 1979, Cilla and I visited Dean Close School in Cheltenham to view the accommodation for girl boarders. Douglas Graham, who had first recruited girls when he was Headmaster of Dean Close, arranged the visit – we stayed with Ann and him at Lockeridge – and his successor Christopher Turner welcomed us warmly.

At Portora, the girls slept in a room adjacent to the Headmaster's House, but with more girls enrolled a different arrangement was needed for 1979-80. The old wooden 'San', located at the top of the drive, was therefore adapted for the purpose. I saw this as a temporary expedient only and pressed for a more realistic and congenial solution. To adapt the Headmaster's House – part of the main building – for the girls was an obvious way forward; but the situation was delicate and produced much tension at Board meetings. In the event, Cilla and I were requested to view a house outside Portora's gates as a potential residence. (It is in the foreground of Colin Gibson's painting, *Portora Royal School*.) We turned it down as unsuitable – thereby saving the Board considerable capital outlay. From 1981, we lived at Rossfad at our own expense. The wing that we had vacated was, however, not then made available to the girls.

The selfless commitment and pastoral care given by my senior colleague Bill Barbour and his wife Ann ensured a high level of morale in the girls' boarding community. After I had appointed Bill housemaster, Ann and he shared the cramped accommodation and spartan existence of the girls at great personal inconvenience. My resignation in 1982 would afford the Board opportunity to appoint a successor whose circumstances permitted of his living in Stepaside, the house within the Portora estate that my predecessor and his family had occupied. That opportunity was taken, and the Headmaster's House at last made over to the girls. Meanwhile, we had recruited more daygirls and the entire complement of girls had become a visible and viable element in Portora's life.

The closure of the Masonic Boys' School in Dublin presented a challenge to Portora. To attract boys from Masonic would strengthen the boarding community, an opportunity to which other schools – notably Armagh Royal – were also alert. Faced with such competition, we knew that we must present our case with both professional integrity and pastoral sensitivity. The Bursar and Senior Tutor joined me on a visit to the doomed headmaster of Masonic School. The key players, however, were the mothers. With some governors and senior staff acting as hosts, we laid on a reception for them. As well as lunch and a tour of the School, presentations were made on facets of life at Portora. Skilled presentation backed Portora's inherent appeal, with the Senior Tutor giving one of the most telling; Robert Hort had also organised the event with his usual thoroughness. Given the claims of rival schools, we were gratified when most mothers chose Portora.

The boys from Masonic School settled well and justified our confidence in our capacity to integrate them into the Portora community. In the wider constituency, I established a good working relationship with the chairman of the Masonic Orphans' Welfare Committee, Mr J. F. Burns, and often met with him in his home at Belmont. As I look back now on this saga, I recall the tribute unexpectedly paid me at the end of the long day in which we had won the hearts and minds of the parents: 'Well done, Headmaster, you did not put a foot wrong all day!' That negatively couched commendation was the only affirmation I ever drew from Capt Mervyn Winslow, the Hon Secretary of the Portora Board.

II. PORTORA AND ITS WIDER COMMUNITY

1. Old Portorans

It was important to regain the confidence of Old Portorans and I knew that I had to work hard to woo this disillusioned constituency. I attended the annual dinner of the Old Portora Union

(OPU) in Dublin in January 1979, when Paddy and Jill Moss invited us to stay with them at Ballybrack. I had called on Paddy in Dublin the previous autumn – he was Chairman of Weir & Sons in Grafton Street – and Jill had been our guest at Portora in December. Their son Philip was then a boarder and his sister Helen came to Portora later. Paddy and I mistook the time of the Union's AGM that preceded dinner in the University Club and missed the generous welcome extended to me by the outgoing President, George Good, the Dean of Derry. This was an unfortunate start; but it helped that the President, Bishop Sam Poyntz, and I knew each other. At the invitation of the Warden of St Columba's, David Gibbs, I refereed next morning the annual football match between Columba's and Portora. I earned some OP points for that – even more when Portora won! My chief impression of the dinner, however, was that most Old Portorans were reserving judgement until they saw progress to match my rhetoric.

If that was true of Dublin, it was even truer of London. Michael Pierce and I shared a cabin on our way to the OPU London Branch's annual dinner in March 1979 – it was customary for the Head of School to attend. The venue was the RAC Club in Pall Mall. Some two-dozen OPs received me rather frostily. I was conscious of a weary scepticism – they found a second Headmaster from Campbell hard to stomach – and I was even mildly heckled during my speech. The saving grace was the presence of Douglas Graham whom I first met there. We agreed to meet next morning, when we discussed Portora's traditions and prospects. When Douglas and Ann were our guests at Portora later that month, Douglas addressed the school at my invitation. In October 1979, I sent him a telegram: 'On the occasion of his 70th birthday, Portora salutes one of its greatest sons, and one of its great Headmasters.' Roger Ellis, the Master of Marlborough, who was helping him celebrate, told me that this text had made Douglas's day.

Several of my initiatives helped to win over OPs in general. The most approved was the return of the VIII to Henley – made possible in part by OP financial support. The London dinner in 1980, in the Garrick Club, was very different from that of 1979 both in attendance – it had tripled – and atmosphere: it was warmly supportive. I was given a standing ovation. The occasion represented a major achievement, in that the attendance at the OPU London dinner was the envy of many English Public Schools. We had flown to London with Paddy and Jill Moss. John Jackson brought Cilla and me to his home in Buckinghamshire on Sunday – we met him before service at All Souls, Langham Place – and on the Monday, Paddy Moss took me to meet the distinguished London art dealer, Leslie Waddington, who had been his contemporary at Portora.

We engaged with OPs in Cork also. One of their most eminent, Frank Jacob, had told Douglas Graham of his initial difficulty in accepting my appointment: he had seen me as a thorn in the side of the Church of Ireland establishment! But Frank Jacob set aside his reservations and graciously invited me to lunch at Arbutus Lodge in Cork when at Hallowe'en 1978 my family stayed at Ballymaloe House Hotel. We enjoyed a good rapport to match an excellent lunch. Frank was a prime mover in the reception that Cork OPs gave for Cilla and me a year later in the Metropole Hotel – owned and managed by Old Portorans. Bishop Poyntz presided; Cilla charmed Frank Jacob with her vivacity and wit. As a social event the evening was a great success. As I said in my speech, however, Portora had no boarders from the province of Munster. In conversation later, I learned that in former times a boy and his trunk boarded the train in Cork and eventually arrived at Enniskillen railway station. The loss of that facility had been one reason for the drying-up of the supply of boarders from Cork.

Old Portorans of distinction visited the School. John Conlin, Bishop of Brandon in Manitoba, preached at Sunday chapel. The academic and author Vivian Mercier came to lunch with his wife, the novelist Eilis Dillon. They presented us with a copy of *Victorian Dublin* to which they had both contributed. Dr Denis Burkitt came to lecture on the different diet of people in Africa and – with copious slides of stools! – showed why they avoided 'western' diseases. (It was before Aids ravaged that continent.) General Sir Charles and Lady Jones stayed with us when the General was Guest of Honour at Speech Day in 1980. A telegram of good wishes to Sam Beckett in Paris was sent in the joint names of Sir Charles, avowing himself Beckett's half-section at

Portora, and of the School. In reply, this most famous Old Portoran expressed his thanks and extended good wishes to Sir Charles and Portora. His telegram, addressed to 'Headmaster Acheson', is the only contact that Sam Beckett had with his old school in more than half a century after he left Portora. Sadly his telegram cannot be traced today.

2. *Twinning with Clongowes*

Early in 1980, I received a letter from the Revd Philip Fogarty SJ, Headmaster of Clongowes Wood College in county Kildare. Fr Fogarty informed me that he and his colleagues wanted to enter a twinning relationship with a school in Northern Ireland of different tradition, and had decided to approach Portora. I placed this proposal before my Common Room and we resolved unanimously to accept the invitation from Clongowes. So began a relationship between two great schools that has found ongoing expression in worship, sport, culture and various informal ways. It was first made public at Portora Speech Day in May 1980. Fr Fogarty attended and responded to my welcome to him and the Clongowes initiative. Thereafter staff in both schools organised fixtures for football, debating, chess and other shared interests, and overnight exchange visits. Both schools had a strong rugby tradition and each an Irish Schools' player in 1980. They had in common the remarkable Father John Sullivan – an Old Portoran who had taught at Clongowes.

In point of literary fame, Clongowes had educated James Joyce as Portora had Sam Beckett. Once the relationship had evinced its viability, the two Old Boy associations, acting in concert, inaugurated the annual Joyce-Beckett Award. It is presented to the entrant from either School who has, in the judgment of the external adjudicator, shown the greatest literary ability. Seamus Heaney was the adjudicator when Fr Fogarty and I were first together at an Award ceremony, in Dublin in 1997. Although long since retired, we have maintained our personal friendship over the years. We are both gratified that the relationship that we began has continued to prove its worth to both Clongowes and Portora. For myself, I am proud to have taken sole authority for Portora in this initiative, with the support of my Common Room. Had I referred the Clongowes proposal to the Governors for decision, they would – I have reason to believe – have declined it. As it is, the twinning of Clongowes and Portora has been an integral part of the experience of two great schools for more than a quarter of a century.

3. Town and gown; cassock and county

I cultivated relationships within the local community. The Headmaster of St Michael's College, Fr Macartan McQuaid, became a personal friend. I got to know Ronnie Hill, the Principal of Enniskillen High School, in the context of the Rotary Club, where I mixed weekly with the business and professional leaders of the town. The Principal of the Collegiate School, George Young, welcomed Cilla and me publicly at an evening event there, before Portora's active recruiting of girls put relationships under strain. On two occasions, Cilla and I were guests of the Commandant of the RUC Depot in Enniskillen at a Passing-Out Parade. We were happy to share one such occasion with the Headmaster of Royal School Dungannon, Stanley Forsythe, and his wife Joan, whom I had taught in Ballyclare High. On a snowy day in January 1979, I preached in Enniskillen Methodist Church at the invitation of the minister, George Good – 'like a Methodist', according to fellow Portora governor Crawford Little. I preached in Inishmacsaint church also for Archdeacon Skuse. As I was often away on Church business, however, I turned down invitations to preach in Clogher diocese – other than St Macartin's Cathedral, which Portora boarders regularly attended.

Dean Clements invited me to preach on Remembrance Sunday 1978. I recall vividly the imposing presence of the Duke of Westminster, three months before his death, and pews full of uniformed men and women, drenched by the pouring rain in which they had marched from the War Memorial. On the same occasion in 1987, they were to be denied even that consolation when the IRA's bomb caused carnage at the Enniskillen War Memorial and left Ronnie Hill in a coma until he died in 2000. The Cathedral engaged with Portora in both our gladness and sadness. It hosted our annual Carol service, the more appropriate in that the greatly talented William McBride was Director of Music both in St Macartin's and at Portora. Through his energy and enthusiasm, and incorporating music of his own composition, William made the event an uplifting and joyous experience.

There was one very public Cathedral occasion that we could have done without: the funeral of Paul Maxwell, who had died in the explosion at Mullaghmore in county Sligo that claimed the life of the Earl Mountbatten of Burma and members of his family. Paul had been engaged for the summer as the boatboy. His was the first funeral after the atrocity. Despite their own great loss, members of the Mountbatten family attended Paul's funeral. The Dean invited me to read the lesson and I chose Rev 21: 1-7, prophetic words with power also to comfort. Paul had died on the August bank holiday in 1979. When term began a week later, we mourned him as a school family in a simple, moving service in the Steele Hall attended by Paul's family. In my address I quoted Milton's *Lycidas*, its great lament including the words, 'For Lycidas is dead, dead in his watery bier.' As on all such special occasions, I drew much strength from Desmond Kingston's calm, efficient and thoughtful ordering of our worship, whether in sorrow or in joy.

Archbishop George Simms called me on the day of Paul Maxwell's death to express his sympathy to Portora. On that terrible day (27 August 1979), eighteen British soldiers had also been murdered – at Narrow Water in county Down. These atrocities, I realised at once, affected the sensitive Dr Simms deeply. He spoke to me out of great anguish of spirit.

There was a happier, private occasion that autumn. Viola, Dowager Duchess of Westminster, had attended Paul Maxwell's funeral. Days later, she invited Cilla and me to dinner at Ely Lodge, to meet Lord and Lady Ballantrae. The Duchess confessed to me that, although he was a distant relative, she stood in awe of Lord Ballantrae, a former Governor General of New Zealand, and flattered us by saying that there was no one else in the county whom she could confidently invite to meet her formidable house guest. For my part, I had read *Beyond the Chindwin* and other books that Lord Ballantrae had written, as Brigadier Sir Bernard Fergusson, about the war in Burma, and looked forward to talking with him. On the night Cilla was instantly at ease, I a shade nervous. Lord Ballantrae asked me about

Portora's history. I began with the founder, King James I, and commented 'King James the Sixth, of course, to you, sir.' He roared with laughter and mistook me for a diplomat! The ice was broken, and the atmosphere relaxed and happy. Lord and Lady Ballantrae were clearly devoted to each other; besides their son, they and we were the Duchess's only guests.

Tragically, six weeks later in early December 1979, we learned from the BBC's Nine O'Clock News that the storms in Britain had claimed two more lives, one being Lady Ballantrae who was killed when a tree fell on the car being driven by her husband on their Scottish estate. I wrote to Lord Ballantrae to express our sympathy. It was many weeks before I received his reply, written in his own hand. He apologised and explained that his son and he had already replied to an avalanche of letters of sympathy, more than a thousand of them from New Zealand alone. He added, characteristically, that they were being sustained by their Christian faith, which they were finding to be 'literally storm-proof'.

Portora attracted many distinguished visitors. Ulster's poet of Planter tradition, John Hewitt, gave a reading in the Seale Room. John Biggs-Davison MP came to lunch with us when on a fact-finding tour of Ulster. David Robertson attracted prominent speakers to Portora Historical Society. With the VIth forms of the other three grammar schools also crammed into Portora library, the atmosphere was at once intimate and electric. During the same School year the Rt Hon J. Enoch Powell MP and Dr Garret Fitzgerald TD came there. Dr Fitzgerald and his wife Joan were dinner guests of David and Elizabeth Robertson, and stayed overnight in our house; fireside chat late in the evening was stimulating, to say the least.

Enoch Powell, for his part, declined to stay and set off at a late hour to drive, without escort, to his home in Loughbrickland. Cilla had rejected my craven thought that our children should not dine with this apparently austere politician. In private, he was nothing of the sort: relaxed, considerate, and interested in the children. When Karen asked to be excused, our guest enquired where she was going and was told 'to do my Latin homework'. Mr Powell responded 'you lucky, lucky girl!' The Duchess of Westminster and Bishop Heavener came to meet

Mr Powell before his lecture. With the privilege of proposing the vote of thanks on both occasions, I used the opportunity to acknowledge Enoch Powell's commitment to the besieged people of Ulster and Garret Fitzgerald's analytical grasp of their situation. Dr Fitzgerald's lecture lived on in public notice as his 'Portora speech'.

4. HMC and AIB

My being Headmaster of Portora opened many doors, both social and professional. I was invited to join the Tyrone Knot of the Order of the Friendly Brothers of St Patrick, and enjoyed social interaction with men prominent in the life of counties Tyrone and Fermanagh. I was a guest of the Commanding Officer NIBD at a Passing-Out Parade – not quite home ground to me, as the Depot was now at St Patrick's Barracks, Ballymena. My visit to the Regular Commissions Board, still at Westbury, was particularly gratifying for me. I took issue with senior officers over the degree of subjective influence that clearly informed the Board's proceedings, in marked contrast to the polity at the Admiralty Interview Board. My attitude did not deter the Commandant, Major-General David Houston CBE, from according me the place of honour at the formal Dinner Night during my visit. This able and affable Irishman, and a Faugh to boot, despatched me next day in his staff car to visit Biddy Scott, widow of Major-General Pat Scott, late of Rossfad.

I had regular contact with Preparatory Schools including Headford School in Kells, county Meath, when travelling to Dublin. The Headmaster, Sir Lingard Goulding, was welcoming, but we both knew that there was not much mileage for Portora among his ascendancy pupils. This was emphasised when I asked the boy beside me at lunch what Public School he would go to and was told 'Eton, of course!' I was invited to become a governor of Rockport Preparatory School at Craigavad, and stayed in the Headmaster's house after Board meetings with John and Rose Agglarge. During these years I kept up my General Synod commitments. In one speech I asked why Catholic-Nationalist support in general was withheld from the RUC when they had smashed the Protestant murder gangs in mid-Ulster. *The Impartial Reporter* made it front page news. Two headmaster colleagues affirmed me. Louis Lord commented that it was time someone had said it. Fr McQuaid that I had articulated his own thinking.

My regular platform, however, was in the Steele Hall at Portora. When asked at interview in Sydney what my hardest task as headmaster had been, I replied: 'To speak to my School with pastoral sensitivity during the years of Ulster violence.' Many pupils had family, neighbours or friends serving in the Ulster Defence Regiment and the RUC Reserve. Many uniformed personnel were killed in these years, particularly during the IRA hunger strike. On some mornings there was evident tension in the School. I tried my best at Assembly and hope to this day that I afforded some comfort and support to a brave but beleaguered community.

I took seriously membership of The Headmasters' Conference. The annual HMC meeting alternated between Oxbridge and provincial universities. I enjoyed an agreeable sequence: Exeter, Cambridge, Edinburgh, Oxford and Durham. To my delight, John Frost was honoured with a personal invitation to the Cambridge meeting in 1979. HMC was organised in regions, with its eight Irish members in the North West Division. The divisional chairman, Peter Watkinson, was the Headmaster of Rydal School. Lyn and he became personal friends and we were to see them often in Colwyn Bay when Karen and Philip boarded at Rydal, and later. I made a point of attending one divisional meeting each year, and so visited magnificent Stonyhurst. David Gibbs was our host at St Columba's in May 1979. English colleagues greatly enjoyed their extended visits to Ireland. They came to Portora in May 1982. At Peter Watkinson's suggestion, I invited Sir John Hermon, Chief Constable of the RUC, and our colleague Dr Jim Kincade, the Principal of Methodist College Belfast, to address us. They spoke respectively of the role of the police and of the influence of Ulster schools in the tragic situation then obtaining in the province. We dined at The Sheelin, with Viola, Duchess of Westminster, as the Division's guest. The Duchess had invited members for a cruise on Lough Erne the next morning.

At the reception for new HMC members at Exeter in 1978, Philip Johnston had introduced himself to me – we had a mutual friend in Bishop Brian Herd. Philip was Headmaster of Queen Elizabeth Grammar School, Blackburn. His wife Cynthia and he offered us their holiday home at Long Preston, where we enjoyed a family holiday in the Dales in summer 1979. Philip Johnston was a member of the Admiralty Interview Board (AIB), and encouraged me to visit the Board with a view to being invited to join its Headmasters' Panel. The AIB was in *HMS Sultan*, an on-shore establishment at Gosport in Hampshire. I went there in March 1979 after the OP London dinner, and stayed with the Flag Officer AIB, Rear-Admiral Waddell, in Trench House. Over a late night whisky (my host was a Scot), we discussed my joining the Board. I was later invited to join its Headmasters' Panel. (Alan Reynolds of Dalriada was its only other Irish member.) Security clearance was as usual protracted and my first Board was delayed until October 1979. It was hard work: my President was an ancient submariner who made no allowance for the rookie who was, formally, his Board's educational adviser. Somehow I survived. One headmaster colleague from the two other Boards kindly acted as my mentor.

The highlight of the week was the Trafalgar Day dinner in the capacious wardroom of *HMS Sultan*. The President introduced the three headmasters and said something distinctive about each of us. My helpful colleague had been decorated with the DSC. My own distinctiveness was opportune, if accidental: I had been born on Trafalgar Day. As this feat was announced, I was aware of a commotion at the far end of the wardroom. I learned later that it was in response to the comment of a WRNS officer, 'I didn't think that anyone was still alive who was born on Trafalgar Day!' At least she knows now.

Before dinner, I had been introduced to the Vice-Chief of the Naval Staff, Admiral Sir Anthony Morton. He asked the name of my school. I thought that he might then ask if Portora were in Mozambique. With instant recall he instead said, 'I know your Bursar, John Cartwright, a personal friend of mine'. (Captain John Cartwright RN was a former Bursar.) Admiral Waddell informed me later that the Second Sea Lord, Admiral Sir Desmond Cassidi, was delighted to learn that the Headmaster of Portora was a AIB member – his son Ruiri was an Old Portoran. Admiral Cassidi invited me to see him at the Admiralty. I suppose that his staff had scheduled 15 minutes for our meeting. Two Ulstermen, however, talked for 40 minutes 'of days that are gone, while the whole population of (Whitehall) looked on'. If looks could have killed when I emerged, I would have been dead before I reached the lift. During 1979-82, I sat on six or seven Boards. I loved the AIB's work and consider it one of the most satisfying facets of my career. Sadly, it was lost to me – like so much else – when I went to Australia. My engagement with the Royal Navy was all too short, but an honour for an old soldier.

III. ENDGAME

1. The home front

From 1945 until 1982, Portora had the good fortune to have the wives of successive Headmasters engage with its life. Ann Graham, Mary Rogers and Sheenagh Garrett made their own distinctive contributions. Cilla Acheson, though we did not then know it, would be the last Headmaster's wife to identify fully and intimately with Portora.

Cilla's involvement was exemplary: she took lunch with boarders and dayboys, got to know the domestic staff, befriended female language assistants, and was, as always, an excellent hostess. Parents from Belfast stayed in our home when their son was in the Erne hospital. The three girl boarders in 1978 had free range of our kitchen, as evinced in a photograph in *The 1608 Royal Schools*. One of Cilla's great qualities was that, like Hardy's heroine in Casterbridge, she 'thought she could perceive no great personal difference between being respected in the nether parts of [Portora], and glorified at the upper end of the social world'. At one event, a lady who had been introduced to her later told Cilla ingratiatingly that she had not known that she was the wife of the Headmaster of Portora. Cilla retorted, 'Should it make any difference?' Cilla was kind to Bert, a retired servant of the school who lived in its nether parts, and visited in hospital Mrs Judge of the domestic staff who had been injured by a terrorist bomb. Her wrath was kindled, however, when Pat, the school gardener (known in our family as 'aye, surely') dug in the spinach she had planted – he did not know what it was!

103

Although our children had settled well in Gloucester House and the Airedales were enjoying Fermanagh, especially when they escaped from the house, Cilla was deeply unhappy. She missed the fulfilment of her playgroup and the loveliness of Kilnacarra. She loathed the arrangement whereby access to the Headmaster's house was through the school office. I had seen Joan Forsythe at Dungannon Royal in control of her front door: she received visitors and acted as the link with her Headmaster-husband. But as I failed to introduce this scheme at Portora, relations between my wife and my secretary were at best strained. When Donald and Isabel Mills stayed with us early in 1979, Donald saw that Cilla's unhappiness denied me her full support and spoke to her about it. Donald was fond of Cilla and showed sensitivity, but as a former Bursar he knew the score and understood how much I needed support. The Lenten mission led by Old Portoran Cecil Kerr also challenged Cilla, and matters improved. Or so it had seemed. In September, I returned from an afternoon's trekking with Miles Hulme to find that Tara had bitten the postman, with Cilla accusing Jean Clarke of deliberately letting her out. Solomon's wisdom eluded me. With my hand forced, I took the right decision for the wrong reason. I moved Miss Clarke (who was close to retirement) to an inner office and the new post of school secretary. This change afforded my family privacy, but at a price. Some colleagues (and some spouses) who had hitherto been supportive of Cilla distanced themselves from her. Every cloud has a silver lining. Months later I appointed Caroline Armstrong as Headmaster's secretary. As with other excellent staff that I selected, Caroline (Melanophy) has served Portora loyally for over 25 years.

I was fortunate in having trusted friends in whom I could confide. Douglas Graham, Donald Mills and Robert Glover of HMC evinced sound understanding and provided wise counsel. So did Kaye Marshall and Liz Orr in Dublin, Deborah Pollock at Old Mountjoy, and Norma Caughey, with whom I stayed when visiting Rathgael House. My closest confidante, however, was Gertrude Matthews, who often stayed with us. Her perception was that I was 'fighting a war on two fronts'. On one occasion when she looked after the children and found them confused, she reassured them that I loved them deeply and explained the pressure I was under at Portora. In 1981, Gertrude conspired to get me away to England at the end of an exhausting summer term.

External disasters took their toll also. Our two cars were written off in accidents. In late September 1979, Cilla crashed into a sand lorry that careered across her main road in rural Tyrone without stopping. A second either way, the lorry would have hit the Renault 16, or the car would have gone under its well. Instead, car impacted cab, and so saved the lives of my wife, two daughters, and one of our Airedales. All were badly bruised and shaken but mercifully sustained no serious injury. The RUC brought no action against the lorry driver. During 1980, Cilla was often in Portstewart to help Gertrude nurse her mother during her final months. We drove to Londonderry where she caught the train to Coleraine. On one such journey, on 2 June, we were in head-on collision with another car and ended upside down in a field. Our powerful Audi 100 had saved us from serious injury but lost its life in the process. I was convicted of careless driving: impulsive headmasters, it seemed, were worse than unseeing lorry drivers. Reflecting now on these experiences, I recall the support given by caring people. With the first accident, John Mills was calmly reassuring when he telephoned me to Campbell College – I was there with our football teams. Caroline, realising that something was amiss when I did not return in June, took charge of our children, and Sam Burnside wisely insisted that I take the family away while we recuperated. David Hewitt acted with his wonted empathy and efficiency as our solicitor.

In 1981, Biddy Scott sold her beloved Rossfad House jointly to her tenants, John and Lois Williams, and us – Cilla and I took a 40 per cent share. The First Trust Bank, newly into the mortgage business, turned down our application despite the fact that Dr Williams, the consultant physician in the Erne Hospital, and I headed the salary league in county Fermanagh. We secured a loan through a broker in Scotland who made his living from inflated medical salaries, and abandoned it expensively when the Northern Bank, of which John Williams and I were both customers, belatedly agreed to finance us. We ignored the loan condition that we physically separate the agreed division of the house, if only because the Bank did not accept that division. Rossfad was a Georgian house with a Victorian wing and 20 acres bordering Lower Lough Erne with a private jetty. I was perhaps the only member of HMC who was driven home by his boys on water.

2. 'Change and reappraisal'

In January 1980, I presented a policy paper to the Board of Governors. Dean Clements commented that it was the first attempt in years to address strategic issues. At *HMS Sultan* earlier that month, I had invited my colleague Ron Merrett, the Headmaster of Plymouth College, to read my paper. He was fascinated to find many similarities with the situation that he had inherited – lack of vision, stagnation, and vested interests – and encouraged me to be resolute. Through the instrumentality of a friend, and without cost to the school, I had had an informal survey made by a Belfast firm of consultants. Two things were clear: major capital investment was urgently needed, and Portora would be able to raise its requisite share of capital for any project approved by DENI only through disposal of the Gloucester House site. Though this reorganisation was the *sine qua non* of my proposals, some Board members assured John Mills that the *status quo* would be maintained. I met at Rathgael House in Bangor with the Department's Senior Chief Inspector in order to clarify my authority over the Preparatory School. I failed, however, to persuade the Board to act proactively.

In another initiative, I created a Priorities Committee to research in depth the options open to Portora and to recommend to the Board a critical path. I chaired it myself and drew its personnel from every constituency in the wider school community: governors, staff, parents and Old Portorans. At my invitation, the Board nominated its Hon Secretary and Gordon Wilson as members, and also its solicitor, Rainey Hanna. I found excellent men elsewhere: John Collinson, Colin Noble, and Frank Storrs, parents of boarders from greater Belfast; Old Portorans E. I. (Teddy) Johnston and Lt-Col M. R. H. Scott, the father of a dayboy; John Burridge, a former headmaster; and Robert Hort, the Senior Tutor. These men offered a wide range of skills and experience, a willingness to place these voluntarily at Portora's disposal, and a commitment, in the case of most, to travel to Enniskillen to attend meetings. At the first meeting, I traced Portora's history and traditions and stressed the imperative need to reassess its current situation. There was value both intrinsically in the committee's deliberations and in the interaction between the Board members and my own nominees. This co-operation, however, was not to last. First Mervyn Winslow and then Gordon Wilson resigned inexplicably from the Priorities Committee.

Dr Gordon McMullan succeeded Bishop Heavener as Bishop of Clogher and became Chairman of the Portora Board in October 1980. With Chairman and Headmaster for the first time graduates of Queen's, I requested that the University be represented at Speech Day 1981 and the Vice-Chancellor in response deputed Professor and Mrs Blair to attend. Portora needed a Chairman of Dr McMullan's ability and total engagement. He evinced strength of character, firm resolution in action, and humility: he was willing to learn. I arranged for both of us to meet with Dr Jim Kincade at Methody. Dr McMullan also accompanied the Senior Tutor and me to a meeting with parents from the Belfast area. It was held in the Stormont Hotel, owned by Billy Hastings, whose daughter boarded at Portora. The Bishop shared his early impressions of the school – he was himself a Portora parent. As to the Board, Dr McMullan had made his own assessment of its fitness to govern and taken the significant decision to attend and chair meetings of the executive committee, so displacing the elected chairman. He also created a finance sub-committee of the executive. And he moved the time of Board meetings from late evening to the afternoon. In his relationship with me, the Chairman was circumspect. He knew of my proclivity to confront the Board and as Lord Erne once said to me, he had 'to carry his Board with him'. Any disappointment that I felt was tempered by my acceptance of Dr McMullan's need to be, and to be seen to be, independent. During his first year, however, I concluded that it would be in the best interests of Portora, the Chairman and myself, that I should seek a new situation. I believe that the Bishop did not fully share that conclusion, but with his knowledge I applied in May 1981 for another position in England, and later that year in Australia.

With my headship in its lame duck phase during my final year, Bishop McMullan became effectively executive chairman of the Board. He took critical decisions himself. At his initiative, the Western Education and Library Board was enlisted to advise the Board on policy matters, including a building programme at Portora and the sale of the Gloucester House site. Its Chief Officer, Michael Murphy, also assisted the Portora Board over the appointment of my successor. Throughout the long year 1982, Dr McMullan guided Portora with assurance and authority. With my co-operation he involved Richard Bennett as Headmaster-elect in the policy discussions with the Western Board. There was one false step. The Hon Secretary and Bursar, appropriating the Headmaster's authority, had earlier appointed an accountant who, undetected by them, had forged his testimonials. (They had not sought references.) Dr Kincade warned me that Portora had made a bad mistake and a former business employer offered to give evidence, if necessary in court. The Chairman, however, decided to take no action, and advised the Hon Secretary, the Bursar and myself accordingly. The School was to pay a heavy price in consequence before the employee in question departed.

Transformation of its Board was an imperative for Portora. I had earlier talked matters through with Archdeacon Skuse, an independent-minded member. The archdeacon, who was supportive of me at meetings – he was a member of the executive – deplored a situation where the Board was dominated by what he called 'the Enniskillen clique'. Change began with the new Chairman. In a reversal of its inhibiting policy that its members be Fermanagh residents, the Board invited one of my Priorities Committee, John Collinson, an accountant, to become a governor. He accepted on condition the finance sub-committee meet frequently. Its members lived locally; he had to travel from Belfast. When the commitment he sought was not forthcoming, John Collinson withdrew his acceptance of Board membership. Let down in this way by members of his Board, Bishop McMullan was obliged to recruit one of his Clogher clergy, Victor McKeon, a former accountant, to provide the expertise that the Board needed.

3. By the way, Headmaster

My own take on Board membership was that the ability and expertise so widely available in Fermanagh were not being harnessed for Portora. The responsibility to identify such potential rested with the Department of Education. It, however, was negligent of that duty in that in practice it allowed the Portora Board to select, and appointed without question those nominated to it by the Board. Both Portora and the public interest deserved better. I resolved to challenge DENI's surrendering to the Portora Board the power to select governors for the School, and did so by letter. An Assistant Secretary, Ken Clark (whom I knew only as a fellow rugby referee), invited me to meet with him at Rathgael House. He made a facetious comment as to where 'hot' letters such as mine were filed. Behind this façade, I detected anger, not so much that I had charged the Department with negligence, more that I had obliged it to take remedial action.

The sequel was instructive. Normally the Department's inspectors called at Portora when they were hungry; now I had a succession of visits at all hours. When we had discussed the weather, the attractions of Fermanagh, and the fact that education was on the whole a good thing, each inspector made to depart. But not before asking 'By the way, Headmaster, could you recommend any persons suitable for nomination to the Portora Board?' I affected to ponder deeply, then offered names from my Priorities Committee and of others equally well qualified. My nominees were presently advised to the Board of Governors as the Department's appointees. There was consternation at this 'unprecedented' action by the Department but no alternative to acquiescence. The day had been carried. The transformation of the Portora Board was assured.

I had some interest in the choice of my successor: John Burridge, Robert Hort and David Robertson were applicants. I did not believe that Robert Hort's appointment would be in either Portora's or his own interest. My confidential reference made it difficult for the Board to appoint him. Later I wrote a supportive reference for Robert Hort when he applied successfully for the Headship of the unique Brymore School in Somerset. David Robertson, for his part, withdrew when he was appointed Headmaster of The King's Hospital School in Dublin.

The strongest applicant for the Portora headship was Dr Gordon Donaldson, Vice-Principal of Wallace High School in Lisburn. His wife Joyce and he – both former pupils of Sullivan Upper – came to lunch at Rossfad. In the light of my experience at Portora, Gordon at once withdrew his application. Ironically, my successor was the only applicant whom I did not know. I came to know Richard Bennett when he was Headmaster-elect and to believe that – to return his compliment – he too would have 'significant impact' as Headmaster.

Despite her enervating ordeal late in 1982 (revealed in the next chapter), Cilla gave receptions at Rossfad for senior Portora staff and their spouses, junior staff and their families, and friends in Fermanagh and beyond. We saw Duchess Viola Westminster then for the last time. She had been a steady friend to us. She died tragically in a car accident soon afterwards. Shortly before we left for Australia, we were guests at the reception given by the Duke and Duchess of Abercorn at Baronscourt for Admiral Sir Desmond Cassidi and Dr Deborah Pollock on the occasion of their marriage. We took our leave of the unique Portora community with mixed feelings. Bishop Gordon McMullan's farewell letter thanked me for facilitating my successor's involvement in policy issues. Richard Bennett joined us for the final event of my headship – the annual Carol Service in St Macartin's. Dean Clements courteously processed before me, so that as before I occupied the place of honour in his Cathedral. For a fifth year I read, in the majestic prose of the King James's Bible, the Christmas gospel. It was, agreeably, my final public duty as Headmaster of Portora Royal School.

CHAPTER FOUR

The King's School

Lamh foisdineach an uachtar. (The motto of Sullivan Upper School. It translates as 'The gentle hand uppermost'.)

Loyalty, honesty, responsibility are not however simple virtues. I have seen too often in my life the errors that arise from so regarding them. (Sir James Darling, *Richly Rewarding: An Autobiography*, Melbourne 1978, p 169.)

I. IT'S A LONG WAY TO PARRAMATTA

1. TKS

Founded in 1831, The King's School (TKS) is the oldest Independent School in Australia. Its Headmaster had, by tradition, always been an Anglican priest, except for Denys Hake (1938-1965). His successor, Canon S. W. Kurrle, was in post when the school celebrated its sesquicentenary. The President of TKS Council is the Archbishop of Sydney. In 1981, The Most Revd M. L. Loane KBE presided, while Messrs P. T. Nicholson and Lyn Arnold as Chairman and Treasurer chaired the Council's executive committee and its finance sub-committee respectively. Mr B. J. Johnstone was Bursar and Clerk to the Council. As for other Anglican schools, the diocesan synod elected councillors, as did TKS Old Boys' Union. The Council had power to co-opt. It met monthly in St Andrew's House, the church house of Sydney diocese. It owned three schools: The King's School and King's Preparatory School, both at Gowan Brae in North Parramatta; and a second preparatory school, Tudor House, located at Moss Vale in the Southern Highlands. The King's School Foundation had its own Board, with Council oversight through nominated councillors. The Council as beneficiary of a trust had appointed another board, again including councillors, to run a 12,000-hectare grazing property, known as Futter Park, near Harden, NSW.

Some 900 boys were distributed in twelve houses. Of the eight boarding houses, four had a complement of 80, four of 64 boys. The names of the houses reflected the School's history and ethos, as with Bishop Barker and Broughton, named after 19th century Bishops of Sydney, or recalled strong Headmasters, as with Waddy and Hake. TKS adhered to its founding traditions. Its uniform was first adopted in 1866 with no substantial change since 1874. King's was one of seven in Sydney that comprised the Greater Public Schools (GPS). They engaged in competitive sports: cricket, tennis, rowing, rugby football and soccer. The Headmaster was an associate member of HMC and the School exchanged staff with English Public Schools. It enjoyed a special relationship with the oldest in England – The King's School, Canterbury, where its founder, Bishop Broughton, had been educated.

In July 1981, I received a round robin from Peter Nicholson advising that the Council had embarked on a worldwide search for a Headmaster. He requested HMC members to encourage promising men to apply. I replied that I was thinking of encouraging myself and duly received the TKS information pack. I applied after consulting two Australians who were with me at ACC-5 in September: John Denton and Maurice Betteridge, the Principal of Ridley College, Melbourne. Both knew the School's history and Betteridge had been a councillor. My referees were Bishop Heavener, Douglas Graham and Robin Morgan. References were not formally taken up. Instead, W. J. Pickard, the former Bursar, spoke to my two headmaster referees and relayed their comments to Peter Nicholson, at whose suggestion I had lunch in London with Bill Pickard and his wife Kath. The Council's invitation for interview soon followed. Anticipating that, I had asked Bill Pickard to query the plan for the appointee to stay on in Sydney – during term at Portora. The Chairman acknowledged to me later that in his planning he had considered only the interests of the School. It was a revealing comment.

Peter Nicholson pursued his own agenda. Married into an Evangelical dynasty in Sydney, he saw his TKS role as a sacred trust. For myself, he instituted a private line of inquiry involving the General Secretary of the Belfast YMCA, Michael Perrott, and an Enniskillen schoolteacher (not at Portora). This unilateral initiative by the chairman was a breach of confidence. Again, his plan for our visit was bizarre. He decided to lodge us with the Headmaster and Mrs Lorna Kurrle but neglected to tell them. Canon Kurrle objected when he found out – I had written to thank him. But worse was to come. When, late in the day, Peter Nicholson booked our hotel, he telephoned Portora instead of Rossfad. As I was not available, he left the information with a junior member of the Bursar's staff. She, fortunately, thought that it related to a family holiday and did not grasp its full import. As to travel detail, I booked and paid for our economy class flights as instructed by the Chairman and advised the cost. He responded 'that doesn't sound like much to me'. Nor was it, by his decision. In the event, Cilla and I endured a 28-hour flight. We had arrived late into Heathrow and were offered the only non-smoking seats left – in the back row of the jumbo, behind a solid smoking bloc and beside the toilets. Things worsened when we could not disembark at Muscat. This ordeal, late in an exhausting term, was undignified and depressing.

They did things differently in Melbourne. Within weeks of withdrawing his application for the headship of Portora, Dr Gordon Donaldson was short-listed for the post of Principal of Scotch College. The Chairman of the Council visited him in Lisburn. It was agreed that Gordon and Joyce would fly to Melbourne during their summer holiday. Scotch College made the arrangements: the Donaldsons flew business class with a stopover in the Shangri-la hotel in Singapore. Their comfort and convenience were the paramount consideration. Scotch College issued the mandatory Employer Nomination within days of Dr Donaldson's appointment. As I was to discover, in this regard also they did things differently in Sydney.

2. Interview and after

But much was done well in Sydney. Our visit lasted for five days, with formal interview in St Andrew's House on Monday, 30 November. A member of Council, Stephen Harrison, met us at Kingsford Smith airport, drove us to the Sheraton-Wentworth hotel, and gave us lunch later at the Bennelong restaurant at Sydney Harbour. Next day Peter Nicholson brought us to Gowan Brae where we toured the School and had lunch with the

Kurrles. At dinner in the Australian Club that evening, our hosts included Bishop D. W. B. Robinson, who was to be elected Archbishop of Sydney in 1982, and Mrs Robinson, Lloyd Waddy QC and his wife Edwina, and Stephen and Jenny Harrison. It was a relaxed occasion. Lloyd arrived late, took his place beside Cilla, and asked 'How have you found Sydney?' As rubbish was lying in the streets because of a strike, she replied 'Very smelly!' Lloyd was charmed, as were all, by Cilla's elegance and natural ease in conversation.

My first interview on 30 November was in the morning with final interview in late afternoon. I had prepared thoroughly and was relaxed. Cilla joined the Council for lunch. (We did not meet other applicants at any time.) Archbishop Loane rang later to say that Council offered me appointment as Headmaster. Peter Nicholson then read the terms and I took notes. It was agreed that Cilla and I would meet next morning with them to complete the formalities. At a social occasion that evening, Lloyd Waddy presented us with his beautifully produced sesquicentenary history *The King's School, 1831-1981*. His inscription expressed the author's hopes for the future of the 'national treasure' that had been entrusted to us.

My contract covered salary and superannuation; provision of house, car, domestic help, and entertainment allowances; flights and transport of our household effects; and an allowance towards Karen's travel from UK – at thirteen, she was resolved to remain at Rydal. Cilla and I were to visit Independent Schools in the USA during the summer of 1982, a daunting prospect from a family perspective. During lunch in the Australian Club hosted by Peter Nicholson, however, Canon Kurrle questioned this plan on the ground that I would have no standing with schools overseas. I thought this specious: I was Headmaster of Portora, a member of HMC, and Headmaster-elect of TKS. I sensed that Canon Kurrle did not want me involved before he retired. The Chairman's letters to me early in 1982 persisted with the USA plan and a visit to Parramatta also. But the Headmaster had locked horns with him – and prevailed. Whatever his motives, Stan Kurrle did us a service. The Council's plan was abandoned and our family summer protected. Abandoned also, however, was the proposal that I be salaried from September 1982, that is, for one term before I became Headmaster. My notes record that the Chairman had verbally included that offer but it did not inform my contract next day. Whatever lay behind this omission, it was unfair to Portora and to my family. Our living on at Rossfad until days before we flew to Sydney meant that removal of our furniture was delayed until the last minute. We would therefore be without our furniture at Gowan Brae for more than two months after arriving there.

Back home in freezing Fermanagh – it was one of the coldest Decembers on record – five intensive days in Sydney seemed unreal. I began to believe that I was Headmaster-elect of a great Commonwealth school only when I read it in 'Court and Social' in *The Times* for 22 December 1981. A call from the *Sydney Morning Herald* infused reality. I affirmed that I was an Irishman and added that I usually describe myself as an Ulsterman. Published on 8 December, my provincial label was interpreted as identifying me with Dr Paisley! Not only did I not learn of this libel but remained unaware of controversy also. My appointment had provoked criticism in letters to newspapers of the anti-foreigner and anti-Pom variety. The Council was obliged publicly to defend its decision. That such controversy was rife was unfortunate; that I was kept in the dark was inexcusable.

From Sydney, meanwhile, Dr A. J. Rae, Chair of the Association of Heads of the Independent Schools of Australia (AHISA), and Dr Iain Paterson, Chair of its NSW branch, sent good wishes. Tony was Headmaster of Newington College and Iain of Knox Grammar School; they remained personal friends after I had left King's. The Bursar and I corresponded about various matters including the terms of Philip's enrolment. Despite Lloyd Waddy's advocacy at Council, our Airedales were not considered family. Tara, in response, took herself off to die and Tanya thought about transfer to the Williams household. Lloyd Waddy visited London in January with Hugh Nivison, the 1981 School Captain, who talked shrewdly with me about the School as we walked on the Mall in winter sunshine. TKS personnel came to Rossfad during 1982: among them the Nicholsons and the Senior Master, Jon Wickham. With Parramatta banned to us, I had asked that the Senior Master travel to us instead – Canon Kurrle initially opposed even that request. Jon was an easy and gracious guest and we valued the opportunity of getting to know him. He related well to my senior staff and the Brandons invited him to Castletown Manor on the evening of their daughter Lorna's wedding.

Another summer visitor was London-based Anne Woodham of the Australian Consolidated Press. Her mission was to write a major feature about us for *The Bulletin*. A Belfast photographer, Stanley Matchett, accompanied her. They spent a day at Rossfad, and we gave them lunch and dinner. Anticipating publication during 1982, Anne and I agreed to avoid policy issues and that no opinion about TKS would be attributed to me. Mr Matchett came later to complete his work. He sent us his 'left overs' – nineteen 35mm and four large transparencies. In the event *The Bulletin* published a 170-word article in its 'People' feature (18 January 1983). It stated the obvious and carried one photograph: all in a day's work, it seemed.

My HMC colleagues were helpful in a variety of ways. Patrick Tobin at Prior Park provided a fascinating insight into life at TKS: he had exchanged for a year with Jon Wickham when a housemaster at Tonbridge School. Ian Jones of Bedford School, who had visited Australia with his cricketers, told me that he had found the atmosphere at King's more unrelaxed than at other Independent schools. On a tour of leading Public Schools in July, I first visited Haileybury, whence my penultimate predecessor in both headships had been appointed – Denys Hake to King's and Val Rogers to Portora. Both had served Edmonstone House, Hake from 1926 as housemaster and Rogers as assistant. David Summerscale gave me sherry in the Master's Lodge and the Senior Master lunch in the Common Room: Mr Cobb had been a colleague of Rogers and had met Hake when he visited Haileybury.

I drove on to Harrow School, where Ian Beer generously spared me time from his end-of-term schedule. At my request he talked about Harrow Services Ltd, the foundation of which he was the Managing Director. He explained also how the staff annexe to the dining hall functioned, with its club facilities for staff, their families and guests. He disclosed too that although, unlike Lancing (his previous headship), the chapel at Harrow was too small to be a school centre, the voluntary daily Eucharist was well attended. Roger Ellis at Marlborough, for his part, talked helpfully with me as we walked through his College grounds. Then at Wellington College, Dr David Newsome counselled me not to have a complex because, like himself, I had not been a housemaster. It was a pleasure to relax on a summer evening in the Master's garden with the author of *The Parting of Friends*.

Finally, I spent a weekend at Charterhouse with Peter and Sandy Attenborough, whom I had got to know when Peter was Headmaster of Sedbergh in Cumbria. They shared with me their experience in the six months since their move from a rural northern school to a leading institution in the cosmopolitan south. Peter discussed his relationship with housemasters in applying discipline, in particular the ultimate sanction of expulsion, his plan to address a weekly assembly, and the need for club facilities for resident staff and families – his Brook Hall had dining facilities for bachelors, but none for women, except on Ladies' Nights. On Sunday morning I attended the voluntary Eucharist in the chapel, with more adults than pupils present. I left Charterhouse with much to think about.

There was one omission from all that went forward so agreeably: the vital matter of our immigration. I had of course applied for permanent residence in Australia. On 28 April 1982, however, the Australian Consul in Edinburgh informed me 'that to date The King's School, Parramatta, has not lodged an Employer Nomination on your behalf'. Not in five months, that is. The Consul requested that TKS Council lodge the requisite document in Sydney with the Department of Immigration and Ethnic Affairs. It was, apparently, a long way from Parramatta to Chifley Square. The letter awaited the Chairman on his arrival in Enniskillen in May. The Consulate was difficult to reach by telephone and my secretary Caroline did well to establish contact. Peter Nicholson almost blew his opportunity. In my hearing, he took exception to speaking with a 'Ms', then suggested that the Employer Nomination was a bureaucratic intrusion. This bizarre conduct aside, Council's negligence meant that we could not visit the Consulate until August. I had originally planned to go to Edinburgh during the Easter holiday (at less expense to the Council).

Although lovely Fermanagh and the Rosses had been as heaven to us during the Portora years, we visited the Continent and England before going overseas. The Morgans in Guildford repaid our hospitality of 1971 and in Norfolk the Murphys welcomed us to Sandringham rectory. Gerry had been Guest of Honour at Portora Speech Day in 1981, when Joy and he, with daughters Geraldine and Felicity, stayed with us. Gerry baptised Rachel in Sandringham church. Rachel was intrigued that her name was entered in the register of Baptisms not many entries after that of Lady Diana Spencer. In July we camped in France and Switzerland.

3. Immigration impasse

With the paperwork from TKS at last lodged, we were invited to attend the Consulate on 25 August. Its programme consisted of interview, a film on Australia, and advice on the medical examination. In September, we attended a doctor in Irvinestown while our house guest Jon Wickham visited the graves of Australian airmen in the churchyard: they had lost their lives while flying from Castle Archdale the seaplanes that patrolled the Western Approaches during the Battle of the Atlantic. The doctor expressed his concern about Cilla's vision. Unable to identify the problem, he referred Cilla to the Belfast ophthalmologist, Charles Maguire, whom we knew – his daughters Amanda and Sara were Portora boarders. When we telephoned him, he anticipated no serious problem. During his examination, however, Charles became evidently concerned and said that he must refer Cilla to his neurological colleague, Dr Victor Patterson. He in turn admitted Cilla to the Royal Victoria Hospital (RVH) for intensive tests. It was by now late October.

To read the copious correspondence of that time is to relive the anxiety born of uncertainty. Our situation was complex: we had to relate to medical consultants and the RVH on the one hand, and to TKS Council and Australian Consulate on the other. The latter could not decide on my application for residency until it received a definitive medical report. That report was delayed until after Cilla had undergone brain scan, lumbar puncture and other tests, Dr Patterson diagnosed her condition as multiple sclerosis. On 2 November, the Consul wrote to me:

Your medical results have been considered carefully but unfortunately your wife does not meet the health requirements for migration to Australia.

I regret therefore to teel [sic] you that your application has not been approved.

The stark finality of this curt communication, eleven months after my appointment as Headmaster, was not unexpected. If the preceding weeks had been nerve-wracking, the weeks that followed were agony. The support of friends helped in enduring it, even if their advice was sombre. Peter Watkinson, having concluded that I would not now be going to Parramatta, drew my attention to the advertised post of Director of Studies at Bloxham. Lloyd Waddy, who had telephoned every Sunday throughout the autumn of uncertainty, caring, compassionate, and clear-sighted as always, now gently cautioned that if I were unable to fulfil my contract, it would *ipso facto* fail. All depended on what TKS would do. To its credit, there was resolve, clear and determined from the outset, that the Edinburgh decision must be reversed. However idiosyncratic in handling other matters, Peter Nicholson was strong and single-minded in this crisis. He never wavered either in support of us or in his mission to secure our entry to Australia. I am not aware of all the detail but I know that he gave leadership of the highest calibre in a situation of great difficulty for the school. For whatever reason, however, he consulted only the executive. Lloyd Waddy, who was not a member, was inhibited from raising the matter at Council given that I was his source of information.

Mr Doug Anthony, a TKS Old Boy, and at the time (during Malcolm Fraser's illness) the Acting Prime Minister of Australia, was kept informed. I believe that he was not asked to intervene but his sympathetic interest cannot have been without its influence. Philip Ruddock, MHR for Dundas, gave advice and encouragement. (Ironically he later became Federal Minister for Immigration under John Howard.) The crucial factor was the Council's bonding itself to indemnify the government. On 13 December 1982, the Consul wrote: 'I am pleased to inform you your [sic] application to settle in Australia has been approved.' The letter was datelined Edinburgh, its heading (for the first time) 'Australian High Commission London'. I was asked to forward passports and instructed not to finalise travel plans until I had received 'the visaed passports'. It was by now mid-December; we were to fly out on 7 January. Taking no chances with the Christmas mail, I flew to Edinburgh. It would have taken some strength to prise the 'visaed' passports from my grasp.

In the three weeks before departure, everything that had been on hold was now concluded: flights, removal of our household effects, and a tenancy agreement for Rossfad. I had requested Brian Johnstone not to settle the Qantas account – it included a short stopover in Singapore – until he had clearance from me. With time running out, his letter seeking clearance was postmarked 13 December, the same date as the Consul's letter. It gave me to wonder about communication between TKS and the Chairman's Sydney office.

We slept off some of our exhaustion in Portstewart before staying at the Royal Horseguards Hotel on the Embankment. Robbie Burns (Cilla's uncle Walter) and Beryl were also in London and gave us dinner at the Ritz. We watched the film *Gallipoli*, a timely reminder that the Anzacs had fought and died alongside the Dublin and Munster Fusiliers and many other British and Irish regiments. On 10 January, Karen returned to Rydal. We watched her walk down the platform at Euston. She did not look back. She was fourteen then and in 26 years since, has still not looked back. We enjoyed Qantas's club facilities. Peter Nicholson had waived the Council's policy that its employees fly economy class – he hardly needed to remind us – and we flew business class. I attributed his decision to the Scotch College factor (of which I had made him aware). The Chairman did not, however, see it as appropriate to meet the expenses of our two-day stopover. After many enervating months, we needed at least that. We slept throughout, even during the bus tour of Singapore! When The King's School had last brought its Headmaster from the United Kingdom 45 years before, the Hakes had travelled by ocean liner with weeks to rest and reflect, a break denied to us when most needed. Instead we kissed the ground at Sydney airport on 14 January 1983.

To look back on the final months of 1982 is to revisit their torrid uncertainty. It is also to recall Cilla's great courage and dignity.

She had not only to come to terms with the brutal reality of her multiple sclerosis but also to live life normally. This involved both final engagement with Portora (detailed in the previous chapter) and also TKS duty. Cilla met with Marjery Tobin at Prior Park in Somerset. She then joined me at Monkton Combe School – we were the guests of the Headmaster and Mrs Meredith. We met at dinner Peter and Brenda Spencer on exchange from TKS. We left early for Heathrow: Cilla flew to Belfast while I drove to Canterbury.

I had spent the previous week at the Admiralty Interview Board where Cilla had been the guest of Rear-Admiral Richard and Mrs Hill during her visit to Gosport. Two incidents remain from my final week at AIB, when I was privileged to serve on No. 1 Board. Preoccupied as I had been, I was behind with my sermon for the Sunday service at The King's School, Canterbury. In the minibus on the way to work, a young WRNS officer proferred her volume of Sir John Betjeman's poems and I was able to incorporate his moving *And is it true?* The second incident was at dinner in Trench House to honour the Headmaster of Eton, Dr Eric Anderson, who was to observe No. 1 Board next day. (We had first met when he was Headmaster of Shrewsbury.) Mrs Hill had of course placed her distinguished guest on her right at dinner, myself on her left. When I told her that I was to preach at The King's School, Dr Anderson said, 'Alan is being very modest: he means that he will be preaching in Canterbury Cathedral.'

I completed my sermon amid the winter snow, before a roaring fire in a pub off the M2. I made it to Canterbury at last, dined with the chaplain, gave an interview to *The Cantuarian*, and finally lodged in the Headmaster's House. I had a sense of unreality: I still did not know if I would be taking up appointment at TKS. But I experienced sheer joy as well. Canon Peter Pilkington and his lovely wife Helen received me in their home with warmth and love. The view from my bedroom early on Advent Sunday was awesome: the grandeur of the ancient Cathedral was enhanced by its serenity in the pristine light of a cold winter morning, the effect heightened by the deep snow all about it. I experienced a deep sense of peace and of the presence of God despite the anguish of the hour.

1. L of a difference

The hot summer of 1983 began for us, then, on 14 January. Nationally, drought was severe, and fires devoured property and claimed firefighters' lives. When Cilla and I drove to Tudor House, we found the scorched earth aspect disturbing. With March registering its hottest day ever, at over 42°C, we recalled that Sydney's first missionary thought he had 'landed on the borders of hell'. We had much to do: opening accounts, buying uniforms, adjusting to city traffic – Irish driving habits made us feel at home – and meeting colleagues. Jon and Sal Wickham gave a reception for non-residents; resident families invited us to barbeques. With the kind loan of a holiday house at Pretty Beach we escaped the inferno of Parramatta to swim in the sea and relax. I prepared addresses for the staff chapel service, the Old Boys' Union (OBU) dinner, and School Assembly. On return Philip and I enjoyed a day/night match at the Sydney Cricket Ground. Phil was thrilled to watch his hero Derek Randall. We had the privilege later of having the England captain Bob Willis in our home – his brother Dave Willis was on TKS staff. I played golf at Royal Sydney – my first ever Sunday golf outing – in company with Canon Kurrle and two councillors, Lyn Arnold and Paul Mazoudier. I gave an interview to the *Sydney Morning Herald* on the day I arrived and before term began attended my first executive meeting, where I observed the interaction of strong personalities and the Chairman's unobtrusive control. Commemoration Day, the first Saturday of term (5 February), after the OBU dinner the night before, was a dawn to dusk marathon. Charles Moore, the OBU President, guided us throughout with courtesy and thoughtfulness.

Having addressed staff and Old Boys, I spoke to the School in Futter Hall after worship. I gave a pen portrait of myself to 911 expectant boys. I told them that I had spent many happy hours cheering for my country against the Poms. When mention of Holywood evoked the anticipated reaction, I responded:

It's not the Hollywood that some of you are evidently thinking of. In Latin, Holywood is *sanctus boscus*, meaning 'sacred wood', and is pronounced, not as holly–, but as holy–wood; there is an L of a difference.

This was well received, by contrast with some of my later attempts at Irish humour.

The first normal Saturday of term was a very wet day and slid into disaster as the GPS cricket and tennis schedule, involving hundreds of boys in matches at home and away, was thrown into chaos. There was clearly bad management of a major logistical operation, breakdown in communication, confusion, frustration and loss of morale. Determined to know why, on Monday I appointed a Board of Inquiry with precise terms of reference, and required it to report and make recommendations to me by 8.15am on Thursday. Hugh Rose, an ex-Wallaby, was Board President, with Peter Philpott, the former Australian cricketer who had managed the Ashes tour of England in 1981, and the admirable School Captain Brian Tugwell, as members. Their clear, concise and comprehensive report revealed a lamentable state of affairs in a key area of school life, and pronounced it unacceptable given that rain on Saturdays in February was normal in Sydney. The Board's practical and wide-ranging recommendations were mostly accepted and implemented, with obvious improvement in management and morale. My showing determination at the outset in directing the complex and vibrant school community was noted.

Two Saturdays later (26 February), not a ball could be either bowled or served at Gowan Brae. We were marooned indoors with our guests, Jika and Marj Travers. It was a bleak 13th birthday for Rachel. Jika was the austere Headmaster of Sydney Church of England Grammar School (known as Shore).

Our domestic situation was bleak too. The shelving of the Council's original plan meant that our furniture would not arrive until March. Nobody had thought that we might need to sit down. With one exception: Lloyd Waddy arrived unannounced on Sunday evening with a vanload of furniture. The Chairman had asked Cilla to choose soft furnishings (Joyce Donaldson had done that six months before in Melbourne) and then criticised her choices. The house had no air-conditioning system and we sometimes slept downstairs in the only room with an ancient conditioner. At least we had got rid of the rat and the fleas. But then Mrs Kurrle announced that we would look after their dog while they were overseas. Cilla has always been kind to the poor but temerity of this order beggared belief. At least the dog did not suffer the fate of the peacocks. When the pair had been presented to the Kurrles, the Common Room had, without much originality, christened them 'Stan' and 'Lorna'. They patrolled the staff carpark beside the Headmaster's garden and often left their mark on the cars. That indiscretion sealed their fate. One after the other they disappeared. It was a chilling and ominous episode.

I perceived the danger that nothing would be achieved during my first year – as in the two preceding years, with 1981 given to the sesquicentenary and 1982 in farewelling the Headmaster. An entire year's programme of welcome – at TKS, in Sydney, and throughout NSW – offered diversion from primary duty. I resolved to avoid that trap: to find time to think and devise a strategy. The first priority, however, was movement. If my goal at Portora had been to have a great school believing in itself again, my goal at King's was to have a great school working for itself again. Two roles needed review. Brian Johnstone as Bursar had, like us all, his strengths and weaknesses. He was a loyal servant of the school, a man of integrity and industry, painstaking and meticulous; but he was neither a decision taker nor an effective line manager. Excellent staff like Mike McKanna, the Property Manager, often lacked direction. Jon Wickham as Senior Master was discerning, sensitive and wise. I bade him report on the myriad experiences that made up the first week of term and recommend how these might be better handled. His report (17 February) was informed by clear analysis, its recommendations by the practical bent of his mind.

Like Robert Hort at Portora, Jon Wickham quickly gained confidence in my delegating significant authority to him. It left me free to focus on policy matters. Throughout 1983 and into 1984, every hard decision that I took – and there were many such – had Wickham's unqualified support. He regularly gave me, in his phrase, 'ten out of ten'. And he extended the same measure of praise to Cilla for her ubiquitous presence throughout the school community. Staff had evident confidence in the new regime. We made the weekly Common Room meeting short and efficient – it had previously been tedious and unstructured – and sometimes dispensed with it. We revived the Education

Committee with the Senior Master as chair. He and I were also seen to act together in the matter of senior appointments, some vacant through demoting ineffective staff.

My first report to Council (25 February) ranged more widely than the usual measles and rugby football. To routine matters such as the numbers in School and the 1982 HSC results, I appended the Wickham and Rose reports both for information and as revealing the skills and organisational flair of colleagues. My own report looked to the future from three perspectives: problems requiring immediate action, matters for short-term research and report, and issues for resolution in the long term.

Within the second category, I cited Council-staff relationship, staff development, and relations with the OBU; admissions policy and liaison between TKS and the two preparatory schools; the corporate nature of the school, with particular regard to its expression in chapel; and the Headmaster's role as chief executive. These policy issues were all taken up in my first year. With matters for immediate action, I identified the lack of a middle management structure and reported that I had established a Management Committee 'to provide centralised coordination of the detail of the school's administration'. Chaired by the Senior Master, it would meet monthly, minute its proceedings, and report to me. As to the pastoral care and accommodation of families, I pressed Council to review the purpose, design and functions of the proposed new dining hall complex in order 'to provide club facilities for all residents'. During discussion, I intimated dismay at the evidence of neglect within the Gowan Brae estate. On Lloyd Waddy's proposal, Council approved $100,000 to be applied at my discretion. I at once committed $40,000 to upgrade the flat of a resident family in TKS Preparatory School, the standard of which had been scandalously inadequate. In another report, I pronounced unacceptable the lack of cottages for resident assistants in two of the eight boarding houses. Council in response authorised the building of two cottages.

Meanwhile, two unrelated issues had tested my nerve. Cam Stewart had been acting housemaster of a boarding house during 1982. He asked me if he would be appointed when a housemaster next retired. I sounded out senior colleagues, several of whom were, like himself, committed Christians. I saw the consensus against him as prejudice. I felt, however, that I could not make a commitment to Stewart without the support of his peers and told him that with regret. I was concerned for his future but need not have worried. Gordon Donaldson flew to Sydney. He had left Melbourne early and I introduced him to my Common Room at morning break. Gordon appointed Cam to a senior post in Scotch College.

The other issue was the place of the school chapel. Under OBU initiative, it had been dismantled when TKS left its founding site and been reassembled at Gowan Brae. There was strong emotional attachment to it. Many Old Boys were married in chapel. Its current use in the school was that the eight boarding houses in rotation attended the Eucharist on Sunday morning. One housemaster told me bluntly that he and 80 per cent of his boys regarded religion as 'codswallop'. His own religion was sport – I had pointedly challenged the sport-is-God culture of TKS when I preached in chapel at the staff service. That boys, especially the codswallopers, should be force-fed with the Sacrament was repugnant to me. I decided therefore that from the start of second term attendance at the weekly Eucharist would be voluntary. Worship in Futter Hall, however, remained compulsory: at Assembly for the School, and on Sunday evening for boarders.

2. Professional and personal

Entries in Who's Who in Australia 1983 and Debrett's Australia and New Zealand reflected my status as Headmaster of TKS, as did membership, financed by the Council, of the Royal Sydney Golf Club and the Australian Club. Lyn Arnold was my golfing partner, though 18 holes with him was work in a different environment – as was breakfast at the Australian Club after a meeting of his finance committee. But Lyn was helpful as well as obsessive: he insisted on meeting in full our initial expenses – in effect an Army-type disturbance allowance. We were reimbursed at last for the Singapore stopover, school uniforms and much else. I set a precedent by attending the finance committee, leaving home at 6.00am to reach its city venue. These regular sessions, like the monthly meetings of both Council and executive, were time consuming, but integral to my role.

Away from School, I met severally at lunch with Headmaster colleagues Tony Rae, Jika Travers, and Alistair Mackerras of Sydney Grammar. The annual conference of the National Council of the Independent Schools (NCIS), attended by Council members, bursars and senior staff as well as heads, was held in May. I flew to Melbourne with my colleague Rod Kefford, who was soon to take up a headship in Western Australia. Cilla joined me afterwards to visit schools in Victoria. Nigel Creese, the urbane Englishman who was Headmaster of Melbourne Grammar, involved us in lunch with his prefects and introduced the careers advisor whom he had recruited from industry. When we called on Sir James and Lady Darling, our host reflected for us on his experiences as Headmaster of Geelong Grammar. I reported to Council:

> The experience overall was of very considerable value. The progress made by the Melbourne Schools in point of Career Guidance, Development, and a computer-based Service Bureau, is most impressive and highlights our own relative backwardness in these fields

Melbourne provided an agreeable private experience. At the NCIS meeting, the Revd Dr Davis McCaughey had given the keynote address. He was an Ulsterman who had been Professor of Old Testament and Master of Ormonde College in the University of Melbourne. When he found out that I had been educated at Sullivan Upper, he summoned his wife Jean, a Sullivan Old Girl. I quickly collared Gordon Donaldson and the four of us transported ourselves to Holywood. Dr McCaughey invited me to play golf at Royal Melbourne before Cilla arrived on Monday evening. I was well beaten by a very fit septuagenarian and entertained to lunch at the club. I in turn invited the McCaugheys to dine with us at a restaurant of their choice. Characteristically, they chose one run by recent Vietnamese immigrants whom they were supporting. We were to be very thrilled that Dr McCaughey's retirement ended in 1985 when the Premier of Victoria, John Cain, recommended him to the Queen for appointment as Governor of Victoria.

The representational aspect of my office was heavy, though lightened by Cilla's being often with me. We took our place in the VIP enclosure during the visit of Prince Charles and Princess Diana: many of my boys were in the massed choir that sang for them on the Opera House steps. We were guests of the Governor of New South Wales and Lady Rowland at a musical evening and of Archbishop Donald and Mrs Robinson at Bishopscourt, where we prayed in the chapel before dinner. I was Guest of Honour at the annual dinner-dance of the British Public Schools Association. At the Annual Ball at All Saints Bathurst, the debutantes were formally presented to me: a charming event in the best traditions of the country schools. I preached for Canon Peter Loane at All Saints, Parramatta, at Sunday chapel at Frensham School, Mittagong, on the invitation of the Headmistress, Cynthia Parker, and at Sunday chapel in Tudor House – as I did every term. Under the title *Irish Mists*, I lectured on the Northern Ireland situation at the Dean of Sydney's monthly luncheon club. Lodge The King's School invited me to dine – the only Masonic occasion in which I have ever participated – as did Old Boy members of the Union Club in Sydney, including Sir Marcus Loane and Sir George Halliday.

Most of these engagements involved an address, whether speech, sermon or lecture: I recorded 25 during the three terms of 1983, or two major speaking engagements every three weeks. I include important occasions at Assembly, but not shorter talks given there or at staff meetings, parents' evenings and other routine functions. Happily, there were experiences where speeches were not required. I rowed on the Colo river when visiting the TKS Prep School camp, wine-tasted with Jon Wickham during our visit to the Cadet Corps camp in the Hunter valley, and flew by light aircraft to a remote location to observe boys engaged in adventure activities.

Our engagement with the TKS community was constant. We took lunch with the Common Room twice a week. The boarding houses in rotation invited the family to dinner each week in first term, the day houses to parents' receptions. Cilla gave lunch to School visitors and evening receptions for members of Council and Common Room. We welcomed boys from Forms 1 and 2 in our home on their birthdays. GPS sports duty absorbed many hours on Saturdays. We were guests on the Women's Auxiliary harbour cruise, at the City-Country reception of the OBU during the Easter Show, and at the annual dinner of the OBU rugby club. At least on such occasions we could sleep in our own beds. We were often away from home, when Sal Wickham supervised Rachel and Philip. They had Elsa for company, our newly acquired Airedale. We attended OBU regional meetings at Dubbo, flown there by my colleague Jim Ward in his light aircraft, at Newcastle, and at Toowoomba in Queensland. We went to Futter Park for a three-day visit.

Professional duty made calls on our time too. We had attended our first AHISA branch event at Trinity Grammar, where we sat at dinner with James and Shirley Mills – Jim was Chairman of Council at Trinity. The national conference was held in Brisbane. After Cilla arrived, John Day of Stockport School gave a dinner party for the Lewises of Geelong Grammar, the Donaldsons and us. At Tony Rae's invitation, I gave a short paper – *First Impressions*. I quoted the visiting HMC Chairman who had said at an earlier conference that Australian Heads were all excellent people, and might be effective also if they had not so many meetings to attend. I was glad to enjoy rapport with Max Howell, our Brisbane host and the AHISA Chair-elect, and to talk again with Sir James Darling on the fringe of things.

We had ample opportunity to relax away from TKS. Frank and Beatrice Watts invited us to their home at Carlingford – Gwen and Marjorie Williams had told them about us. They were an interesting couple: Frank had worked for the ABC and Beatrice with Sir Brian Hone at Melbourne Grammar. One of our happiest outings was to the *St Matthew Passion* in the concert hall of the Sydney Opera House as guests of Jonathan Persse. As we dined on the terrace, *Canberra* slipped her moorings and sailed majestically past. Colin Tunbridge and I had lost contact: he visited us at Gowan Brae and invited us to stay with Dorothy and him in Canberra, where Colin was rector of Christ Church, Hawker. In this May holiday also we were guests of Geoff and Janet Ashton at Markdale, where we enjoyed their charming home and beautiful garden. I had dismissed the school with *The Lake Isle of Inisfree* and on return replaced Yeats with Dame Mary Gilmore, whose poetry we had first read on a plinth at Pejar. On other holiday outings we stayed in the hospitable homes of TKS parents John and Bev Allen and Bill and Dimmity Davy. John

Allen, a grazier like so many Old Boys, gave us a tour of his Berridale property. It seemed as extensive as Fermanagh.

In the August holiday, when Karen was with us, we were guests at Cassilis station of another Old Boy, Ellick Busby. We knew of him too through the Williams sisters, and had had early experience of his kindness when he left a leg of lamb in our porch on his way to Sydney. Our hilarious stay with Ellick, a bachelor of singular idiosyncracy, preceded that with David and Min Montgomery on their Strangford property. Both of well-known county Down families, and TKS parents, they knew that we needed a break in seclusion and looked after us with great thoughtfulness. By then, not only had the drought broken; perversely the land was under water. But for the loan of David's 4-wheel drive, I would have had a problem getting Philip to hospital in Moree where he was detained overnight. Surgery, however, was not then necessary. Our family doctor, Dr Neville York, removed Phil's appendix later, with his wife Jean as his anesthetist.

Among Irish visitors to Gowan Brae were Sheila Sleator, the widow of Colonel Jim, and Derek Shaw from Gilford who had business interests in Australia. James Morrow arrived from Enniskillen in December. I had arranged for him to assist in Tudor House for six months before he went up to Cambridge. James spent part of the Christmas vacation with us. A visitor from within Sydney was Kerry Packer. At a luncheon given to thank him for his benefaction to TKS, he and I had hit it off so well that the great man thought to enrol his son James. While the Packers were being shown the School, the chauffeur told me that James took these decisions himself and that he was averse to TKS. He was right; we heard nothing further.

3. Policy and style

As 1983 progressed, policy changes were implemented. I addressed the critical area of admissions by creating the post of Registrar and appointing Hugh Rose. We thus brought the School's annual intake under control. In practice, the two Preparatory School Heads had enjoyed autonomy, as had the deputy head at TKS: established criteria and consultation had been absent. As it was, the 1984 intake would be too large, with unacceptable class sizes of 30-plus – the consequence of commitments made at too many reception points. Admissions apart, the general lack of coordination disturbed me. Some housemasters had never met Bob Darke who supplied them with boys from Tudor House. This absurdity was now rectified. Again, TKS Council had minimal face to face contact with the headmasters of the junior schools. On my proposal, each now attended one Council meeting every term to speak to his report, and the Senior Master one Council meeting and all meetings of the executive. The Council also determined that the Headmaster become chief executive, with the Bursar in a staff appointment. The Finance Bursar (a new appointment) and the Property Bursar (a new title) were among those who now reported to the Headmaster.

In the management of boys, several issues were vexatious. We still sought the ideal balance for chapel and decided that there would be only three Sunday evening services each term in 1984. As to discipline, there were expulsions late in 1983 for vandalism, theft and drugs. But they were isolated cases due in part to decisive action. Far more widespread was the ugly practice of bullying. Too easily condoned as tradition, it was particularly rife in the boarding houses. The Senior Master had early in 1983 alerted housemasters to the evidence of severe bruises presented by some boys in 1st Form – it came to light in the Gym. Jon Wickham worked hard in conjunction with housemasters to combat this cancer and we expelled boys for bullying. On 25 October I addressed the School about the 1984 intake:

> I want to stop the tradition … that boys coming in in 1st Form should be harshly treated in any way. If that is a tradition of the school, it is a damnable tradition; it is one that we want to get rid of. Those boys are … weaker, they are more exposed, they are more at risk [than you]. Let us resolve that we will treat them with courage. What did the chaplain say in his prayer just now? 'True courage is gentleness.' Let us get that into our thick skulls, mine as well as yours. Let us be sure that our attitude is more gracious, more gentle, more tolerant, more welcoming …
>
> Let us resolve – and these are my last words to you – to

treat boys who join us next year, not as you yourself were treated when you came to the School, but as you would have wanted to be treated. If we can bring about that change in attitude and behaviour, then we will change the experience of the school. Someone has wisely said that it takes a year to create a 100-year tradition. If we can [achieve that] we will have a more healthy, a more positive, and a more Christian School, manifesting courage and manliness, and the qualities of tolerance and good neighbourliness and commonsense while we are at it.

Jon Wickham and I were generally of one mind. With one initiative, however, he did not agree. It was on the morning that Australia won the America's Cup. When I asked Jon to convene a special Assembly to celebrate this victory, he astonished me by saying 'We do not do that sort of thing here.' He in turn was taken aback when I said 'We do, while I am Headmaster.' When the School assembled – the VIth Form, normally exempt during their final term, attended – I addressed it on what I declared 'a very great and a very proud day for this nation'. I said that I had only once known an atmosphere akin to that now gripping Australia. Recalling the August day in 1953 when England had regained The Ashes, I said:

I am not an Englishman, but I was in England on that occasion, and I remember the atmosphere: it was electrifying, the whole nation was agog with excitement and elation and a sense of pride. Well, I sense and see that same atmosphere around me today, and I am very proud to participate in it, and proud to be in Australia, and I am proud in a sense to be an Australian in this day of great triumph … [It] was that crew, their skill, their guts, that won the day, and I am sure that the whole of Australia is proud of them. That is why I thought I would share my own thoughts and my own emotions with you, knowing that in some sense I personify yours, and I've tried to express what I know boys and staff will be thinking.

I discerned too much of a tendency at TKS to think of itself as a place apart, aloof from community or even nation. Such a mindset seemed to me unhealthy, unwise or even – as on this occasion – unpatriotic. I am glad that I challenged it that day, and proud that I encouraged The King's School to identify with the nation's elation.

III. ALL HELL

1. Feeling the heat

The year 1984 was pure Orwell. It was foreshadowed in the third term of 1983. I went again to Victoria. John and Vibeke Lewis received me at Geelong Grammar with the same warm hospitality and helpfulness shown by the Attenboroughs at Charterhouse. John had been Master in College at Eton (and would return there to succeed Sir Eric Anderson as Headmaster). His experience at Corio, as a recent arrival from UK, was apposite for my situation. Another commitment was to assess the service offered by Management and Skills Training (MAST). Nigel Creese and five other Victorian headmasters welcomed me to a weekend seminar under its auspices. Subsequently I invited MAST to conduct a two-day seminar in April 1984 for some councillors, senior staff, and the President of TKS Foundation, with the school's long-term prospects and planning needs as agenda. I soon became aware of criticism that I was often away from Gowan Brae – the Newcastle and Futter Park outings were in this term also. And I faced hostility over my choice of Speech Day guest of honour. With his retirement imminent, I wanted the school to honour Jika Travers, controversial figure though he was. Council agreed. Several of my senior colleagues, however, as refugees from Shore, were resentful.

It was now that I first conceived an ill-defined feeling of uneasiness. The impression was sharpened when, at the executive meeting on 23 December, Lyn Arnold proposed a vote of thanks for my first year's achievement coupled with a warning that opposition to me was mounting. That mixed message left me tense during the long vacation, with Gertrude, who was with us for six weeks, bearing the brunt of my unrelaxed state. She herself was given to think when the Kurrles invited her to lunch without Cilla and myself, as her hosts. She saw significance here deeper than breach of etiquette.

It is important to view criticism of my initiatives on its merits. I was aware of the opposition of some Old Boys to my policy on chapel, but I had carried councillors, both clerical and lay, and housemasters with me. My attitude to TKS uniform also caused excitement but was misunderstood. My concern was to protect the uniform, much as the Army had had to protect Service Dress after it replaced both 'Blues' and battledress. I had taken the matter up in my Speech Day Report. The need for action was reinforced when, accompanying the Inspecting Officer among the ranks of the Cadet Corps, I saw the shabby state of the uniform of many senior boys. I was wrong, however, to speak about it at the AGM of the Women's Auxiliary. It was perceived as adding insult to injury. Again, my new role as chief executive was causing anger. This fundamental policy change ought to have been commended to the Common Room by the Chairman as Council policy. Bill Pickard (who had in effect chosen me as Headmaster) made Peter Nicholson aware of his hostility to it. Within the School, there was a perception that Brian Johnstone had been wronged.

I began to see, not that I had done too much too quickly, but had not consulted enough. The impasse induced by earlier inaction had made prompt remedial action imperative. I had acted with decision but not always with consensus. The sound advice that Sir Marcus Loane had sent me through a third party in 1982 now seemed ironical. He had advised that I should do what I deemed necessary in my own way, rather than become 'the victim of strong advice, often conflicting, from many quarters'. In that way, Sir Marcus had opined, I would avoid being 'seen to be captive to any particular point of view or group in the early formative period'. In the event, the only strong advice that I had heeded had been my own, and I had been captive only to my own intuition and judgement. I had seriously mismanaged change in the organisation. I paid a heavy price. The controversial import of innovative policies and my absorption in my chief executive role combined to undermine confidence in my leadership.

In first term 1984 my personal situation was unusual. With School commitments detrimental to family life, we had enrolled Rachel at Frensham and Philip as a boarder in Broughton House

– he had been a dayboy in TKS Prep. Cilla went back with Gertrude. After her heroic efforts throughout 1983 she deserved a break – the Council paid her travel expenses – and she was absent all term. The hot summer of 1983 had badly frightened her; ironically, that of 1984 was much cooler. In my wife's absence, I stopped travelling other than to Tudor House, declined all outside speaking engagements, kept meetings to a minimum, and worked to consolidate the policy changes. In my report of 24 February to Council, I took up the broader issues flagged twelve months earlier. Within the school, I still met younger boys on their birthdays though less comfortably (for them) in Cilla's absence. But with the new timetable devised by Wickham – it now rotated on a six-day basis – I was cut out of teaching. I had less contact with colleagues also. As our domestic help still came every day, I lunched at home to give her something to do! With a heavy heart, I felt bound to relieve Jonathan Persse of his housemastership of Waddy, a decision made easier by Jonathan's dignified acceptance. Of the several applicants for his post, Peter Philpott impressed me most. He had recently remarried, and I appointed Judy and him to Waddy. Jon Wickham again concurred.

While on my own for two months, I enjoyed the support of friends within and beyond TKS. Sal Wickham was always ready with advice, practical help and her endearing smile. Tricia Bell travelled to Frensham with me on Rachel's birthday Sunday – her twin daughters boarded there. Graeme and Helen Lowe offered their holiday home at Kilcare to Phil and me for half term. Jill Friend hosted a lunch party for Dr and Mrs Rae and other Newington guests on a GPS Saturday. Mrs Irene Ashton invited me to dine in her elegant home in the Eastern Suburbs; I drove Dave Willis, another guest, back to Gowan Brae. James Morrow spent a weekend with me. Of my new friends in Sydney, Paddy and Maggi Morgan invited me to a dinner party where I first met Ken and Annabel Baxter. I had been on my feet all day at GPS events and retired for an hour's sleep during dinner.

I played golf on four occasions: twice with Lyn Arnold, and twice with the Captain of Royal Sydney, Ken Chapman. The first outing with Ken was early on Saturday so that I could watch GPS action at Scots College afterwards. It was a typical Saturday in February and all sport was cancelled – we had golfed just in time. The second outing was during Robbie and Beryl's visit when the Captain of Royal Sydney honoured Robbie by partnering him – Robbie Burns had represented Ulster at golf before he joined the RAF on the outbreak of War.

After I had left TKS, a management consultant opined that, feeling unsettled, I had subconsciously undermined my position – a well-known behavioural phenomenon. The theory has some merit. My union with TKS was a mismatch: spiritually, I felt that I was in the wrong school, many there that I was the wrong Headmaster. The culture of bullying upset me. I knew that I could not crush it: the power of an evil tradition was too strong. As for the GPS mentality, I had challenged the deification of sport from the start. Again, King's claim to be a faith school was specious. Key staff with no Christian conviction had been recruited for other reasons, particularly prowess in sport. When Archbishop Robinson dedicated the new Preparatory School building early in 1984, he spoke of TKS as 'unashamedly Christian'. Sitting on the platform beside him I saw the bemused expressions of senior colleagues. In a different context, when the Council voted to fill a vacancy on the executive, the OBU and clerical nominees received equal votes. It was a rare opportunity to elect an able cleric (Ian Mears) to this Old Boy stronghold, but the President declined to give a casting vote. The OBU nominee was elected later.

It may be that all of these misgivings inclined me to self-destruction, and that my behaviour was perceived as bizarre, even reckless. I cannot be sure. But when Sir George Halliday telephoned his colleague Dr Allan Bryson – whom I had not met – and asked 'Why has the Headmaster resigned?' he was told, 'Because they think he is bonkers'.

2. Hell hath no fury

They thought too that I was at once ruthless and weak. My demotions of some senior staff inspired fear. My intention to move against the practice of regular drinking by resident staff was known – that it took place in the boarding houses was unacceptable to me. My weakness consisted in not caning boys. Wickham did not cane either, but his was a different case. Again, after I had apologised to a colleague at a staff meeting for biting his head off, Dave Willis told me that he had read contempt on the faces of others – apparently only the weak apologised. Fear and contempt were a lethal combination, expressed in hostility. In mid-term the Senior Master advised me that housemasters had requested a meeting with me. I considered that much of their criticism, in an atmosphere at best strained and at worst antagonistic, was unfair. That I was out of touch with boys was evidently untrue and was implicitly rejected by the boys at my final Assembly. But at no time, amid much relentless sledging, did my housemasters object to me as a person, whether in point of my predilections, habits or morals. The fact that the meeting had taken place at all, however, was used as a propaganda tool. The perception that I had lost the confidence of my staff now became widespread.

Opposition to me, on whatever ground, allowed those who had been against the appointment of a non-Australian to say 'We told you so'. They included members of Council, Common Room, and the Old Boys' Union. They had simply bided their time. Their goal was to replace me with Jon Wickham. Back in Enniskillen, the shrewd Renee Benson understood. She told me that when I had introduced her at Portora to the 'tall, handsome, alert Australian' – she alluded to Jon Wickham – she knew that my headship would be in trouble. Meanwhile, the overt hostility of some had been matched by the eerie silence of others. The Chairman had told me in 1982 that Council expected us to meet weekly. He met with me only once during my final term. Jika Travers had vanished too. When I told Dr Paterson that I was in trouble, he was astounded – he had heard nothing. But Knox Grammar was neither Anglican nor GPS. Shore was both and Jika had heard everything. He told Iain Paterson that there were 'ructions' in the Church and the Old Boys' Union; but he had said nothing to me.

My detractors were not above cynicism. The charge that I drank too much was specifically put about after the 1984 Head of the River. Stephen Harrison had been with me there, and neither of us had tasted alcohol all day. What he did to counter the slander, I do not know. It hardy mattered: the farce that heavy whiskey drinkers at TKS should charge me with their habit was played out with straight faces. Archbishop Robinson came to our home after I had resigned and said that he knew the charge was false. It was in effect an apology; but the damage had been done. It was charged too that I engaged in improper relationships. A watch was kept on my personal mail. The School Captain, Andrew Ashton, was asked who Mrs Irene Ashton was. As she was his grandmother, he asked the reason for the enquiry. I had of course written to thank Mrs Ashton for her hospitality. The rumours were so legion that at the OBU City-Country reception, my friend Bruce Hood offered his own with the facetious comment that I had worn my green (rugby) jersey too often.

The Ashes had acquired new meaning at TKS. A memorial Garden conceived for reception of the remains of Old Boys had not yet been completed. Deposited remains had found a temporary repository in the recesses of the Headmaster's study. We enjoyed a ghostly rapport. If all Old Boys had been as these, I reflected ruefully, I might have rested in peace.

Loss of support for its Headmaster, for whatever reasons, was a serious situation for TKS Council. With my position untenable, in a tensely unsettled atmosphere, Council had an unenviable duty to discharge. Termination of my headship might have been achieved on rational grounds, with decency and integrity. Instead, underhand *ad hominem* tactics brought matters to a head. A personal letter was removed from my out-tray and passed around at a meeting of the executive of which I was not notified. This illegal expedient led to a special meeting of Council. Two days before it, Paul Mazoudier asked to meet with me as the President's emissary to discuss the format of the meeting. I consulted Dr Paterson, who interpreted this offer as civil and helpful. Neither of us suspected that it was a trap. Paul Mazoudier's purpose was different from that advised. He bluntly offered me the options of resigning for 'personal reasons' with six months' salary, or of being 'crucified' and left empty-handed at the Council meeting. As we had been unable to fix an earlier time to meet, it was by now close to midnight. Cilla was to arrive into Sydney airport at 6.00am.

On her return Cilla learned of the charge that she been away too long. Jika Travers picked it up and the executive took it up at its fateful meeting. During 1983, at her insistence, Cilla's multiple sclerosis had not been made widely known in the TKS community. The price of privacy was loss of understanding: she had drawn cruel comment about the way she walked, as now about her absence. She spoke with a trusted friend at Gowan Brae and was told, 'The knives came out for Alan before you went away.' It was cold comfort for her.

Before the Council meeting began, the President received from me my letter of resignation and then offered prayer. I had asked to address the Council. While I was awaiting admission, one clerical member reputedly demanded to know what I had done. It will have been an interesting moment, for the questioner had swapped wives – permanently – with his churchwarden. For myself, having not been there during the first part of the Council's business, I did not know what information (or misinformation) had been placed before it. When I rose to speak, I first expressly said that a personal friendship to which exception had been taken had afforded me strong support. I then detailed the working relationship recommended by NCIS for Chairman and Headmaster, insisting that it had not obtained at TKS. Lloyd Waddy told me that he was proud of the dignity and openness of my performance.

My resignation took effect five days after the Council meeting, on the last day of term. Jon Wickham had been appointed Acting Headmaster. Though debarred from any contact with the school, I spoke at the final Assembly. When I took my place, Wickham asked if I had cleared my intention with the Chairman. I replied that as Headmaster I needed no one's permission to address my school. I spoke to the boys from my heart. I scorned the charge that I had been remote from them. I told them that I intended to stay in Australia and that I hoped to find the courage that so many of their families manifested in the hardships of drought, fire and flood.

When I concluded, 900 boys rose to their feet as one and gave me a standing ovation. It was a moment of deep emotion that I shall always cherish. I broke my bail again when I invited the School Monitors to my house. They articulated the school's instinctive understanding of all that I had stood for. One appeared to express their mind by saying that if the school's future lay with

Wickham and Rose, they were glad that it was their last year.

We had the five vacation weeks to pack, store our furniture and leave. I bought an ancient Holden. In six months it never broke down and I had the later satisfaction of having Mike McKanna accept it for Gowan Brae. One evening we packed as much into the Holden as it would hold with Elsa and ourselves. Sixteen months earlier we had arrived to an empty house, our furniture on the high seas. Now the house was empty again, our furniture – after barely a year's occupation – in storage.

3. Life beyond hell

We had strong affirmation from within the TKS community. Sir George Halliday gave us lunch in the Union Club on my last day as Headmaster, Lloyd and Edwina Waddy dinner after we had left Parramatta. James and Susan Ashton expressly confirmed their invitation for the family to spend Easter at Millamolong. Ken and Marilyn Chapman had us to stay in their holiday home in the Southern Highlands in June, Mac and Jill Halliday in their home in the Eastern Suburbs. We lived in Ron and Robyn Arnold's home at Kenthurst for the six weeks that they were overseas, and again in Graeme and Helen Lowe's house at Kilcare. After Cilla and Philip had left for Ireland in July, some TKS families invited me to their homes. And Ken Chapman and I were able to get around Royal Sydney without my having to worry about time out. Ken commented on the marked improvement in my golf!

I was made aware of support too in the wider community. Kerry Packer invited me to see him and when we met urged me to stay because Australia needed me. I tested his judgement with job applications and was interviewed for senior executive positions in Sydney in both a major charity and a hospital. Though unsuccessful, I learned that a perception was abroad that I had been unjustly treated. It helped that my referees were eminent men: Sir George Halliday, Dr Iain Paterson, and Ken Baxter, then the high profile Chairman of the Egg Marketing Board. With the precipitate haste of my resignation from TKS, residual matters had to be taken up. I retained the highly respected firm of solicitors, Hardings, and they in turn the distinguished Senior Counsel, Simon Sheller, an Old Boy of TKS. Mr

Sheller was clearly angry that TKS Council had learned nothing from previous crises and contemptuous about the Archbishop's praying over my resignation. My solicitors strove for months on my behalf, to no avail. They and Mr Sheller waived all charges for their services.

One of the saddest aspects of our ordeal was that rumour and slander had leapt 12,000 miles. *Schadenfreude* was rife in both Belfast and Fermanagh and was thoughtfully shared with our families. We learned who our friends were. Lois Williams at Rossfad silenced all gossipmongers within her hearing. Colonel Ronald Greeves countered one in Belmont thus: 'What you are telling me about Alan Acheson is so contrary to the character of the man as I know him that I refuse to believe it.' Dr Jim Kincade, in a warmly supportive letter in his own hand, reminded me of Oscar Wilde's adage that there was one thing worse than being talked about – not being talked about. Gerry Murphy wrote re-assuringly from Sandringham rectory in the same week. He re-called how the Englishman, Archbishop Hugh Gough of Sydney, had been 'sent away' 20 years earlier. I derived comfort too from the experience of a professor at the University of Sydney – an Englishman – whose guests we had been at dinner in the Australian Club. He wrote that he had had to fight off attempts to destroy him during his first two years in his chair.

One reported incident, however, gave me utmost comfort. In autumn 1984, before their match with Ulster, the Wallabies trained at Sullivan Upper. David Hewitt, then Chairman of the Board of Governors, introduced himself to the coach, Alan Jones. One of the outstanding centre threequarters of all time thus met one of rugby's most successful coaches. David brought my name forward. Alan Jones gave a spirited response, the gist of which was that I had been treated outrageously. He well un-derstood: he had been Head of English at The King's School and had resigned in circumstances that afforded him an insight into my experience.

The Heads Association was unable to elect my successor to membership until it received assurances from TKS Council. Its national Chairman, Max Howell, corresponded with me for 12 months after I had left King's. Although vexed that neither Dr Paterson nor I had consulted him before I resigned, Max's support meant much to me afterwards. He knew that Iain Paterson and I had been deceived about my financial severance, but he had no more success here than my lawyers. At Max Howell's request, I provided a report of my experience during my final term. He discussed it with Nigel Creese before presenting it to his Standing Committee in November 1984. They understood that I had been unable to fulfil my membership obligations, in that I had not been the sole channel of communication between Council and staff and that meetings had taken place without my knowledge. The Heads Association therefore sought assurances that, were it to elect Jon Wickham to membership, he would not be so treated. To that end Max Howell invited Peter Nicholson to meet with him. They met in Brisbane early in 1985. Max told me in his letter of 20 March 1985 that he had achieved nothing in my interest but everything that he had sought for my successor's protection.

Note: after the thematic Chapter Five, chronological narrative resumes at Chapter Six.

CHAPTER FIVE

Why the whistle went

Judging from his decisions it appeared that referee Jonathan Kaplan was embracing St Patrick's Day as enthusiastically as the Irish supporters. During [the first half] Ireland scored three tries and each of them owed much to Kaplan's green-eyed view of the match. (Mark Reason at the Stadio Flaminio in Rome: *Sunday Telegraph*, 18 March 2007.)

To make one mistake was unfortunate, and two careless; but even Oscar Wilde might have been at a loss in defining the referee's third. Or have pointed out that the report tells us more about the writer than the referee. In some forty words, the reporter has given one fact: that there was a referee in this Italy *v.* Ireland match. And come to think of it, it is the one indisputable fact in every game of rugby, wherever and however it is played.

After leaving Sullivan Upper, I played only briefly for Holywood RFC: at under 10-stone, I was not an effective flanker. John Ellams coaxed me in 1962 to play at Eglinton midweek – I refereed on Saturdays – and in 1964-65 at Wilton Park, Beaconsfield. My experience at full back for the Brigade Depot was torrid. I was badly concussed in a match with Limavady Grammar and after our one-sided match with Foyle College, had nightmares in which I was overwhelmed by hordes wearing Foyle colours. I fared better in Guyana in 1966. Despite my initial intention to stick to refereeing, I played for both the Middlesex Regimental XV and its Sevens side. In tropical heat – we played our matches during the last hour of daylight – and against lightweight, mostly non-European opponents, my fitness and mobility counted, just as they had at SUS. I played with Lt Harry Barstow, soon to be selected for the Army XV, and under Capt Peter Cheesman's shrewd and genial captaincy. I made the initial mistake, however, of playing on when the battalion returned to the mud of Ulster.

My refereeing career, by contrast, spanned 44 seasons. My first match was in September 1961, my last in October 2004. My involvement was not continuous: I had two breaks, each of about five years' duration. But I enjoyed more than 30 years of active engagement and handled over 700 matches. I was 23 when my refereeing career began, 67 when it ended. I had been a member of the Ulster, Army, and Sydney societies, and officiated in three continents and six countries. My career had three phases: its dawn in the 1960s; high noon 1974-79; and a long twilight from the 1990-01 season until that of 2004-05. The very ordinariness of my experience may hold some interest. I tell it as it was, with some reflection. Whether of interest to others or not, however, refereeing has been an enriching part of my life – challenging, engrossing and satisfying – and one of my oldest and most enduring loves. It has produced good friendships: these, and my memories of richly varied experiences, have made it worthwhile.

I. DAWN: 1961-1969

1. Ulster referee

I took up the whistle at Ballyclare High. My first outing, an under-14 match in 1959, was an unmitigated disaster. I could only improve, and next year refereed the 1st XV with confidence. My colleague Sam Bell saw my potential and had me referee an inter-club friendly in April 1961. I applied to join the fledgling Ulster Society of Rugby Football Referees (USRFR) – founded in 1950 – and refereed out of Ballyclare RFC in the 1961-62 season. (Brian Stirling, an international referee, was the club's most distinguished referee.) Curiously, I never wore the Ballyclare RFC colours – I preferred jerseys of plain colour. When I went to buy the club socks, I came away with a pair of Collegians' socks. Although I wore these for over 30 years, no one ever noticed. Before my first match I enquired about training courses for new referees. As there were none, 'Paddy' Patterson advised me to 'go out on Saturdays with a whistle and learn from your mistakes'. (W. J. Patterson was President of USRFR in 1962-63.) As both my teaching and driving had been launched on the same basis, I took Paddy's point. I learned from my mistakes with chalk, steering wheel and whistle, after the fashion of the 1960s.

My first match, in the 4th Division, featured two Belfast clubs. As Malone was the 'home' side, and the club had more teams than pitches, the match was played somewhere in Newtownabbey. If I ever find a lake in that amorphous borough, I shall rediscover my pitch, for play was held up for ten minutes while the ball was fished from the lake. A reserve ball was not part of the scene 45 years ago. Somehow, relying on public transport and encouraged by Tom Rothwell and the lovely Marlene Culley at Ulster Branch – the office was then in Howard Street – I got through my first season. Perhaps the secret resides in words that I wrote in 1962:

> I decided, while refereeing a 4th Division match at Carolan Road in wind and rain, with two spectators, no touch-judge, and one team down to 13 men, that I loved this game of rugby football.

During my year at Eglinton, I was selected on occasions by the autonomous NW District branch. On 20 October 1962, I refereed Limavady *v.* City of Derry. It was my most senior match and sternest test to date, tense rather than enjoyable. I had not yet learned to stop players 'talking at' the referee. The severe winter of 1963 put paid to rugby in the province for almost three months. My match at Banbridge on the last Saturday of 1962 was my last until mid-March. In the autumn of 1963, when teaching at Sullivan Upper, I refereed all of the 1st XV's home matches, going on to referee a club match on Saturday afternoons – a tight schedule on early kick-off days. After my last match the SUS team lined up outside the new War Memorial pavilion and sang 'For he's a jolly good fellow', one of those simple gestures that mean so much. At their match with Boys Model, Ernie Davis, as a good headmaster, was there to support his XV. He said to me afterwards, 'It is always good to see a match so well, and above all so impartially refereed.' He added that that seldom happened at country schools. Two seasons later, when I was refereeing at Sullivan from nearby Palace Barracks, Ernie was again on the touchline. Without recognising me, he paid me precisely the same compliment. I took it that the 'country schools' had not improved!

2. Army referee

During that 1965-66 season, I was a member also of the Army Rugby Union Referees Society (ARURS). I had been classified on joining as Grade 2 (rather than Grade 3 – the Army's top referees were Grade 1) on the strength of Harold Jackson's report to ARURS. I had recourse to Harold because the Ulster Society had failed during five seasons to assess me. Harold had watched me referee at Sullivan Upper when his son Peter was playing for the 1st XV. I owed more to Harold Jackson than his formal support. He was an early encourager of my career and I learned much from his own refereeing – to interprovincial level. Immaculate in his NIFC jersey and socks, tall and neat in build, Harold was one of the finest referees that it has ever been my privilege to observe.

Colonel Jim Sleator at HQ Northern Ireland Command was another encourager. On my return from Guyana, he appointed me to several inter-regimental fixtures. In one match at Ballykinler, I discovered that a Welsh regimental XV, composed mainly of Other Ranks, could make a referee's life very difficult. Colonel Jim groomed me for promotion and in March 1967 I was selected to referee an inter-Corps match: RAMC *v.* REME, at Aldershot – a most enjoyable experience. In the light of my Army status, the incongruity with my position in the Ulster Society was glaring. By October 1967, I had been a member for six years. Although there had been gaps in continuity when I was in England and Guyana, I continued my involvement whenever I was in the province and refereed in aggregate for four of the six years. Even during the pressure months of early 1966 pre-Guyana, with soldiering, research and romance in competition, I still found time to referee. Marlene calculated my expenses and sent the Branch's cheque out to Atkinson Field. Despite this record, however, I had never been advised of my grading, nor been assessed or promoted. I had attended the Society's monthly meetings, held in the NIFC clubhouse at Shaftesbury Avenue. At one meeting, Alfie Jamison challenged the management on policy issues. He showed courage, not least in his criticism of selection policy. (G. A. Jamison became an international referee, but was never elected President of the Referees Society.)

For my own part, I had not only refereed to Army inter-Corps standard but had handled two local international matches in the Caribbean – the *Guyana Graphic* had reported favourably on my performance. On return from Guyana I wrote to the Hon Secretary of the Ulster Society, Hugh Scott of Dungannon. I outlined my record with the Army Society and enquired about my USRFR grading. I said that I was aware only that Frank Humphries had once looked over his shoulder at me when observing another referee at Ward Park. (F. C. Humphries was President of the Ulster Referees Society in 1966-67 and H. M. Scott in 1967-68.)

I received no reply from the Society. Before the next season began I had left for BAOR. I refereed there for some 18 months but without enthusiasm. During the 1968-69 season I hung up my boots. My experience of the Ulster Society had been such that, on return to Northern Ireland in 1970, I had no interest whatever in resuming as a referee. Indeed, I had thrown away all records of my refereeing during 1961-67, an uncharacteristic action that I regret. So it was that, during my last year with Rhine Army and for four years back in Ulster, I enjoyed the first of my two five-year breaks from active refereeing. My children were young and I was glad to spend Saturdays with them.

II. HIGH NOON: 1974–1984

1. The road to Ravenhill
My return to refereeing was perhaps suspect in point of motive. I availed of the tacit understanding that members of the Common Room at Campbell College who engaged in club rugby were exempt Saturday afternoon duty. (Classes ended at 1.00pm; sports continued until 5.00pm.) Thus in September 1974, I joined three colleagues who were already on day-release: Jack Ferris and Nick Jones, who played for Civil Service and NIFC respectively, and Tom Patton, a distinguished referee. Ashley Armstrong, then with Collegians, joined us later. Like Tom Patton, I had initially no club affiliation. On those occasions when we both refereed Senior League matches, 'Campbell College' was given after our names in press notices. This was very proper in that most of our refereeing took place in College

147

time. The Ulster Branch, however, directed us both to join a club – I believe to ensure insurance cover. We both chose nearby CIYMS, the club where Tom had been a player.

Although I was starting *de integro*, I was pitched into the Junior League right away. As in 1961, I refereed a Malone team in my first match: their IIA side, captained by Brian Lally, had Carrick IB as opponents at Cherryvale. To follow up with CIYMS II *v.* NIFC II, and a Schools' friendly, RBAI *v.* Grosvenor High, was a gratifying start. As I still lacked assessment by the Ulster Society, however, it was an agreeable surprise to be selected in December for the Towns' Cup semi-final match between Ballymoney and Dungannon. Ironically, my two 4th Division fixtures of that season fell on the Saturdays before the semi-final, an instance of what Tom Patton deemed poor selection: it had happened to him before Senior or even Representative matches – Tom was on the inter-provincial panel.

The Towns Cup match was played at Ballymoney RFC's ground at Balnamore, a rough field distinguishable from the farmland around it only by the goalposts. A large crowd attended in festive spirit – it was the Saturday after Christmas – and was rewarded by a fine contest played in an excellent spirit. Dungannon won, but were well tested by the home side. My friends in Ballymoney RFC reminisced with me 25 years on as though the match had been played the previous week. Good experiences in Ulster club rugby linger on. Andy Irvine, the incumbent Scottish full back, was among the spectators: he was spending New Year with his fiancée's family in Ballymoney. For myself, I was aware that none of the players had seen me before and grateful that they accepted me with courtesy and evident confidence.

When I asked Brian Baird, the Society's president, why I had been selected, sight unseen, for such an important match, he replied 'We had good reports of you.' Brian thus acknowledged that, thirteen years since my first selection, the Ulster Society had yet to assess me formally. That situation changed early in 1975. After I had refereed two matches in the Schools Cup, I took on the Medallion Shield match, BRA *v.* Regent House, at Castle Grounds. Ike Kerr spoke to me afterwards. I attempted the impossible in persuading Ike to be brief – Cilla and the children were in the car en route to Portstewart – and he rewarded me with his parting shot, 'You know how to read a game.' Of all the advice that Ike was to proffer over the years, this generous comment is all that I can recall. (Isaac Kerr was President of the Ulster Society in 1977-78.) That autumn, another assessor observed me – Ray Williams, whose outstanding international career had recently ended. Ray watched me at Shane Park during a Crawford Cup match. Ike and he appear to have concurred in their appraisal of me, and for 18 months – from October 1975 to April 1977 – I lived rugby on a different plane.

A succession of cup matches in various competitions culminated in my selection for the final of the Crawford Cup at Ravenhill in 1977. I was appointed also to the interprovincial match between Leinster and Connacht Junior sides at Mullingar, a contest that lacked the creative tension of Ulster club rugby and was flat as a refereeing experience. I had one match only in the Boston Cup, played under floodlights at Bangor RFC. I remember the occasion well, not so much because I had difficulty seeing the ball, but because Ike Kerr pinned me verbally against the changing room wall afterwards. It was ten minutes before I dared attempt to remove my boots and twice as long before I could access the shower, pursued by Ike's steaming commentary. Ike's passion for the game, ubiquitous presence, and penchant for correcting referee peccadilloes, ignored mere practicalities.

Youth rugby was always enjoyable. The annual Senior Schools Sevens tested fitness and speed, and the Schools 2nd XV competition, with successive matches to referee, stamina and concentration. Of numerous Schools Cup matches, two stand out as hard-fought contests worthy of that prestigious trophy: Belfast High School v. BRA, played in January mud that made jerseys indistinguishable, and Ballyclare High v. RSD, when I had to clear excited spectators from the pitch. Of my 32 matches in the 1976-77 season, eleven were played on Wednesday – the Campbell College dispensation covered that sports afternoon as well as Saturday. Some involved Representative youth teams at Ravenhill. I refereed Ulster Under-19s against Ulster Juniors, the Under-19 final, the interprovincial Under-19 match Ulster v. Connacht, and Ulster B against Ulster Colleges.

A particular highlight was the annual Dudley Cup fixture between Queen's and Trinity played on a glorious February day, sunny and windy, in 1977. My friend Trevor West had travelled with the TCD team, so enhancing both my enjoyment of the occasion and his own commitment to Dublin University Football Club (DUFC), whose 150-year history he was to edit for publication in 2003. Trinity were clear favourites. In 1976 they had regained the Leinster Senior Cup after many years, defeating Blackrock in the final after a replay. With Michael Gibson (of Leinster) as captain, their DUFC Colour Team of 1976-77 included present and future Irish internationals in John Robbie, Ollie Waldron, Donal Spring and Gibson himself. But Queen's beat them convincingly. Apart from Robbie's skills on the losing side, I recall most vividly the incident when Gibson regained his feet from the bottom of a pile-up, found that I had given a penalty to Queen's, and asked wearily 'What is it this time, ref?' Somehow the moment epitomised a lacklustre performance on Trinity's part, with Queen's more hungry to win.

In 1977-78 my season began with a Senior League match at Branch Road, Derry and ended with the Towns Cup final at Ravenhill. After the match at Derry, Tom Patton asked our colleague Ashley Armstrong, the visiting Collegians scrum half, how my performance had been and was told 'Bloody marvellous!' Alfie Jamison, who had travelled to City of Derry to assess me, was neither as cryptic nor as uncritical. He was bothered about my running angles and at Donaghadee some months later expressed concern that they had not improved. I never did quite get the point here. Alfie apparently wanted me to achieve economy of movement; but there was no reason for anxiety. In some eyes, I was the speediest referee in the Ulster Society and was envied in particular for my capacity to run backwards at speed. These attributes may have gained me the nod for the Towns Cup final in 1978, between Armagh and Ballyclare. I was appointed only after several preferred referees had cried-off with late season injuries, the selectors turning to me – so I was told – with the enigmatic affirmation, 'Acheson will not let us down.' A strong wind dominated at Ravenhill that Easter Monday, blowing straight down the pitch. Ballyclare won because they made better use of the wind.

My bread-and-butter in these years was, however, the Junior League, and especially its high quality Section 1 Teams. These represented Ulster club rugby at its ruggedly attractive best during the pre-professional era. After 30 years, my memories remain strong and vivid. Twice in the same month, I refereed North II at Carolan Road and was gratified to overhear Paddy Patterson say to his touchline neighbour, with evident comfort, 'The same venue – and the same referee.' It seemed that I had learned from my mistakes. One remarkable match lingers in memory: Armagh IA *v.* Ards IA, at Palace Grounds. It was a hard-fought, physical contest, primarily between two resolute, very fit packs, with the big, strong Ards forwards held tenaciously by their lighter opponents. With no try scored, it was a close, tense battle of the sort where it is vital for the referee not to make a mistake, and so deliver victory to one side or the other. With the score level at two penalties apiece, the likely draw promised a fair outcome to a titanic struggle. It was not to be. A blatant offside offence by an Ards player gifted a late penalty to the home side, and their kicker converted it with clinical precision to give Armagh a 9-6 victory. It had been one of those days when, listening to the pre-match hype – I had changed in the old, wooden pavilion with the teams – I quaked at the prospect of controlling thirty players of such fiercely determined intent. But such thoughts always evaporated on the pitch, not so much due to self-belief as to the attitude of the players of that era: courteous, encouraging, and grateful, and within that mindset, inclined to accept refereeing decisions without question. That afternoon at Palace Grounds was no exception. I think upon it every time I visit the City of Armagh.

2. Traumas and trials

The Ulster Referees' Society of the 1970s, with some 150 members, was more open and better managed than in the previous decade. Backed by dedicated office staff, volunteer General and Selection committees carried out the Society's essential business. Weekly selection meetings heard reports from assessors and appointed referees to all listed matches – these now included Schools 1st XV fixtures. The Society was represented on the Branch's Reports Committee, which dealt on a weekly basis with disciplinary matters, mostly instances where players had been 'sent off'. The Society's monthly meetings, held at Cooke RFC at Galwally, though well attended, were typical of the 1970s in that they were dreary and pedestrian, and lacking in imagination. The usual format was for a senior referee to lecture on aspects of law – scrummage, lineout, offside, foul play. While some speakers were respected, others lacked credibility: the worst was a referee who had had a dozen fights erupt in a recent Senior League match – a notorious instance of loss of control.

I found pre-season courses helpful, particularly one directed by John West of the Leinster Referees Society, then at the height of his illustrious international career: his experiences and insights were fascinating, and his laid-back commonsense approach to refereeing refreshingly different from prevalent attitudes within Ulster. Again, Tom Patton and I were among the 20 Ulster referees who attended a residential course at Carnlough under the direction of Norman Sansom of the Scottish RFU. I learned much from another skilled international referee of quiet authority and engaging personality. I persuaded Tom to drive back to Belfast over the Big Collin, which overlooked the lovely Glenwherry valley.

Ravenhill's influence, however, was not always supportive. Days after a Junior League match at Ward Park, Ike Kerr (again) accosted me with 'You made a mistake at Bangor!' He was alluding to my checking a spectator for strident verbal abuse. It was not a mistake, rather an advised intervention on my part. It proved effective: it silenced the miscreant. Had he persisted, I would have ordered him away from the playing enclosure. The referee controls that area in law: why not, then, in practice? The offender was an official of the Bangor club, though I had not known that when I intervened. My action drew support from the Bangor players, voiced by Dick Milliken, the Irish centre, who was playing for Bangor IIA on his return from injury. Dick thanked me for my initiative, and said that the players were often embarrassed by the offensive behaviour of the official in question. My impression was that no one had tried to shut him up before that afternoon.

If that was a minor incident, worse was to follow. I attended the meeting of the Reports Committee after I had, for the first time in eight years of refereeing, ordered a player off. It happened during the Towns Cup match on 25 October 1975 between Omagh and Dungannon, a local derby in county Tyrone. That rivalry, enhanced by Cup fever, made for a spirited atmosphere among the large crowd. The drive from Belfast – I had left Campbell before classes ended – had settled me, and I was consciously at the top of my form in fitness, mental alertness, and self-confidence. The match began in a lively spirit, but the players settled quickly, as my players always did once they had taken measure of their opponents – and the referee. The young Dungannon scrum half took a heavy blow early on. I was concerned for his safety and instructed his captain George Armstrong to watch him closely. An opponent, however, was more aware of his vulnerability, for minutes later the Dungannon player was poleaxed when he was in a defenceless position and had to be carried off the field. He took no further part in the match. Neither did his assailant, an Omagh prop. His assault was both vicious and deliberate. I paused to establish that I had already cautioned him for foul play and then ordered him off. My action was instinctive, my judgement clear, my decision grounded in law. It defused a potentially explosive situation, for the Dungannon players were incensed. I spoke with both captains and had them address their players, before I allowed play to resume. There was tension in the air but no further trouble. I had expressly warned Dungannon players not to take the law into their own hands; to their credit, they heeded me.

In conversation after the match, a senior member of the Omagh club – a prominent businessman in the town – told me that, in view of the player's unsavoury record, it was time for the club to ask him to move on. That opinion, though interesting, was not relevant to my report to the Reports Committee. I doubt, however, that the Omagh club's representative will have advanced it to that committee.

After a player was ordered off, the referee had first to notify the Hon Secretary of USRFR, at that time Jim McBride, then submit a written report of the incident within 48 hours to Ulster Branch. He had then to attend the Reports Committee hearing at Ravenhill. While waiting to be interviewed, I became aware that I was overhearing the committee's discussion in the adjoining room and that the chairman was reading my report aloud. In a somewhat world weary tone, he punctuated his reading with such comments as 'Where have we heard that before?' Clearly, an incident that was unique in my career was a routine matter to the disciplinary personnel of the Branch. They seemed also, when I appeared before them, to treat my verbal evidence with scant respect, indeed scepticism. In law, a referee must take into account, when determining dangerous play, both 'the defence-less position' of the one player, and 'the apparent intention' of the other. How to define these phrases in post-match analysis, and how to defend one's decision, were other issues entirely. But I found myself obliged to define and defend. It was as though I were the guilty party, and not the offending player. In short, I found the attitude of the Reports Committee of the Ulster Branch unsympathetic and inappropriate. I was not sur-prised to learn later that the player had been given two weeks' suspension: a sentence not only derisory, but negligent and irre-sponsible also.

I wrote to the Ulster Referees Society expressing my dismay and advising that I thought of quitting as a referee. I added that colleagues at Campbell College shared my reaction. The Society in response gave me to understand – verbally, not in writing – that my discussing the matter with colleagues was not approved of, as it was none of their business. On the contrary, it vitally concerned men who devoted much time to rugby football, whether as players, coaches, referees or administrators, and who had a duty of care towards hundreds of boys who played rugby. They shared my alarm at the signal sent out by the Ulster Branch in the face of assault upon, and serious injury to, a de-fenceless player. The support of Common Room colleagues at that time meant a great deal to me. The Society's verbal repri-mand was, apparently, the sole result of my representations. But the ultimate outcome was gratifying. Although neither Branch nor Society intimated the intelligence to me, my understanding is that this episode in 1975 was a turning point, in that the Ulster Branch's sentencing of players guilty of illegal and dangerous assault became thereafter more realistic and responsible. I had not protested in vain.

There was to be a reassuring sequel – almost two decades

later. I had refereed an Omagh team at Limavady, and recognised a forward now 'playing down the club' who had taken part in the Towns Cup match in 1975. In conversation at the bar afterwards, we recalled that day, and I reminded him that I had ordered off his teammate. There ensued a county Tyrone pause – it seemed like five minutes – before he said 'He was good value for it!' Out of the mouths of players ...

It was not only the Ulster Branch that, in my experience, gave referees a hard time; some club members had nothing to learn from Ravenhill. In March 1977, I handled at Shane Park the late season Senior League match between Instonians and Derry. Instonians had few points to date and badly needed a win. The match was a tense, dour battle, which the home side managed to win by a converted try to nil. Neither Instonians players nor supporters could relax at any stage and their relief at the final whistle was palpable. John Hewitt, the former Irish out half, was evidently still living on his nerves when he bought me a pint. It was the prelude to a post mortem that I was not wise enough to avoid. 'Tosh' Taylor, whom I knew from a professional context, abetted Hewitt in this inquisition. My decisions were questioned, one in particular relating to a deliberate knock-on by an Instonians centre. The most bizarre criticism, however, was that the match had lasted 92 minutes, that is from kick-off to no-side. It was as though I had committed an offence. Had my critics never heard of half time, or of the referee's obligation – not an option in law – to add on stoppage time? Were they aware that the referee was the sole judge of time? Their impertinence could only be explained by the nervous tension of men who had longed for the end of the match, and for whom every stoppage had been an agonising delay. But to charge the referee in effect with mismanagement, and to do so after the match, was without precedent in my experience. Whatever the tensions and frustrations of players and spectators during play, it was a convention in the sport – and a healthy one at that – that all was forgotten once play had ended. That convention was violated, and hospitality sullied, on that afternoon at Shane Park.

With rugby central to its history and ethos, Campbell College was a good environment for a referee. There was regular midweek engagement, whether with intra-College or inter-School fixtures, and interaction with coaches; and training was a joy in the magnificent grounds at Belmont. For the College's annual matches against the Old Campbellians, I usually refereed the 2nd XV – I was never offered the senior match. I regret one experience, however: refereeing a match between a Common Room XV and a College XV. I was uncomfortable, with my decisions disputed by colleagues and mistakes compounded under their criticism. I realised too late that there is a peculiar psychology whenever men play against boys, and had not allowed for it.

Coaches did not always appreciate my application of law either, as one incident recalls. In a match on Fox's Field within the College estate, I penalised the Campbell 1st XV centres for 10-metre infringement at a lineout. With the eyes in the back of my head, I had watched them edging forwards from the start of play, and when they blatantly infringed, glanced in their direction to determine the mark for the penalty. Denis Grant, the 1st XV coach, misread my glance as a belated decision after the lineout had ended. An opportunity to correct a basic flaw among the backs was therefore missed through his drawing the wrong conclusion. Soon afterwards, Campbell played BRA in the Schools Cup at Castle Grounds. The backs were penalised in front of their posts early in the match. It came as no surprise to me that their offence was 10-metre infringement at a lineout. This early setback unsettled the team. They played badly, lost their confidence, and were beaten by a margin of embarrassing proportions.

3. Out west and down under

When he visited Portora with RBAI teams, Jim (Jesse) Page presented me with a Five Nations tie for 'keeping the flag flying in the west'. He had a point. Distance was a deterrent, given that I had a lot of travel from Enniskillen for reasons other than rugby. Over the years I have admired those headmasters who kept up their refereeing: Steve Hilditch, an exceptional international referee, and Vic Outram, an All-Ireland League (AIL) referee, and an Enniskillen principal to boot. Neither, however, had to cope with boarding school commitments. For myself, I decided during a difficult second year at Portora to curtail my refereeing, thus effectively ending my burgeoning Senior League career. But in my first year at Portora, I had resolved on 'business as usual'. After a quiet start to the season, I was selected to referee the historic first Senior League clash between NIFC, one of the oldest clubs in Ireland, and newly promoted Ards; it was deservedly won by Ards. A week later I travelled to Galway for a Senior Friendly, Galwegians *v.* UCD – Sean Beverland, an Old Campbellian, propped for UCD. I decided not to stay the night, and with snow falling kept mostly to the coast on the return journey. I was relieved to see home that night and was in my place in Portora chapel next morning.

Philip often accompanied me during that season (though not to Galway). He was with me when our car 'put its leg out of bed' on the M1 after leaving Shane Park. Cilla had to drive to Lisburn to rescue us and we were late for the last evening performance of the annual school play. Phil was with me again at Branch Road in March 1979 for what proved to be my last 'big' match, a Towns Cup semi-final – played closer to the final than in 1974. I had a rare moment of joy when the Ballymena pack leader spoke to me as we left the pitch. He clearly did not want to be overheard, for without turning his head he said conspiratorially as he drew level with me, 'I always enjoy my game when you are the referee' – and with that strode impassively on.

Thereafter, until we left for Australia in 1983, I refereed only intermittently. At the final of the Army Major Units competition at Thiepval Barracks, Major Bill Mirehouse RMP, the father of a Portora boarder, saluted as I arrived to officiate. It was like coming home. I was presented also with a commemorative plaque, a rare event for a rugby union referee. In my final term at Portora, I refereed the 1st XV's match with RBAI, which Portora won. The large contingent of 'Inst' parents and supporters thanked me sportingly.

My most memorable match was that between a composite RUC XV and a Welsh regiment XV, played at Palace Grounds. It threatened from the beginning to degenerate into a brawl, with the Welsh evidently spoiling for a fight. That they did not provoke one, or even a skirmish, was due to the iron discipline of their RUC opponents. They refused to be provoked and tried to play rugby. The Welsh vented their frustration on the referee, subjecting me to verbal abuse and jostling. Then Jimmy McCoy spoke to me. Although he was an Old Portoran, we had not previously met. He said quietly, 'If anything happens to you, you will be looked after.' Seldom have ten words afforded me so much comfort, such sense of protection. The match proceeded, uneasily, to its finish, but without assault or mayhem. Although relieved, I was a shade disappointed that nothing had 'happened' to me. It would have been something to witness fifteen policemen responding to a 'ninety-nine' call in the interest of the referee! Jimmy McCoy was selected at prop for Ireland after I had left for Australia. Match programmes at Lansdowne Road described him euphemistically as a civil servant. Jimmy had been that to me in Armagh.

Whenever I reflect on the purple patch in my career during the 70s, I see that my refereeing priorities were clear. The first was to be there: to know what had occurred, and to take appropriate action. I achieved that goal through physical fitness, positional awareness, and intuition – knowing 'how to read a game'. The second was to be impartial. Players know that referees make mistakes, just as they do, and accept those mistakes the more readily if the referee knows what is going on and is even-handed in his application of law. A fit referee who keeps up with play, is there at the breakdown, and sees everything, is a referee whom players trust, respect and obey. I made mistakes in every match I handled, and often had irate coaches doubting my paternity. Just as regularly, however, I enjoyed player indulgence of my fallibility, given that I tried not to offend in the crucial areas of awareness, fitness and impartiality. There was one exception to this general rule. I never knew, and what is more, never wanted to know, what went on in the front row of the scrummage. My attitude was that front row forwards looked after themselves and that a referee who intruded was inviting trouble. It was more sensible to trust the players. This approach always worked: my scrums seldom collapsed, no front row player was ever seriously injured, and players did not try to hoodwink me. I knew that, with my laid back approach, good eye contact was vital; given both, scrum management was straightforward.

Another guideline that I followed was to compensate for player interference. By that, I mean that if players tried persistently to influence my decisions, I accepted that I was being influenced and looked for opportunities to nullify that influence. On one occasion a former Irish player tried to referee a match for me. His side was behind, and he badly wanted to kick at goal. I heard comments such as 'What about the deliberate knock-on?' (Actually, thanks to John Hewitt, by late 1978 I thought I knew one when I saw one.) My response was to determine that, unless murder was committed in front of the stand, I would not readily award a kickable penalty. In short, the only equitable way to handle an intrusive player who tried to deny me the right to decide was to deprive him of power to direct.

I never got 'into' refereeing in Australia. Although I joined the Sydney Referees Society, I did not engage at club level – because of King's School commitments in 1983-4, and from lack of interest thereafter. I wore the 'Sydney' badge on my navy jersey, however, throughout Ulster from 1990! My refereeing in Sydney was confined to the Greater Public Schools (GPS) scene during 1983 and briefly in 1984, with some matches at Knox Grammar in 1985. I never watched rugby union in Australia. I identified instead with Philip's passion for rugby league and his support of the Parramatta Eels. Phil played for the 1st XV at Rydal School but maintained his interest in the other code. I used my brother Paul's press pass in 1988, when Janice and he were in Australia, attended most of the Eels' matches, and sent my notes to Phil. My disillusionment with GPS football had killed my interest in rugby union down under, an experience that I shared with hundreds of boys from GPS schools.

Of my few matches in 1983, the first was Sydney Church of England Grammar School (Shore) *v.* Shore Old Boys. Headmaster Jika Travers, a former Oxford Blue and Wallaby, commented on differences of interpretation between the hemispheres, as when I allowed the ball to bounce off the full back's chest without adjudging a knock-on. This was not the family's only engagement with Shore Old Boys. Bowling his leg breaks, Phil was to take five Old Boys' wickets when he played against them for the Shore Common Room in 1991. On the White Oval, I refereed TKS 1st XV 's match with Oakham School during the English school's 'Australian Tour-1983' – the legend on the tie presented to me at the reception. The Oakham captain expressed there his relief that, after problems of interpretation in previous matches, I had presented 'like an English referee'. So much for my

159

protestations that I was not a Pom! In the GPS competition, I refereed the 2nd XV's fixture with St Ignatius, also on the White Oval. In a tight match, King's won narrowly, a result that the visiting coaches attributed to the bias of the referee. They were too thick to appreciate that, when handling his 'own' side, a referee invariably leans the other way (except of course in 'country schools'). Their gerning attitude was in marked contrast to the grace shown by the RBAI coaches when they had lost to Portora the previous autumn.

Another match of note involved King's16As against GPS opponents. (I have forgotten which school, but it scarcely matters.) The match was watched by hundreds of supporters from both school communities. Although they were roped off from the playing enclosure, it was yet a cauldron, the atmosphere charged and menacing. As a contest it was fierce, as a spectacle, deplorable. The noise level was alarming, the degree of intimidation disturbing. There were grounds for abandoning the match, and to this day I regret not having done so. It would have registered my contempt for this type of atavistic behaviour, hosted by a Church school. My final engagement with the GPS scene was in April 1984, in a calmer atmosphere. I refereed, in succession, King's 15As and 15Bs on the White Oval. In that ample setting, spectators were at a remote distance, and both matches were relaxed and agreeable affairs. It was the morning after I had resigned as Headmaster (though my resignation was not yet public knowledge). After the trauma of that event and the stress of recent days, I needed the release of physical exertion, and the sense of peace that this essay into refereeing afforded was as balm in Gilead.

III. LONG TWILIGHT: 1990 – 2005

1. 'Another 20 seasons'
When I rejoined the Ulster Referees Society in November 1990 on return from Australia, I was 53. I refereed my last match two days after my 67th birthday – on 23 October 2004. During fifteen seasons, I handled 240 matches: as divided into 5-year periods, 110 in 1990-94; 87 in 1995-99; and 43 in 2000-04. My reduced commitment during the final five years indicated neither declining

powers nor waning enthusiasm, but upheaval in personal life and lengthy visits to Canada from November 2001. Throughout these years, I was one of the Society's most travelled referees, excluding AIL-panel referees who travel throughout Ireland. I travelled from the North Coast for ten years, and then – after I had left Ballycastle in June 2002 – from the Dublin area, whether Howth, the Theological College at Rathgar, or Brittas Bay. The selectors respected my seniority by allowing me often to nominate the venues, sometimes even the matches, at which I wished to officiate. I was thus able to visit clubs where I had not been in earlier periods and ultimately refereed at almost every ground in Ulster. Sheephaven Bay was an elusive exception. Although selected for several matches there, because of cancellations I never made it. I asked to referee Sullivan Upper *v.* Portora Royal before I retired, and was twice appointed to this nostalgic fixture, the first having been cancelled. David Hewitt honoured me with his presence on the touchline.

Ironically, my return to refereeing had not begun well. My first season was difficult: I had several unhappy matches, felt unsettled, and questioned whether in my mid-50s I should continue. Then late in the season I went to Neilsbrook to referee Randalstown *v.* Enniskillen 2. Dr John Stewart told me that it was the most sensibly refereed match that he had watched all season and that the players had never known where I would turn up next. Such encouragement has power to influence: thereafter I was both clearer about my commitment and more confident. Bill McBride's gracious hospitality at Eaton Park two weeks later, when Cilla was with me, clinched matters. During each of the next two seasons I refereed 27 matches, more than in some seasons in my prime. Throughout all fifteen seasons I kept my 1A grade, which qualified me for matches up to Intermediate league and cup, and all club under-19 matches also. For my final four seasons, section 5 of the Junior League was added. In practice, however, I was often switched to fixtures at higher levels, particularly Schools 1st XV. Jill McCullagh at Ravenhill made sensible use of my being available at short notice, and during my peripatetic phase was adept at locating me.

Many assessors were old friends: I was always glad to see Jim McBride and Roy McGarvey on the touchline. Another old friend, Robin Hogg (President of the Ulster Society in 1994-95) captured the spirit of things in 2002 when I was in my 65th year. After watching me referee Enniskillen 3 *v.* Donegal 2 at Mullaghmeen, he reported:

> This was a thoroughly enjoyable, hard fought match played in a good spirit. Alan looked well up to it, and good for another 20 seasons.

Without ever asking permission, I trained on the underused Gaelic pitch near my home in Ballycastle, with its magnificent view of Knocklayde. During the season after it was regrassed, I trained among sheep even closer to the mountain, in fields that now support hundreds of homes. Although I travelled to most Belfast and all county Antrim clubs, the ideal fixture for me was west of the Bann. I went via Coleraine and did our weekly supermarket shopping there. I travelled to all the Tyrone clubs and was always glad to return to Fermanagh, even on the raw March day at Mullaghmeen when my fingers were so numb that my colleague Nigel (now Sir Nigel) Hamilton had to untie my bootlaces. I enjoyed most my outings to the hospitable county Donegal clubs – Inishowen, Letterkenny and Ballyshannon; and Donegal, where Harry Trimble, the local rector, was always welcoming. In the Dublin-based years, I travelled to grounds that were now closer than from Ballycastle: Virginia and Monaghan, Armagh and Newry.

I was happiest when visiting Carndonagh, home to Inishowen RFC. I had first come upon the team, with Padraig Kelly as captain, when I refereed at Kilraghts Road on 19 October 1991, my first match that season on return from overseas. I saw them again on 30 November in their 'home' match with RUC 3 – for security reasons it was played at Limavady. Padraig and I developed one of the best friendships that I ever made through rugby. His teammate John Merritt became another good friend.

In the mid-90s I joined Armoy RFC. I had rejoined CIYMS on return to Ireland but paid a hefty fee for the privilege of never visiting Belmont. The Armoy club, by contrast, not only levied no fee but also paid my annual subscription (initially unknown to me) to the Referees Society. Tom Christie and the other Armoy members looked after me proudly at the club's annual dinner and on other occasions. The pre-season tournament hosted by the club was a fine event, full of open, spirited football. Sadly, my whistle went there in 1998 for a poignant reason: to mark the start and finish of the silence observed by the assembled teams for victims of the Omagh bomb, one week before. Ballymoney RFC was my second home. I was often free to help out Bill Nicholl, the club's match secretary – Bill always brought me a pint while I showered – and was privileged to attend his retirement dinner at the Ballymoney club.

I enjoyed too my engagement with Woodvale RFC, until the club's sad demise. I refereed some of their matches at Ballysillan Leisure Centre – it was close to mother's home in North Belfast as was the club's social centre. When Tommy Taylor became a referee, he reminded me of an incident in Woodvale's match with Cavan at Cherryvale in which he had played. He and I were pursuing a lofted kick upfield when Tommy said 'Ref, do you realise that a civil war is going on back there?' He said that he would never forget my reply, 'Never mind – they will soon discover where the real action is.' And they did: sixteen forwards trooped sheepishly after us seconds later. It is a good example of my response to occasional flare-ups – I simply ignored them. Referees who gesticulate inanely and blow their whistle dementedly only prolong these situations.

2. Hugs and punches

I enjoyed Schools' matches as thoroughly in my 60s as I had done in my 20s. I refereed a fine match between Rainey Endowed and Portadown College for the Doyle Cup, and saw the Portadown XV again at Portora – a welcome return visit there, enhanced when I called with the evergreen Renee Benson. I refereed at Belfast High, with headmaster Stephen Hilditch present, and at Ballyclare High on a day so dangerously cold that some club matches were abandoned when hypothermia struck later. I went too to Omagh Academy, to Strabane Grammar for their match against Dalriada in the Schools Cup, and several times to Dalriada School. I was always on call for Dunluce School in Bushmills. After Regent House was well beaten by a strong Ballymena Academy home side, the Regent coach thanked me for protecting his young players and my stout clerical friend Terry Kerr, who was present as a parent, envied me my engagement.

Occasions at Coleraine Inst (CAI) were always full of interest. At a Medallion Shield match, my grandson George caused the crowd some amusement by exclaiming 'Grandad is wearing no trousers'! When I was living in Dublin, Jill switched me late one Friday to a 1st XV match at CAI. I accepted on condition that both coaches agree to a late kick-off (as they did); but as I left Ballsbridge at 6.30am, I easily made the scheduled time of 10.30am. I was rewarded when the Headmaster of CAI, Stanley Forsythe, commended my fitness and sharpness, and more especially when Joan Forsythe hugged me warmly at half time. Another visit to CAI involved their semi-final match with Belfast Inst in the 2nd XV Cup – by now a knock out competition. After two early tries by CAI, the turning point in RBAI's fight back came when I adjudged as illegal the 'flying wedge' type of penalty kick that they attempted. David Harkness, the home touch judge and a Senior League referee, told me that RBAI had deployed that tactic all season but that no referee had hitherto had the courage to call it illegal.

Club rugby offered rich rewards also. I refereed at Kilraghts Road the Ulster final of the interprovincial Under-16 competition and was happy that Ballymoney won. When I was selected for the annual Boxing Day fixture between the Waterside and Cityside players of City of Derry RFC, I enjoyed the relaxed occasion so much that for several years I repeated it by request. Albert Austin and other Derry friends from the high noon era treated me right royally on these and other visits. I relished above all, however, my experience at Neilsbrook when I entered the dressing room of the losing team, never the happiest of venues. I was solemnly told by one of the Randalstown players – 'Ref, most of the referees we get are younger than you, some of them still in their 20s.' (I was then 65.) Only slightly shorter than a county Tyrone pause, a county Antrim pause ensued. I waited. And then heard, 'But none of them covers as much ground as you did today.' It was worth the wait.

The new professional era in Ulster rugby affected club rugby adversely, if indirectly. In a league match at Eaton Park with Instonians as visitors, Ballymena RFC failed to provide me with a touch judge: potential flag bearers were in the stand watching a vital All-Ireland League match. In the new order of things, the Ulster Society was able to attract sponsorship and its referees were rigged out in appropriate attire. I was able at last to shed my Collegians socks! I was less taken with other novelties and never carried – and so did not use – the new red and yellow cards. Nor did I ever 'bin' a player. But essentials did not change, and especially the friendships that the game evoked. On a bitterly cold, wet day in January 2004, when all matches at both Ballymoney and Coleraine RFCs were cancelled, my match at the University of Ulster survived. As I was still shivering badly after a hot shower, Tony Morrison, an assessor and old friend, brought me to his home in Portstewart and sensibly gave me hot whiskey before we joined the others for our meal in the Anchor Bar.

There were remarkably few unsavoury incidents over fifteen years. Of three that I record, two happened at Clogher Valley RFC, a club founded when I was in Australia. In March 1999, Clogher Valley 2 played North 5 in the league. They had expected to win, and were miffed when North, a vastly experienced side with greater skills and discipline, took control and won the match. The losing side's frustration was vented on the referee. Ugly mutterings that NIFC was 'a wealthy Belfast club' inferred that I had been bribed to favour the visitors. One of the most unpleasant on-field experiences that I had ever endured was compounded when neither thanks nor hospitality was offered to me.

In February 2004, I returned to Fivemiletown for the replay of the regional final of the Under-19 Cup between Clogher Valley and Monaghan. In a highly charged atmosphere, both coaches incited their teams and openly criticised me. The players generally became unsettled and some excitable. Contrary to my usual approach, I kept an iron grip on the scrummage. But I feared for the safety of the young players. After one major eruption, I abandoned the match early in the second half – the only such decision in my refereeing career. I had for years in reports to Ulster Branch expressed disquiet over the evident deterioration in the style and spirit in which Under-19 club matches were being played, but this Cup match was downright dangerous. One of the ironies was that the home coach, a menacing presence on the touchline, had been the most docile of props on the previous Saturday – a wise stance for him to adopt at Inishowen. And not only ironical, but disturbing also in its implications.

The *cause célèbre*, however, had been at Magherafelt on 9 March 1996, when Rainey Old Boys 4 had played Lurgan 2 in a league match. I saw the punch aimed at me by a Lurgan player, turned my head, and received a glancing blow on the side of my face. The offender, whom I ordered off, was not a young hothead but a bank official in his mid-30s who had recently resumed playing. After reporting the incident, I left on a prebooked trip to England. On arrival with Nick Jones at Wellington College, I was greeted with 'I hear you were thumped!' As usual, bad news had travelled fast. The meeting of Ulster Branch's disciplinary committee, postponed until my return, was very different from that of October 1975. Some ten officials and a solicitor were present and the atmosphere sympathetic. I was even thanked for not abandoning the match, a response that had not occurred to me on the day. This incident had sent shock waves through Ulster rugby. The offending player was banned for ten years – effectively a life ban. I could not but reflect that a more savage assault at Omagh two decades earlier had merited only two weeks' suspension. That said, I was sensible that physical assault on a referee strikes at the very foundations of the game; and I welcomed the exemplary justice of the Branch's sentence. Privately, a civil action brought against my assailant reached settlement out of court.

Ironically, I saw little rugby and got to few international matches – my brothers gladly took up my usual allocation of two (paid) tickets. Lansdowne Road occasions stand out in their rarity. Back in 1980 I had taken Philip to see the Welsh match when he was eight: he was thrilled to touch green jerseys at the pre-match photographs. We got to our seats to find that a wide aisle separated them. So Phil watched the match on my knee! Now, years later, Jim, John and I, with Phil and his cousin Peter, saw England well beaten by an inspired Irish team. On other occasions I had friends for company, as Keith Prosser from Bristol and later Peter Barrett. The courtesy of playing the national anthem of the visitors was not extended to the England team at

Lansdowne Road. 'God save the Queen' had last been played at the final international match played at Ravenhill, in 1949. But in 1997 courtesy was shown – and not only to the England players, but the Ulster players on the Ireland XV also. I had been waiting since 1955 to hear my country's national anthem played at Lansdowne Road – and sang it with some emotion.

3. Final whistle

Despite absences in Canada during my final three seasons, I continued to referee whenever I was in Ireland. On return from two months in Vancouver Island, I attended the monthly meeting of the Ulster Referees Society in January 2003. I was gratified when the president, whom I did not know, acknowledged me and asked members to welcome 'our oldest active'. Ironically, when I next attended on my 67th birthday – it was to be my final meeting – no one seemed to notice. Except my friend Mark Orr, who generously hailed me in conversation as a role model and inspiration to our younger colleagues. Neither of us knew that my match two days later would be my last. Two weeks after it, I flew to Toronto. After running at pace in the Ulster autumn, the onset of arthritis in my left hip meant that by winter in Ontario I could hardly walk.

As I reflect on a career with the Ulster Referees Society that spanned 44 seasons, I note the curious fact that the Society had never replied to any letter that I addressed to it – on any subject. (My text has included some instances.) On Roy McGarvey's advice, I had enquired about the Hennessy Awards, whereby – so I understand – retired referees with at least ten years' service are entitled to apply for ticket allocation for home internationals. I wrote twice to the Society about this entitlement without reply on either occasion. It means that, after serving the IRFU's Ulster Branch in aggregate for more than 25 years, I am no longer able to purchase international tickets as of right. More recently, I had taken up with the Society's Hon Treasurer the dual payment over several seasons – by Armoy RFC and myself – of my annual subscription. He must have been comfortable with this double dipping, for again I received no reply.

But even these experiences did not prepare me for the last straw – a sad footnote to my career that I give here for the record. I had travelled in autumn 2004 from either Brittas Bay or Howth, and claimed my expenses as usual. Ulster Branch had paid for my travel from Dublin in the previous two seasons. In 2005, however, I received only 25 per cent of the amount I had claimed. Was this a mistake, a change in policy, albeit without consultation, or a specific decision not to meet my actual expenses? In order to find out I wrote to the Hon Secretary of the Referees Society, Gerry Wright, an ex-RAEC officer like myself, posting my letter at Dublin airport. When I received no reply, I sent a follow-up email from Canada. There was again no response from Gerry. I wrote next to the chief executive of Ulster Branch, Michael Reid, expressing regret that I must refer to him a matter of routine administration. He did not reply – so much for the new professional era. Under guidelines issued by the Small Claims Court, I then wrote formally to Mr Reid, advising that I would take legal action if he failed to reply. There was again no response. On return to Belfast, I applied to the Court for recovery of the amount outstanding. The Court formally notified the Ulster Branch. The Branch at once acknowledged liability and drew a cheque in my favour – it covered my full travel expenses, interest thereon, and repayment of the Court fee. The chief executive signed both letter and cheque.

I had not intended that the five matches that I refereed in early autumn 2004 should be the last of my career, and am glad that I did not know at the time. The first, at Randalstown, was a typical early season match played rather casually in warm sunshine. The second, at Shaw's Bridge, represented a not unfamiliar hiatus, with youth teams from Cooke and Instonians, who shared grounds and clubhouse, booked to play on the same pitch at the same time. The problem was resolved by playing the matches in succession, with reduced halves; I refereed both. The third Saturday, 9 October, was a glorious autumn day. I had set out for Derry from Howth, but when I checked with Jill on arrival in Belfast on Friday, was switched to Omagh Academy's match with Royal School Dungannon. The large crowd responded both to the lovely morning and – I sensed – to my own spirit: I was fit, sharp and relaxed, and clearly enjoying myself. My old friend Jack Reid, the Omagh coach, said of his opposite number – Keith Patton, the Ulster Schools coach – 'I have never seen

Patton so quiet!' It was only later that I recalled having played against Dungannon Royal in the Schools Cup in 1954-55, exactly 50 seasons before. Happily, the fourth fixture was in Holywood, with the added bonus that Ballymoney were the visitors. Inspired by the intrepid 'Tosh' Skelton, they won a clean, robust match against Holywood 3.

My fifth match was at Carndonagh. Had I been choosing the host club for my final match, I would have chosen Inishowen RFC. On a raw day earlier that year Padraig Kelly had made me don my tracksuit top for the second half and fortified me from his hip flask – at 66, both were refereeing 'firsts' for me. John Merritt and Padraig himself, having hung up their boots, were again on the touchline on 23 October 2004 to see Inishowen's 13-year unbeaten record under my refereeing remain inviolate when they easily defeated Strabane 2.

These final five matches epitomised all that I had enjoyed in Ulster rugby since 1961. They recalled refereeing experiences in which, over a span of 45 years, I found enrichment, fulfilment, and infinite joy. I understand very well why the whistle went.

CHAPTER SIX

From Australia to Canada (via Ballycastle)

Success consists of going from failure to failure without loss of enthusiasm. *(Sir Winston Churchill)*

I. SECOND CHANCE, 1984-89

1. *'Not many of your sort'*

Cilla and Philip left for Ireland in July 1984. Cynthia Parker had offered me her *pied à terre* in Mittagong and I tramped the roads on winter afternoons with a happy Airedale, returning to a log fire, good books and the Bodyline series. My job applications were prepared weekly before I drove to Sydney. My host there, Paddy Morgan, an Old Portoran and retired RN Commander, accompanied me when I addressed the Rotary Club of Sydney on Northern Ireland. His staff typed my applications. I was interviewed for the positions of chief executive of Geelong Hospital; regional director with the Health Department in Victoria and regional inspector, based in Newcastle, with the NSW Education Department; deputy chief executive of the Royal Blind Society in Sydney; and secretary in Canberra to the national conference of Vice-Chancellors. I stayed with Nigel Creese in Melbourne, endured psychometric testing, and got to know the intriguing world of management consultancy. The highlight was a hilarious interview in Newcastle with Mr Pickwick (or his double) and his colleagues. While these experiences were affirming, however, I needed the ultimate affirmation of success.

The Australasian Director of Spencer Stuart and Associates, Kerry McInnes, interviewed me for the post of chief executive of Multiple Sclerosis Society of New South Wales (MSSNSW). He informed me that, although I was a strong candidate, he had selected another whom the Society's President, John Studdy, would appoint when he returned to Sydney. I flew to Belfast in September facing the spectre of failure. While I was in

Portstewart, however, Maggi Morgan rang to say that Mr Studdy wished to see me on return. He told me that he had seen the preferred candidate in a different light and that I had replaced him. John Studdy related two significant facts. First, he had sought to ascertain if the Society would be harmed in the market place by my appointment and concluded that it would not. Second, that John Barraclough, a former minister in the NSW Government, had suggested that I deserved a second chance. The President then detailed my salary package. Accommodation apart, it was similar to that at TKS. Status and salary were restored – and the prophets of doom confounded.

In the weeks before starting work I reflected in spring sunshine at Mittagong on the vicissitudes of 1984. I had earlier devoured books on both management and stress, and also the book of Psalms: every facet of experience confronted me there, whether as comfort or counsel. In six months I had had neither need nor desire to attend church and instead identified with what Gerald Priestland termed 'the great church of the unchurched', so free from hypocrisy and cant. After the psalmist, I had never wavered in my expectation. In the end, in God's gentle irony, a new situation had been provided.

There was both occasion for regret, and one moment of pure delight, during the months of waiting. I regretted having resigned from the Anglican Consultative Council. No one in the Church of Ireland, rightly, had suggested it – I was an elected representative, not a delegate. Moreover, it would have given me much satisfaction to speak, as it were, for Australia at ACC-6 (in July 1984) in the absence of Archbishop Donald Robinson who had been refused a visa by the Nigerian authorities. But my misplaced sense of propriety had deprived me. The delight arose when I signed on as unemployed. I had been reluctant to do that until Maggi Morgan persuaded me that I owed it to myself as a taxpayer. (I had paid tax up 60 per cent before Paul Keating, the Treasurer in the new Labour government, reduced it to 49 per cent.) At the exchange a young man with long hair and one earring interviewed me. He did not look up until we came to 'previous employment'. When I replied 'Headmaster of the King's School', his head came up, his mouth fell open, and his earring went flying as he said, 'We don't get many of your sort in here!'

John Studdy had appointed me knowing that Cilla might not return to Australia. She did, however, before Karen and Philip arrived for Christmas. Phil collected autographs of the Wallabies on his flight. Rachel was overjoyed at our reunion: she had for weeks been alone in Australia. The Morgans went to Ireland leaving us with their home and swimming pool. Before they returned we had rented a house at Wahroonga. On the advice of Dr Paul White – the jungle doctor – Cilla and I attended St Paul's, Wahroonga the Sunday after our three children flew to UK – Rachel to visit family. Dr White had simply said 'Go to Brian King'. We soon knew why. Brian, the rector of St Paul's, and his radiant wife Pamela welcomed us with grace and love. On several occasions they invited parishioners to meet us in their home. Brian told me that I was still grieving. His pastoral care was the first offered to us in Sydney. He and I became friends and met regularly after he left St Paul's in Gordon RFC: Brian had played for the club and I was a social member – it was a refuge near my new office in Chatswood. Jim and Shirley Mills (from a previous life) were St Paul's parishioners; Shirley was the Director of Music. They became friends, as did Don and Rose Cameron. Donald, Bishop of North Sydney, lent me the *C. S. Lewis – Arthur Greeves Correspondence*: I had not known of the book, much less that Robin Morgan in Belfast had persuaded the Greeves family at Altona to release the letters for publication.

From 1987, I represented St Paul's parish on Sydney diocesan synod. John Studdy knew how much it meant to me but said nothing when I told him. He had no need to: his characteristic ear-splitting smile and the warmth in his eyes said it all. I was gratified that Archbishop Robinson called my name when I rose to speak at my first Synod.

I had exhausted my six months' terminal payout in paying school fees. To avoid tax, I now diverted much of my salary into the Society's superannuation scheme. To compensate, we sold our wing at Rossfad to John and Lois Williams, retaining only the mews. Karen went up to Leicester University in 1986 but was ineligible for a grant on account of my high salary. Philip stayed at Rydal until 1990. Sir George Halliday urged me to bring him to an Australian school and better provide for our own future. But Phil had been hurt by the TKS fiasco and had settled well at Rydal. We resolved to pay fees and airfares for six years. We did, however, recall Rachel from Frensham and she enrolled in the High School in Turramurra where we now lived: we were tenants of Tim and Jane Hawkes, parishioners at St Paul's, in Catalpa Crescent. Only now did Rachel disclose to us the sadistic abuse that she had suffered at Frensham – the School in further negligence had said nothing about her prolonged torment.

Weekends were now our own, a change welcome to Karen and Phil when home on holiday. Phil and I ran the City-to-Surf event every August. We watched Paul Eddington's moving portrayal of the cuckolded housemaster in *The Browning Version* at the Opera House. We supported England at the SCG, so failing – like Sir James Darling, a lifelong England fan – Lord Tebbit's fatuous 'cricket test'. We had time for overseas guests, including Bishop Heavener, Fr Philip Fogarty and Cecil Kerr, the last exhausted after his healing ministry in Sydney. Desmond and Deborah Cassidi stayed also when Sir Desmond was on Commonwealth Youth business. Sandra Orr and two other nurses from Dublin stayed longer, as did Old Portoran Chris McAuley. Paul and Janice lived with Rachel and me when Cilla was overseas in 1989. Under Paul's influence I ran the inaugural Anzac Day half-marathon but finished way behind this vastly experienced marathon man.

2. Chief Executive of MSSNSW

I must briefly encompass my five years in charge of a highly respected State charity. The society was poised for major advance. As well as day centres in the Sydney suburbs of Chatswood and Kogarah and the outreach of its social work team, it would soon commission a 50-bed hospital for young adults with MS – at Lidcombe in the western suburbs. Federal government funding for operating costs had not yet been secured. In any case, the Society must increase income from fundraising programmes (or marketing – the euphemism then in fashion). The imminent expansion in turnover, services, administration, staff and volunteer complement, required direction and management of the highest quality. The President attracted new directors from public life and business, including John Barraclough and Ken

Baxter. He asked me to report on how best to employ directors' expertise and I recommended that the Board disband its executive committee and appoint Services, Marketing and Finance committees that would meet regularly, minute their business, and report. This *modus operandi* proved effective. The Finance Committee appointed a salaries sub-committee. I made annual recommendations for executives who reported to me.

John Studdy was President of the National MS Society of Australia (NMSSA). John Foley, my counterpart in the MS Society of Victoria, doubled as NMSSA's Executive Director. The two Johns were a formidable team in point of ability and mutual understanding. Studdy served on the boards of many public companies, as chair of several; Foley, previously a party political organiser, was universally respected and listed in *Who's Who in Australia*. Both offered me friendship and support. John Studdy and I met regularly in his city office at 8.00am. Based on openness and trust, our partnership was the bedrock of my chief executive role. While the primary responsibility of NMSSA was funding MS research, the regular sessions of its National Council, each preceded by a two-day conference of State executive directors, allowed wide co-operation. NMSSA was affiliated to IFMSS – the International Federation of MS Societies. Australia hosted in 1986 its annual conference, held in Sydney. It involved much work for my staff, co-ordinated by Diana Pollack. The conference was deemed a success. My reward was to attend the 1987 conference in Washington DC. I ran early one morning there to the Lincoln Memorial and was much moved by Lincoln's Address at his second Inauguration, the text of which was etched on the wall of the Memorial.

Business travel was time-consuming: fifteen flights to Melbourne in five years, first flights to Adelaide, Hobart and Perth, and return to Brisbane. I attended the annual conferences of TAIF (The Australasian Institute of Fundraisers), the first in Christchurch in 1985. On that New Zealand trip I saw uncle Vincie shortly before he died, at my cousin Margaret's home north of Auckland. I had first flown from Christchurch to Wellington, where His Excellency Sir Paul Reeves received me at Government House: we had last been together at ACC-5 in England in 1981. When flying to UK on leave, the Pacific route allowed me to stay in Los Angeles with Billy and Sue – Billy McNinch was my first cousin. Flights via Singapore took 24 hours. Twice I hired a car on arrival at Heathrow and drove direct to Stranraer, stopping every two hours for exercise and fresh air.

Except for statutory holidays, however, I took no leave during my first 18 months. I sought an executive team able to give capable and effective leadership. As Financial Controller, Bill Northcote was exemplary: young, efficient and utterly loyal. He enjoyed the respect of staff in all departments. When I told Bill that I had no grasp of our daily cashflow, he devised a formula for reporting that was later adopted by other State Societies. I perceived that some senior staff needed replacing and dismissed one executive who was unable to tell me what he did! The part-time Medical Director was next to go: a Board member, Dr R. G. (Rocky) McEwin, a former Chief Medical Officer of Health for New South Wales, provided wise support here. I sensed that the Marketing Manager, appointed just before my arrival, was the wrong man but delayed acting until I had evidence. At my request, John Foley came to Sydney and carried out an audit of our marketing operations. I first dismissed the assistant manager whose appointment had shown poor judgement, then the manager. John Studdy's sensitive understanding helped me to handle the stress of this protracted ordeal.

It was a relief to select competent staff. The excellent Dr Rosemary Hanson became Medical Director, and Ken Lewis – born in Belfast but reared in Australia – Marketing Manager. Ken, innovative and inspirational in leadership, matched Bill Northcote in assuidity and loyalty: we formed a close-knit triumvirate. We recruited first-class managers: Karen D'Souza for Internal Services, Sam Tayeh as IT Manager, Jane Scroope as Director of Nursing. I appointed Maggi Morgan as Volunteers Co-ordinator. Her energies and flair were long to serve the Society in upmarket social events also. Fundraising programmes such as MS Read-a-thon needed capable managers. We offered attractive packages including a car. At my instigation the Board disclosed fundraising costs in our annual accounts – previously only net figures had been published. Several directors had objected, fearing loss of public support, but the

Society's openness was widely approved and our Annual Report attracted Awards for its quality and professionalism.

The challenge of integrating the two main arms of the Society's operations – Services and Marketing – was acute. Some health professionals looked on fundraising with distaste, although their very livelihood depended on it. Regular managers' conferences did not always have happy outcomes. I enjoyed good relations with individual Services managers, especially Virginia Adams, head social worker, and Jane Scroope at the Nursing Home. Rebecca Braid, manager of our Chatswood day centre, prayed with me in her office when I was under pressure. Some lighter moments relieved the intensity of our operations. The Art Union (another euphemism) sold 25,000 tickets – at $25.00 – four times a year through telemarketing. We invited a celebrity to make the draw at an in-house reception and then to telephone the winner – the call was amplified for all to listen. We hoped that the top prize would go to an ordinary type. We shook our heads in disbelief on hearing, typically:

> Who did you say you were – Joe Soap? You must be joking! What? It's true then – really? So I've won a BMW! It'll look really good, mate, alongside the Porsche and the Mercedes.

During my third year, the Board was obliged to heed criticism of me. I had, not for the first time, made enemies. Again, I had shown poor people management skills and lost some able staff. Ken Baxter conducted the Board's inquiry. His report allowed directors to retain confidence in me. One recommendation was that I apply for membership of the Australian Institute of Management. I duly applied and, in recognition of my professional career, was elected a Fellow (FAIM). I held my office, if less assuredly, for two more years. During that time the Society achieved all its aims, appreciably increased income, produced healthy balance sheets, added a funded hydrotherapy pool to its facilities at Lidcombe, and raised its profile in the State and its prestige in Sydney. I felt entitled to the five weeks overseas leave that I took in spring 1989. It was a tactical mistake. Sir James Darling wrote that in 30 years at Corio he took a risk every time he went to England. In my case, the Board decided then to retrench me, and search for a chief executive with a background in commerce.

There had been two turning points during my final years. The first was when a new Services Manager was appointed. Dr Hanson and I selected an experienced man, well regarded by the health profession in Sydney and highly recommended. We chose a woman in second place but, confident of our first choice, paid scant attention to her. A group of directors met the two and spurned our preferred candidate when he made an unfortunate comment. It was the first time in nearly ten years as a chief executive that I was denied the right to appoint senior staff. In this case I was thwarted in my bid to complete a strong executive team. As it was, the directors' appointee related to some of them better than to me before resigning within two years. As I had inherited a loose cannon on the fundraising side – he was accountable to senior directors, until Ken Baxter called his bluff – it was irksome to revisit this imbroglio in a different area of operation.

The second turning point came at the final of our Quest fundraising programme, a prominent event in Sydney's social calendar. I briefed Cilla about directors who would be at our table. One was Susie Menadue whose husband John was Chief Executive of Qantas. With a misplaced sense of mischief, Cilla asked John Menadue what he did. When he replied modestly, Cilla retorted: 'So you work for Qantas! Let me tell you about your rotten airline' – and did, in excruciating detail. The story got around the Regent Hotel then and the city by morning. My boss dined out on it for weeks. It was taken as proof of my commercial ineptitude.

I was not, however, charged with nepotism. I employed both Janice and Paul. There was a perpetual shortage of nurses at Lidcombe and Janice was an excellent nurse. Again, we ever sought good telesales staff and Paul – as UTV sports viewers and Ravenhill crowds knew – was a superb communicator. Both proved their worth in the eyes of their managers. So did Chris McAuley: he was told that 'with a voice like that' he could sell anything.

My (almost) five years of service were nicely acknowledged. My severance package included a year's salary, household removal expenses to Northern Ireland, the equivalent of two business class fares to Belfast, office furniture, and retention of my company car until we left Australia three months later. We sold furniture at auction and offered redundant household items to parishioners at St Paul's. Our accountant spoiled the party by referring to a city firm without my knowledge a query that I had raised with him about tax obligations. I received two vacuous paragraphs – and an account for $1000. Our accountant was a friend and fellow parishioner. I seethed, said nothing, and settled the account. The MSSNSW directors laid on a farewell luncheon in Parliament House, arranged by John Barraclough. Lloyd Waddy delighted us when he attended and made a gracious speech: Lloyd linked the two worlds that we had known in Sydney. The Board trawled worldwide for a chief executive and found him in Geneva. After his brief tenure, they turned to John Foley, who readily moved to Sydney. On John's retirement, Bill Northcote succeeded. John Studdy apart, these two men had been my best supporters. Their successive appointments pleased me greatly.

II. LIFE AS A CAREGIVER

1. Ballycastle

We left Sydney late in 1989. Flying with BA, we expected our luggage to be mislaid. The airline obliged and so spared me having to handle our heavy cases – they were delivered next day. We lived with Gertrude for more than a year while John and Doris Matthews generously stored our furniture. Our plan for the mews at Rossfad was unacceptable to John and Lois Williams. With no alternative for us but to sell, they became sole owners of Rossfad, ironical in that they could not have bought the property without us. Remaining friends, we stayed at Rossfad or acted as caretakers when the family were away. Postponing house purchase, we lived from the start of the very cold April of 1991 in George and Barbara's holiday house at Brittas Bay. Friends in Dublin were welcoming: Bishop George and Mrs Simms had us to tea, Paddy and Jill Moss for dinner. Jim Hartin and I talked church history in Castlemacadam rectory and I preached for Roland Heaney in Redcross church.

In October 1991 we moved into our own home in Leyland

Park, Ballycastle. As I was now Cilla's caregiver, financial planning was imperative. Australia supplied £100,000 in severance and superannuation payments, but school fees (in Phil's last year at Rydal School) and car purchase made inroads. Most funds were left in Sydney to be drawn down tax-free at my 55th birthday in 1992. Five years later my pension from DENI became available – less than half of a full pension and based on my 1980-82 salary. (It attracts inflationary increases, not professional awards.) In 1997 the entire lump-sum component was needed to redeem our mortgage. Happily, life assurance policies matured at intervals, when terminal bonuses were still at over 100 per cent. Cilla received basic Disability Living Allowance (DLA) from 1992 and, when her further deterioration merited higher allowances from 1997, I was awarded Carer's Allowance. In our changed income situation Phil received the maximum student grant when at Goldsmiths' College in London. Phil was unique among his peers: he actually lived on his grant.

Ballycastle was a lonely experience for us. Its air of friendliness was genuine yet deceptive: friendship was not readily offered. We lived among good hardworking neighbours but were isolated from the professional end of the town. Apart from Albert and Alicia Duncan in Ramoan rectory, we received no invitations to dine, ironical in that Cilla had spent years giving dinner parties. But as a family we enjoyed Marcella McMullan's hospitality – her beautiful home was suitable for Cilla's wheelchair. Although I was a member of both Ballycastle Golf Club and the Probus Club, I had no golfing partner until, late in the day (for me) Victor Dobbin retired as Army Chaplain-General and came home with Rosemary to Ballycastle. It had mattered less in that Philip golfed when he was home, and Jim in the good years that he enjoyed after being in hospital in 1991. Otherwise I played solo in summer before 6.00am on Saturday or Sunday, getting round in under two hours and home to make breakfast before Cilla was awake: good for both fitness and morale. Twice a week I tramped Ballycastle forest, on the slopes of Knocklayde, without ever meeting another townie in ten years. My friendships with, first, Hugh A. Boyd and then John Bach, chaplain and criminologist at UUC, were inspirational in these years of isolation. Our neighbour Charlie McKinney became a particular friend of both of us, always helpful and good company. Friends from Sydney, Canberra, Dublin and England came to lift our spirits also.

Ramoan parish was a mixed blessing. Until he retired, Archdeacon Duncan was a devoted and sensitive pastor who gave Cilla Holy Communion at home when she became more housebound. Whenever she attended services in Holy Trinity, Cilla was ignored. The caring Sharon Wilson saw her wheelchair acting as a barrier. It was a struggle too to get Cilla into the Quay Road hall: it had no disabled access. It was well we were on hand. After one Sunday evening Eucharist, we invited a Canadian priest for supper and one summer Phil and I brought an American in the pew behind us home for lunch. He was thrilled with Cilla's gooseberry tart.

We were happy that Karen and Philip found good partners. Karen and Mark Sherrington had fallen in love in IVth Form at Rydal. They were married in Holy Trinity, Ballycastle in September 1993 with the reception in the Marine Hotel. Philip and Beth de Rose met in what Phil described in his wedding speech as 'that well-known dating agency, the Goldsmiths' Christian Union' – they were married in Christ Church, Chislehurst in August 1996. Rachel, for her part, had stayed on in Sydney. When she returned to Ireland we realised that she was ill. It was, however, some time before she entered hospital – a time not without stress. She recovered and enrolled in London's Guildhall University, though against her consultant's advice. Her illness recurred in London and she spent two further spells in hospital there. From April 1997 she lived with us in Ballycastle.

We were invited to Portora, where Bishop Brian Hannon hosted a reception and received my (photographic) portrait for the School. Our friends Sam and Marie Morrow were there. Sam, now Secretary of the Portora Board, epitomised the new genre of effective governor that my initiative in 1982 had made possible. We retained contact with The King's School also. Jonathan Persse sent me the school magazine until he retired. Keith Asboe, who had been Director of Music, brought Helen to stay with us – they had married after Keith retired. We were delighted when Lloyd Waddy became a judge in the Family Court of Australia and also Chairman of TKS Council, and when Tim

Hawkes succeeded Jon Wickham as Headmaster. Brian King's becoming Bishop of Parramatta (and a TKS councillor) gave us great joy – as Brian noted in his response to us. Brian King shunned the indoctrination that defined Sydney diocese. I had anticipated his episcopal promotion before leaving Sydney. Characteristically he had asked me to pray that, in that event, pastoral ministry remain his priority. I believe it did.

On return to Ulster initially, I had – more from pride than realism – applied for chief executive positions. North Eastern Education and Library Board did not interview me, but Driver & Vehicle Licensing (DVLNI) did – at Stormont. I did not succeed. Thereafter I sought only pocket money. I applied to the Oxford and Cambridge Board. Its wise arrangements of the 1980s were no more. Its new monitoring sessions were obligatory, but I might not travel from Northern Ireland: I had to register a 'home' address in England. I was never called upon, so much for claims of an examiner shortage in the 1990s. I had more time for my regular commitments and interesting sidelines: when David Hewitt and his colleagues on the Parades Commission came to Ballycastle, I gave evidence at a hearing.

In 1993 I became an Electoral Registration Officer, based in Ballymoney, and for five years had sole responsibility for compiling the electoral register for the two Portrush wards. Most officers were married women. Our remuneration, averaged hourly over the street work and the complex administration, was less than the minimum wage. The attraction for me was that I enjoyed weeks in the open-air in autumn sunshine – I recall only five days of rain in as many years – a delightful situation on the Atlantic, and the discipline of working a 12-hour day. Every year I lost ½ stone, perfect preparation for the rugby season. I worked too as Presiding Officer at elections: for the European Parliament, the Northern Ireland Assembly, and Westminster; and the referendum on the Good Friday Agreement: stationed variously in Portrush, Portstewart, Killowen, Armoy and Ballycastle, and finally Cushendall polling station at the General Elections of both 2001 and 2005, as Senior Presiding Officer for the latter. I got to the last of the mandatory training sessions in 2005 by driving direct to the venue in Cookstown on arrival in Dublin airport from Canada – and slept throughout!

Two comments must suffice. It was my duty to see that each voter was identified by one of several prescribed documents before I issued him/her with a ballot paper. Many senior citizens were in effect disenfranchised by this requirement: mother had no driving licence and in her 80s ceased to have a passport. My attitude was that if satisfied as to the voter's identity, I would use my discretion and issue the ballot paper. The second comment concerns the elections of May 2005. As once before, the parliamentary election was combined with the local authority election. The reward for polling station staff was an enhanced fee, but at a price. To administer two different voting methods, first-past-the-post and proportional representation, was not easy. Throughout the 15 hours of polling (7.00am–10.00pm), I had to instruct each voter in both voting methods, issue two marked (perforated) ballot papers, and guide voters to the appropriate ballot boxes, time-consuming tasks that were virtually impossible to complete at peak voting times. In practice, I relied on the young Sinn Féin agent in attendance all day to point voters to the correct ballot box.

2. Mobility, more or less

While she could still cope, Cilla and I travelled to England. When Phil graduated, Derek and Jean Powell met us, lodged us in Blackmore House, their beautiful home near Brentwood, provided a car for our drive to Goldsmiths', and returned us to Stansted. (Jean – neé Gordon – had been my teenage girlfriend.) On the day after Phil and Beth's wedding in August 1996, in intense heat and with no air-conditioning in our car, Cilla collapsed on the M4. I drove like a fury to Keith and Jan Prosser's home in Bristol and carried Cilla from the car into the cool hall: her relief was heart-rending. The love shown by friends in England meant much at a difficult time. Caroline Smith had given a lunch party at Oadby in 1989 when Karen graduated at Leicester. After Colin moved to another Methodist circuit, we looked after their home in Chapel-en-le-frith while they were in India at Christmas 1997. When our families joined us from London, Cilla first saw there our beloved grandson George. When alone, I repaired to Chapel often and climbed Kinder Scout in the Peak District on each visit, however brief. I was able to attend one OP London dinner with my host in Marlow, James Morrow, and Leo McKinstry's marriage with Elizabeth in Sidney Sussex. When I went to the porter's lodge next morning, I found that James Morrow had been there before me; and over breakfast I met Nicky, his Rhodesian fiancée.

Ireland did not compete. Rossfad apart, we stayed only with the Orrs – our last visit was days before Liz died in a freak road accident in Dublin late in 1994 – and with Donald Mills at Dunleckney Glebe after Isabel's death. During that visit, Peter and Anne Barrett gave us lunch in the deanery in Waterford and Ginnie Kennerley tea in Timolin rectory. We had, too, occasional holidays in the west: Connemara in 1992 (our children's 25th anniversary treat), the Rosses and Sligo. We discovered how appallingly bad was the standard of disabled facilities in Irish hotels. In April 2000 we flew to Harare for James Morrow's wedding to Nicky. The flights – and those to and from the Victoria Falls on Cilla's birthday – were arduous. I arranged with Air Zimbabwe's attendant that when Cilla needed the toilet on the overnight flight, I would drag her along the aisle and he would kick open the door (he sat facing it). Nicky's family had lodged us in the home of friends who were overseas and their servants looked after us devotedly. At the bride's home during the reception, fine young men led by Chris McAuley carried Cilla through the beautiful gardens between the marquee and house facilities. Sadly, we noted early indications of the tyranny that was to destroy Zimbabwe. Our new friends in Harare had no expectation that Tony Blair – 'Mr Blur', as Gerry Adams shrewdly called him – would intervene in this imminent tragedy.

From 1997, Rachel's support had allowed me more freedom. Mother had turned 80 in 1995: we ate often in her favourite pub, Corrs (Corner), and she sometimes came to Ballycastle. I visited old friends such as Sheila Sleator and Lily Hewitt (now living in Holywood), both growing older with grace. In Britain I stayed with friends from Biddy Stevenson in Old Colwyn to Derek and Hilary Gay at West Mersea. When 3rd Holywood celebrated its 50th anniversary in 1993 at the Ulster Folk Museum, I gave the address at the pre-dinner service held in the museum's historic church. Major Ivan Nelson and I met again at a RAEC Association dinner in Lisburn: our paths had never crossed when we were serving. The GOC-in-C Northern Ireland, General Sir John Wilsey, received me in his home before the dinner: we had served together in Palace Barracks in 1965. Twenty years after leaving the Army, I could stay at the RAEC HQ Mess in Eltham Palace. I wrote there the submission that I made about Portora's future [DENI: Proposal 50]. After government sold Eltham Palace to English Heritage, the Corps recovered its use for a Luncheon in the Great Hall. I was proud to escort my daughter-in-law Beth – an Eltham girl – to that function. She was by far the youngest there and carried the day with her charm and poise. I attended the Gallipoli Memorial Lecture in Holy Trinity Church in Eltham on 26 April 1995: 'Churchill and Gallipoli.' Eighty years after Gallipoli, Martin Gilbert's lecture was a vindication of 'Churchill's part in the Dardanelles-Gallipoli story'.

I attended functions held by the Antrim Knot of the Friendly Brothers, to which I had become affiliated. The background here is that, when the Fermanagh Knot was formed while I was overseas, my records had fallen off a lorry between Omagh and Enniskillen – I learned that only on enquiry years later. (My annual subscription, however, had been safely collected every year.) Senior members of the Order worked hard to have me reinstated. I was grateful for their intervention, but intrigued as to why such assiduity was needed to make good a miscarriage.

My most bizarre experiences involved Smith Square where I had last been seen in 1970. Of my sponsors, Nicholas Winterton MP acted with enthusiasm, Brian Mawhinney MP – on the ground that it had been a long time – with reluctance. Sir Fred Catherwood gave me warm encouragement. Andrew Mitchell MP, the Vice-Chairman (Candidates) was supportive at interview – he said I had much to offer. When Andrew moved on, Tim Smith MP became his sceptical successor – his problem was my age. On his abrupt departure, Dame Angela Rumbold MP was the third to interview me. The appointment indeed changed hands so often that at one point Brian Mawhinney was unable to tell me who held it – Brian always replied to my letters. As to the Central Office agent, I had alphabetical misfortune in that I was his first interviewee on a Monday morning. He deemed it impossible that I had sought nomination in North Down as a serving officer. It was of course a matter of record. Attitudes at Smith Square epitomised all that was wrong with the Conservative Party before 1997: arrogant, complacent and power-besotted. Central Office needed the Ulster realism that Brian Mawhinney would inject as Party Chairman. But even he could not see that the game was up. In 1997 I tramped the streets and lanes of Macclesfield in support of its MP's bid for re-election. Nicholas Winterton was committed and hard working. Labour voters told me that they wished he were their man. He was, in that he was re-elected when many, including the gracious, and to me helpful, Dame Angela, lost their seats.

3. Divorce

Northern Ireland had one residential MS Unit. It was located in Dalriada Hospital in Ballycastle. Families drove from all over the province to access the unit. I was able to push Cilla there in her wheelchair. She had excellent care; Rachel and I brief respite. As carers we were on our own. Karen and Phil lived in England. Cilla's brothers were committed both professionally and in church activity. They might have taken Cilla into their homes or on holiday. Such compassion would have meant much to her, but was never offered. It was the same in Guernsey. I visited Robbie and Beryl three times. Although they had bought the house next door to put up family and friends, they were adamant that Cilla might not come there. We applied to Ballymoney Rotary Club for help in purchasing an electric wheelchair. The club was unable to help and Cilla went without. As an absolute beneficiary of her father's will, Cilla was potentially wealthy, but an agreement that would have allowed her to access her inheritance without detriment to her mother's interest was, as far as I know, never considered. It was none of my business to suggest it. Cilla is today maintained by the state – and sustained by Rachel's selfless love and devotion.

Carers and teachers have this in common: they know what pressure is. Others know nothing of the concomitant isolation, relentlessness, and physical and emotional exhaustion. My brother Mervyn and his wife June understood that during the life of their severely disabled daughter Christine. My state was, to my acute embarrassment, evident when I stayed with Leo and

Elizabeth McKinstry: it presented both as loss of confidence and confusion. Ruth Simmonds – she had arrived from Canada on marrying her cousin, Edward Orr – introduced me to a therapist in Dublin who perceived, from dire symptoms, how close I was to breaking point: she had seen others in like situation destroyed. She counselled (why I am not sure) that I confess early infidelity. Ironically, I had long prayed for strength not to confess, knowing both what Cilla's reaction would be and how much she needed me. Cilla, for her part, had for years prayed that my health would hold: she encouraged my refereeing and hillwalking as much in her own interest as mine. I was not mistaken. Cilla petitioned for divorce on the explicit ground of my unfaithfulness during our early years of marriage. But it was more complex. When I told Fanta that we had separated, he said 'I am saddened but not surprised.' As a trusted friend, he understood that there were problems in our marriage, knew too that Cilla had refused marriage counselling. But for Cilla's incapacity we would probably have separated much earlier.

The terms of the divorce were simple. I surrendered my interest in our house but retained my pension income. As it was inevitable that Cilla would be in residential care within a short time – in the event three years – this split protected Rachel, as the house remained her home. But it left me homeless. It was the least of my problems. With the church, as Dr Bryan Follis puts it, 'over-interested in sexual sins', I was rejected by some and, worse, lectured (in pejorative ignorance) by others about my marriage vows. In discovering that divorce alters the dynamics of relationships – with one's children, with in-laws inevitably, and with friends, I learned who my friends were. I could not but reflect that – certainly for the 'guilty' party, as both society at large and the church in particular discern guilt – divorce is treated as a disability. The divorcee is therefore subject to the attitudes that the disabled suffer, whether the disability is physical or mental: lack of compassion, of understanding, of even Christian charity. I had observed Cilla suffer for years from such neglect; had drawn inspiration from her courage. That inspiration was needed now and was not denied me. At Christmas 2004, after our divorce was absolute, Cilla's gift to me was inscribed 'to my gentle ex-husband'.

III. THE CHURCH OF IRELAND REVISITED: 1988-2008

1. Synods, Colleges and Cathedrals
On 14 October 1988 I successfully moved this Resolution:

Synod notes the generous contribution of the Church of Ireland to the membership and leadership of the Diocese of Sydney throughout its history, as recognised in the Presidential Address to Synod in 1987, and as recorded, particularly in the appended clergy lists, in *Sydney Anglicans*.

Synod also notes the steadfast Christian witness in Northern Ireland today, in difficult and distressing circumstances, of the bishops, clergy and laity of the Church of Ireland.

Greetings from the Synod, a copy of *Sydney Anglicans*, and the text of the Resolution were sent to the General Synod of the Church of Ireland.

In May 1991, still on the theme of historical indebtedness, I proposed a Motion of thanks, at the 200th anniversary of his death, for John Wesley's impact on the Church of Ireland through his preaching ministry and his work as priest. The scene was not Sydney, but Belfast: I had been re-elected to the General Synod in 1990, six months after return from Australia, by the diocesan synod of Connor. (That body has re-elected me at every triennial election since then, including those in 2005 and 2008 when I have been resident in Canada.) No trumpets had sounded on my reappearance in 1991; but Houston McKelvey later told General Synod that he was glad to see me back – and at the rostrum. The Diocesan Council of Connor appointed me to the General Synod Board of Education, of which Houston McKelvey was Northern Secretary. In 2001, when seconding the Board's Report at General Synod, I pronounced Houston ubiquitous and indefatigable, and potentially an outstanding Dean of Belfast – he had just been appointed to that office.

The General Synod's Select Committee on Marriage elected me as chair at its first meeting in 1992, with Dr Joan Turner as its very efficient secretary. Members included two clerical married couples, David and Mary Woodworth and Raymond and Bobbie Moore. We all had our agendas and progress was initially difficult. I tried to emulate the courteous firmness of two fine chairmen, Gordon McMullan at Portora and John Studdy in Sydney. I had a visible reminder, as Dr McMullan was, happily, a valuable member of the Committee. (Bishop Walton Empey was the other episcopal member.) After a difficult early meeting, David Woodworth wrote encouragingly, 'You managed admirably.' When David, who was Dean of Cashel, died suddenly soon afterwards, all the elected members of Committee were in Cashel for his funeral. Our work was intensive. At our residential session held in the OLA Convent Guest House in Rostrevor, the Revd John Chambers of the Presbyterian Church was our able facilitator and Kate Turner recorder. As Fanta generously observed, I had been able to knit the members into an effective and affectionate body. Out of our work emerged the Church of Ireland Marriage Council, the creation and financing of which involved me in much intricate negotiation with the RCB and its officers, among whom David Meredith gave wise guidance and firm support.

For ten years I taught part-time in Trinity College, Dublin. After Jim Hartin resigned as lecturer in church history, I chanced to meet Ginnie Kennerley, then on the staff of the Church of Ireland Theological College (CITC), at the Christian Renewal Centre at Rostrevor. Ginnie undertook to tell the Principal that I was willing to help and in response Professor John Bartlett invited me to lecture Year 2 students on the Church of Ireland's Evangelical tradition; later, to be assessor for the auxiliary ministry course. For my 10 o'clock lecture, I left Ballycastle at 5.30am and reached central Dublin in three hours. Inching along O'Connell Street was relaxing after the rapid drive. Canon Billy Marshall thoughtfully alternated with me – we each gave two lectures instead of one – so that I had to travel less often. One year two former Roman Catholic priests from Year 3 attended my lectures: Dermot Dunne (now Dean of Christ Church Cathedral, Dublin) and Mark Hayden. When I lectured on English church history from the Reformation to the 20th century, Maria Jansson, whose degree in theology exempted her from my course, paid me the compliment of attending my lectures.

I was the Church's lay representative at the annual meeting in 2003 of the Irish Methodist Church, held in Ballymena. My request to address Conference was granted and I spoke of my long indebtedness to 'the people called Methodists'. At the annual meeting of the Wesley Historical Society, I was welcomed as an honoured guest. That event took place during Conference, to which the Society's proceedings were reported annually. In the light of that wisdom, I suggested to the House of Bishops that the Church of Ireland Historical Society be made accountable to the General Synod. I had no response from the House. The Society, without even episcopal patronage, remains independent.

Soon after return from Sydney, I requested the Bishop of Connor, Dr Poyntz, to licence me as a Reader in Connor. He refused me, as did Bishop Moore later. Sam Poyntz and Jimmie Moore were Old Portorans and old friends. But each rationalised a decision that I sensed had been taken on other grounds. Not that it mattered. In 1998, Donald Mills asked me to give the address at the Memorial Service for his wife Isabel in St Lazerian's Cathedral in Old Leighlin. The Revd James McMaster invited me to preach on 31 October 1999 at the Civic Service in St Nicholas's Church, Carrickfergus, to mark the 400th anniversary of the arrival of Sir Arthur Chichester in Ulster. A month later, in Advent, I gave the Webster Memorial Sermon in St Finbarre's Cathedral at the invitation of the Dean of Cork, Dr Michael Jackson. And in April 2000, Nicholas Cummins, the Dean of Killaloe, invited me to preach at Bob Hanna's installation to the chapter, in St Flannan's Cathedral. It pleased me that both Deans were Old Portorans. To preach in the space of 18 months in an ancient church and three cathedrals was a feat that only a southern bishop on his enthronement circuit might emulate.

Nor was I quite finished. In 2004, the Very Revd Douglas Stoute invited me to give the Homily during Choral Eucharist in St James's Cathedral, Toronto, at the Patronal Festival on 24 July. It was a long way to go for a sermon but as it was unlikely that anyone else in the Church of Ireland would to be so honoured, I accepted the Dean's invitation. The Cathedral did me proud: two nights in the prestigious King Edward Hotel and a handsome honorarium. Finally, under Bishop Jebb's discerning eye, I preached in St Mary's Cathedral, Limerick for Dean Maurice Sirr, in January 2006.

At the Chichester commemoration, in trying to apply king-dom principles to the Ulster situation, I identified rights vital to the self-respect of both communities. For Protestants, their very presence in the province, discerned in Bishop (later Cardinal) Cahal Daly's fine words in 1972, 'This was and is their home-land: they know and seek no other'; for Catholics, partnership in government. I said:

> That right has at no time, in the 400 years since Chichester, been enjoyed: not under the Ascendancy Parliament, not under the Union, not under Stormont, and not (save for a few months in 1974) under Direct Rule. Yet such partnership is not only a question of natural justice, but a Biblical imperative as well.

As we recessed, Austin Ardill from his pew handed me his order of service. With his scribbled words of thanks he had given a Biblical reference – Malachi 2:10. I looked it up and read: 'Have we not all one father? Hath not one God created us?' I was gratified by Austin's empathy and evident conviction.

I was in Canada when I learned that the Armagh Electoral College had failed to elect to the see of Clogher. During a flight from Toronto to Vancouver I scribbled the reasons why the House of Bishops should now appoint the Dean of Cork and mailed my thoughts to the Archbishop of Armagh. After Dr Michael Jackson was appointed Bishop of Clogher, he wrote to say that it was amazing what some people got into by way of in-flight entertainment! Having 'called' this appointment correctly, I corresponded with the Primate about further episcopal ap-pointments. In the event all of those whose names I brought for-ward (except for one woman) became bishops. Without impair-ing confidentiality, Dr Eames appeared to enjoy our exchanges. I was gratified when he wrote, 'I have given careful consideration to all that you say – I always do.'

2. A History of the Church of Ireland, 1691-2001

Research and writing were both a first love and an activity com-patible with my primary role as caregiver. I spent six months rewriting my doctoral thesis with a view to publication but was turned down in 1990 by SPCK and other publishers. A précis appeared in 1992 under the title *A True and Lively Faith*, published by the Church of Ireland Evangelical Fellowship (CIEF). I contributed articles and reviews to the English journals *Churchman* and *Third Way*; and for *Search*, an article on Bishop John Jebb, drawing on the unpublished Jebb Papers in TCD, and regular reviews. The *New Dictionary of National Biography* (DNB) – it would be published in 2004 as *The Oxford DNB* – commissioned me to revise entries for three bishops of the Established Church in Ireland. The commission came by default: I had been in Australia at the planning stage and no one in Ireland had recommended me. I fared better with the *Blackwell Dictionary of Evangelical Biography 1730-1860* (1995), with some 40 entries (almost 20,000 words). I had written most of these in 1966, but Inter-Varsity Press failed to publish and Dr Andrew Walls returned my articles. They were now dusted and revised. The General Editor, Dr Donald M. Lewis of Regent College, Vancouver, accepted additional entries from me. Given the Irish Church's strong Evangelical tradition, however, and its worldwide influence in the 19th century, the paucity of Irish entries is a serious imbalance in a work of international scholarship. (This criticism is even more apposite in respect to the Presbyterian Church in Ireland.) The Dictionary omits also some Irish pioneers in Canada.

In 1994 a conference of church historians was held in Dublin with the theme, 'Towards a History of the Church of Ireland'. I gave a paper at a session chaired by Dr Kenneth Milne – there was a parallel session – and attended by the Keynote speaker, Professor Patrick Collinson, who noticed my paper in his address, and the late Prof Donal Kerr. Most papers were published in *As by Law Established* (1995), of which Dr Milne was a co-editor. My paper was not included: for what reason I do not know – the editors did not consult me. There was nothing for it but to publish alone. I settled to the task and wrote much of the text in the library at UUC; on some days I wrote 1000 words. Admiringly, Prof Dave Sturdy told me that most professional historians managed 500 words daily. We made it a family affair when Philip got Rachel's typescript of the text on to the computer.

Thanks to the guidance and warm encouragement of Canon Michael Kennedy, APCK's publishing sub-committee took an interest in my project and its then hon secretary, Peter Barrett, the Dean of Residences in Trinity College, was helpful at every stage. Negotiation with The Columba Press resolved that Columba and APCK would publish jointly. Columba's Seán O Boyle met me and proposed a print-run of 750 copies, 250 in hardback and 500 in paperback. When I countered that the market would bear a higher total, Sean retorted that he did not want to end up with 'books under the bed'! But in the light of the strong response to the pre-publication price offered in a flyer carried by southern diocesan magazines, Columba increased the print-run to 1250 copies – in hardback only.

APCK hosted two public launches. With Archdeacon Alan Harper as chair, the Primate launched the book on 22 October 1997. As I had given my appraisal of his Primacy, I had not invited him to write the Foreword. Dr Eames was gracious both in accepting my decision and in quoting Bishop Harold Miller's thoughtful Foreword in his speech. In November, Dr Jacqueline Hill of NUI did the honours in Church of Ireland House, Dublin. The book went out of print in just over two years. In 2002 Columba published a Revised and Updated Edition. I added two sections: an update to 2001 and, because the book's acceptance throughout the Church had in effect conferred official status, a table of the Episcopal Elections 1871-2001. As I had written primarily for Church of Ireland people, I was gratified when Bishop H. R. McAdoo spoke as it were for the Church in his letter to me that the Primate quoted at the Belfast launch. After commenting that the book was 'beautifully produced', Dr McAdoo wrote:

> I am impressed by the clear style, detailed mastery of material and admirable fairness in handling different viewpoints. Your research has made available so much that gives depth to the whole picture of the last three centuries ... I offer you my warm congratulations and the thanks of all of us.

Bishop Donald Caird, who reviewed for *The Church Times*, paid me the courtesy of reading his review over the telephone before publication. Dr Patrick Kelly in *Search* was elegantly erudite. *The Irish Times* declined offers to review: in 1997, by its

Foreign Desk editor, Patrick Comerford, and in 2002, its Economics editor, Jane Suiter. I reflected that the paper had responded in an editorial to my 1972 speech, written in four hours, whereas it ignored a book that had taken four years to write. Colin Armstrong's review in *History Ireland* was surprisingly negative. Colin, an Old Portoran, had had input in shaping the book – I still have his copious notes on my drafts – but did not disclose his interest when he offered his review. Professional historians largely ignored the book. Dr Anthony Malcomson, by contrast, began his magisterial biography of Archbishop Agar by quoting my analysis of the character of the 18th century episcopate.

With my academic interests centred on Dublin, I stayed often in the city – and beyond. Friendships old and new meant much: with Stanley McElhinney, solitary now but as hospitable as ever, and David McConnell, the affable and urbane Vice Provost of TCD – we had met at an examiners' meeting. Far from Dublin, George and Carol Cliffe in Piltown, and Bob and Pat Hanna in Ennis, welcomed me in their rectories.

When working in Dublin, I stayed with Dr Jenny Moreton at Howth. She had good friends there in Peter and Gwen Holmes and Wahid and Stella Mikhail; I taught Stella (now Stella Jones and rector of Clonenagh in Ossory) when she entered CITC. Jenny was an authority on computistics. Peter Holmes and I heard her lecture at Maynooth to eminent scholars including the late Prof Henry Chadwick. Jenny's devotion to St John's Sandymount evinced her Catholic spirituality. Every year she placed flowers on my great-uncle's grave – she had been of St Stephen's, Lewisham, though after Fr Willie's time: she took the train to Portadown, from where I drove her to Scarva. Jenny Moreton introduced me to Diana Macfarlan, daughter of an archbishop, widow of a divinity professor (she had remarried), and an author, who ended her days in a shabby Home not far from Braemor Park. Jenny was often with her. I visited Diana whenever I was at the College and learned much about serenity in adversity. After Diana died, Jenny and I were upbraided for not attending her funeral – we had learned too late of her death – by some who had neither dreamed of going near her in life nor of not being seen at her funeral.

After Jenny Moreton left Howth, Peter Holmes made his apartment at 1 Abbey Street available to me. It was a delight to look down on the yachted harbour and to Ireland's Eye beyond. I was there in 2003 when uncle Jimmie died. Barbara asked me to speak at his funeral. On a glorious autumn day it was pleasant to address extempore the large crowd who stood on the grass and the turning-circle outside the magnificent Georgian door at Athgoe Castle.

I was sometimes the guest of retired members of the Society of Jesus in their House in Lower Leeson Street in Dublin, at Fr Philip Fogarty's invitation. At Mass before dinner, these godly men offered me full Eucharistic hospitality. I found it moving to share in the simple celebration, pared to its liturgical essentials, and to be part of the semi-circle around the altar when bread and wine were passed from hand to hand.

I stayed often at Braemor Park. Dr Adrian Empey, the hard-working (and last) Principal of the Theological College, made me welcome and always found time to offer friendship. By leaving the College at 5.30am I could catch the morning ferry from Rosslare, and by driving the M4 on a Saturday, could reach Earls Court from the Welsh coast in four hours. I made the trip to London often, staying with Phil and Beth in Plumstead and getting to know my lovely grandchildren. The 2nd edition of my History (in 2002) was dedicated to George, Alex and Barney, the year before their beautiful sister Erin was born. On a day outing from Plumstead, we went to the Sherringtons in Brighton and I met my sweet grandchildren, Samantha and Aaron, whom Karen and Mark had adopted after agonising delay and threatened legal action by the natural mother. By twice accepting Lady Stella Durand's welcome invitation to stay in Kiltegan rectory – Stella had been my student in TCD – I was able to leave for Rosslare at a more civilised hour. My thoughts turned to the 19th century rector of Kiltegan, Edward Blake, whose sons were leading pioneers in Upper Canada, in government, university and church.

IV. CANADA 2002–08

1. Comings and goings

On a brief visit to Canada in 2001, I stayed with Ruth Simmonds in Cobourg on Lake Ontario and Mike and Fran Kotchan on Vancouver Island. Ruth had left Dublin soon after Edward Orr and she separated; Fran was related to Cilla's family. From June 2002, I stayed two months each with Ruth and the Kotchans. At a very low point for me – a first Christmas far from family – Mike and Fran, and many of their friends, offered understanding and supportive love. I spent a week also in the Vancouver School of Theology (VST) with opportunity at last to meet Donald Lewis at Regent College. Herb O'Driscoll arranged my stay in VST. I had the pleasure after 50 years of hearing Herb preach again – in Christ Church Cathedral, Victoria – and of visiting Paula and him in their home. There was reunion with another old friend too: Milton Hsu gave me a tour of Vancouver and looked after me for a day. During 2003 I researched the contribution of Irish pioneer clergy and laity to the Anglican Church of Canada. Both Ottawa and London had good archival material and the respective diocesan archivists, Glenn Lockwood and Diana Coates, were most helpful. In London, the Bishop of Huron, Bruce Howe, welcomed my interest. Wendy Fletcher-Marsh at VST had suggested that I stay in Medaille Retreat House of the Sisters of St Joseph. The Sisters and staff received me in love. Dan McNamara, who supported the House professionally and personally, became a valued friend. I had the privilege also of meeting with Dr Donald Akenson in Kingston. I told him of Dr Malcomson's comment (in his biography of Agar) that, however confusing, the most recent historians of the Church of Ireland are Akenson and Acheson.

When Ruth Simmonds and I parted early in 2004, I left Canada, seemingly for good. Happily, my friendship with Peter Walker survived. Canon Walker is the rector of St Peter's, Cobourg. He spent his sabbatical in spring 2004 in Oxford, at St Stephen's House. I drove him to Holyhead, then to Belfast where Raymond and Bobbie Moore were our gracious hosts. Dean Houston McKelvey enthralled Peter with his take on

Ulster realities and Colin Hall-Thompson showed us some of these in East Belfast. Canon Michael Kennedy gave us a hilarious and erudite tour of Armagh Cathedral. Peter preached at St Bartholomew's in Dublin. The weeks after his departure marked my lowest point. I had two car accidents within a week in the Republic. I thought of becoming the tenant of Armagh diocese in a flat near the See House – Peter Walker had wondered if Armagh was big enough for me! But I dithered and remained homeless. In July, when I was in London, Ontario, a caring Ginnie Kennerley committed me to the Armagh tenancy and bade me give the agents a starting date. I complied. Thence to Washego to stay with Sue Kenney whom I had met at St James's and to meet her partner Bruce Pirrie. At my request Sue mailed her *My Camino* to Bishop Richard Henderson who had also walked the Camino Santiago de Compestela. Finally I entrained for Cobourg to stay with Peter and Ginny Walker in St Peter's rectory.

As we left Union Station a flamboyant gent sat down beside me. We got on so well that he invited me to dine in his Cobourg home that day. When I demurred on the ground of discourtesy to my hosts, David Smith said, 'Come for dinner tomorrow and bring your hosts with you.' When the Walkers and I duly arrived, our host showed Peter and me his gallery of 19th century statesmen before introducing me to his wife Heather Smith, then an Associate Chief Justice of Ontario, their son Alex, and their other guest, Mme Ginette Duplessis. It was evident that Peter and Ginette, both talented musicians, related affectionately. Peter had founded the Tallis Choir in Toronto and conducted it for 25 years. Ginette had been a classical singer in Quebec, Europe and the United States. I was attracted to Ginette (on this 7 August 2004) – she would later pronounce it *un coup de foudre*. Our host, however, had other matters on hand. A son of Campbell-Bannerman Smith and a Liberal Member of the Senate, David Smith proposed the toast 'William Ewart Gladstone'. I responded with 'Benjamin Disraeli, Earl of Beaconsfield', and honours were even.

Ginette taught at both the Royal Conservatory of Music (RCM) and the Faculty of Music of the University of Toronto. She flew to Winnipeg next day to examine for the RCM. On her return we lunched, gardened and agreed to stay in touch. In November I returned to Cobourg. Ginette's best friends in Sydenham Street welcomed me warmly: Duane and Pat, Donald and Dodie. Ginette and I were married in the chapel at St Peter's, Cobourg, on Victoria Day (22 May) 2006. Peter Walker officiated with joy. George and Barbara joined our Canadian friends on the day. We enjoyed a week's honeymoon in Acapulco.

2. Oh Canada!

To this immigrant's eye, Canada defines itself in negative, even derogatory terms. An influential former journalist, Walter Stewart, wrote that 'smugness has become a national religion, a national disease'. A modern successor, the *Toronto Globe and Mail's* Jeffery Simpson, avoids the S-word but discerns 'parochial Canada' as thinking it has nothing to learn from other nations: from Norway, for example, about greenhouse-gas emissions, Iceland about offshore fisheries, or the entire industrialised world about health care – nothing to learn in the false assumption that all is well. Canada's commercial prophets descry a culture of complacency in national life. Perrin Beatty, CEO of the Canadian Chamber of Commerce, while extolling Ireland's example, early in 2008 deplored Canada's lack of competitiveness and 'comfortable acceptance of mediocre performance'. In July 2008, the Conference Board of Canada, a business think-tank, reported that Canada's relative competitive position continues to slip. In other areas of national life, the Globe pronounced the RCMP 'horribly broken' as scandal, corruption, excessive use of tasers, and loss of public trust rocked the Mounties. Again, attitudes to Canada's Afghan mission derive largely from a simplistic distinction between reconstruction and military engagement, based on the myth that peacekeeping is Canada's modern role.

Much in Canadian custom is attractive: the priority accorded to pedestrians at intersections, the freedom for motorists to turn right on red on a clear road, and use of dipped headlights in broad daylight. It is depressing on return to Ireland to find most cars without lights in poor visibility. Lives would be saved on Irish roads with the perception that headlights have value primarily, not to allow drivers to see, but cars to be seen. But driving at dusk, or in dangerous conditions, on the 401 is just as depressing. Though cars have headlights on, few show lights at the rear where they are needed. Collectively, Canadians can be as unthinking as we Irish – and that is saying something. Other facets of Canadian life are gratifying. Canadians are good tippers, with 15 per cent being the norm – sometimes more; consciously or no, the Biblical precept about gleaning is followed in this generous national custom. Above all, fallen soldiers from Afghanistan are honoured from every bridge on the 401 – 'The Highway of Heroes' – as their coffins are borne from RCAF Trenton to Toronto in sad and dignified convoy.

That (to my eye) Australians take themselves too seriously and Canadians not seriously enough, has to do with distance: with Australia's remoteness from everywhere, and with Canada's internal vastness. Distance drives Australians to compete with the world and demands success. Australia is not exactly small; but 80 per cent of its population live in five coastal cities, four of which – Perth is the exception – form an arc around the federal capital, Canberra. Ottawa, by contrast, is remote from both the Maritimes and British Columbia. Friends in BC told me that the capital is prejudiced against it. No evidence was produced, nor needed to be: it is an article of faith in the West. Not that much happens in Ottawa. The Parliament elected in late January 2006 did not meet for a month, with time only for MPs to self-congratulate before the Easter recess. During Beijing 2008, there were calls for Canada to emulate Australia in providing more funding and training for its Olympic athletes. Ironically, the Australian press was bronzed-off by the haul of gold medals won in Beijing by the Poms – the best result for the UK since 1908, topping Australia in total medals won also.

For whatever historical reasons, 'English' Canada is paternalistic, producing a docile public and an arrogant official class. Australians can obtain passports at hundreds of outlets; Canadians form queues outside their few passport offices. Alcohol may be purchased only in official premises, in Ontario the stores of the Liquor Control Board (LCBO). Australians and Irish would not tolerate it. The LCBO's monopoly induces complacency: no delivery service is offered – even to its best customers. Officialdom misses the trees for the twigs. In October

2007, the Ontario Energy Board approved changes to the rates Union Gas charges its customers – an annual decrease of 59 cents (of a household outlay of more than $2000). But for an increase of seven cents in transportation costs, the saving would have been a majestic 66 cents! Such idiocy invests more serious matters. As my divorce was registered overseas, I had to employ a solicitor to certify that its terms were compatible with Ontario law. Two sentences would have sufficed. The office of the Registrar General rejected my solicitor's more expansive letter. A second letter informed that I had lived in Australia but included no additional relevant point. It was accepted. This bizarre exchange contributed to a delay of four months in issuing our marriage licence. The same mindset is apparent in business. Letters that I wrote to the Post Office and Shoppers Drug Mart in Cobourg received no reply. Nor is this small town habit. My letter to Manulife asking if my health policy covered a dislocation evoked no response.

Professors Donald Akenson at Queen's, and Bruce Elliott at Carleton, have been pioneers on 19th century Irish immigration to Canada. Don Akenson has shown that the Irish were the predominant ethnic group in Upper Canada (Ontario) from the 1820s to the 1880s; that the ratio of Protestant to Catholic among Irish immigrants was consistently two-to-one, both before and after the Great Famine; and that the Irish settlers, Catholic and Protestant alike, were predominantly a rural people – that is, they did the hard work of pioneering. The spur to large-scale Protestant emigration was the enacting in 1829 of Catholic Emancipation. Bruce Elliott has tracked family migration patterns, especially from Tipperary, by painstaking research on both sides of the Atlantic. Ontario's immense debt to the Irish and its rich Irish heritage do not impinge on provincial consciousness today. Canadian Irish, especially those of the once-predominant Orange tradition in Toronto, have had to hide their diminished heads in the light of pervasive misunderstanding and prejudiced analysis of Ulster's recent history.

Hip surgery
Much public attention in Canada focuses on health issues. Hard facts are scarce. I detail now my positive experience of elective

surgery. Arthritis had invaded my left hip in late 2004. I fell between two public health systems, each with lengthy waiting times before consultant appointments. That in Belfast came too late: I was locked into the immigration process. Five million Canadians are without a family doctor. No doctor in Cobourg accepted new patients – until Dr Philip Stratford returned from the USA. I joined a list that was soon full and so found an excellent doctor and an immediate rapport with him. Dr Stratford referred me to Kingston General Hospital (KGH). Dr Mark Harrison examined me there on 21 November 2006. I was fortunate again. This leading orthopaedic surgeon, an Associate Professor of Surgery at Queen's, is a warm-hearted man, laconic and likeable. His assistant forewarned me that waiting time for surgery was up to a year. Dr Harrison, however, with x-rays showing the need for hip reconstruction, told us that further delay could be disastrous, and said that he would operate early in 2007. On 2 January, his secretary Angela duly advised 26 January as the operative date, with pre-surgery procedures – in the conjoined Hotel Dieu Hospital – a week earlier. Kingston is 150km from Cobourg. Don Pirie drove there in my interest on five occasions, three of them in January: and Dodie and he stayed overnight in our Kingston hotel before my admission at 5.30am.

Hospital had its lighter moments. I had opted for a spinal anesthetic on advice that it would speed recovery. It was just as well: I needed my wits about me in the recovery room. There was consternation that my bed was the wrong way round. Though it had sufficed for surgery, wheeling it in public would, apparently, be sacrilege. So four nurses tried to right it – in vain. I recalled 'the sofa' at Mrs Proudie's reception. A new bed was then ordered. From long experience I told the nurses that it would not appear on a Friday afternoon. It was 90 minutes before they accepted both that I was right and (as I overheard) frustrated. The faulty bed behaved impeccably and I arrived into the ward where Ginette, Dodie and Don had endured a long wait. When they left I found three agreeable ward companions. They were bemused when, as I felt no pain, my morphine drip was disconnected; and amused when the nurse on duty when I first showered, a hearty country girl, bade me wash my 'jewels'. Nursing care by both men and women was of the highest quality. A staff party beside our ward was an invasive contradiction. The din continued until after midnight. All four of us were upset and Russell Hall, who was closest to our (open) door, visibly distressed.

Before surgery I fixed with my local Community Care Access Centre (CCAC) to have home physiotherapy – by Therapacc – on a private, that is self-paying, basis. A nurse at KGH therefore undertook to liaise with Therapacc 'to provide them with orders/ information on [my] progress at KGH'. Her supervisor overruled that with a curt 'client not eligible for CCAC services'. Her impertinence meant that my physiotherapist was working in the dark. That, and my too vigorous exercising, resulted in a dislocation after five weeks. It coincided with the worst snowstorm of the winter. Don was unable to drive. Dr Harrison discussed emergency plans by telephone. Then Duane and Pat learned of my predicament. They at once offered to drive us to Kingston in their SUV – and did so on a deserted 401. The x-rays showed that something had indeed 'popped out'. Dr Harrison needed 90 seconds to 'pop' it in – he knew that I needed no anesthetic. It was another Friday: Dr Harrison began three weeks leave that evening. He banned all exercise in his absence and saw me again the day after he resumed work. Our splendid neighbours apart, two friends did much to lift my spirits. The parish nurse at St Peter's, Diane Froncz, gave graceful support especially at the dislocation crisis. And one week after my surgery Peter Barrett brought us great joy when he came for the day. Ginette and he became instant soul mates.

Having no health card, I paid all medical expenses myself. The accounts department at KGH deemed me a *de facto* resident of Ontario, so reducing the daily rate for my four days in hospital to $1254 (non-residents pay over $3000). I settled also accounts for Hotel Dieu clinics and specialists, assuming – wrongly – that KGH had notified my status. I was relieved to negotiate refunds. In total, I paid $8911.39 for surgery, hospital, and all related fees and charges: five clinics at Hotel Dieu over six months, including pre-surgery, four days in KGH, and the fees of my surgeon, assistant surgeon, and anesthetist. I paid also the fees of three other members of the Department of Anesthesiology who had seen me at pre-surgery, a costly case of overkill. At the sterling exchange rate of January 2007, total costs were therefore some £3950. This compares with the £7500 advised at the time by a private clinic in Northern Ireland.

3. Immigration impasse - again

Ginette and I represent the first European nations: the French who, from Champlain's arrival in 1608, pioneered Lower Canada, with much Irish support; and the Irish who pioneered Upper Canada and peopled its Anglican, Catholic and Methodist churches. We unite two illustrious names. An Acheson ruled in Quebec in the 1830s and a Duplessis was premier of Quebec in the 1950s. But history counts for nothing in 21st century Canada.

Applications for residency go to the federal Department of Citizenship and Immigration Canada (CIC). Stephen Harper's government in 2006 halved the residency fee (from $1000) and collected it at completion rather than up-front. Later the Minister, the Hon Diane Finley MP, assumed power to intervene in tackling the immigration backlog. This controversial initiative evaded the glaring need to reform a process that is, by its absurdities and inefficiencies, hugely wasteful of resources. My 'In Canada' application was within the Family Class with Ginette as my sponsor - inappropriate in our case, but there was then no alternative. To have to provide photographs of our engagement and wedding was insulting. That Ginette must also provide detailed evidence of her finances was - she wrote to the Minister - invasive and humiliating. With some spirit, Ginette added that, despite her Canadian citizenship since birth and her Québecois nationality, the process treated her like 'a recent immigrant from Timbuctoo seeking to bring her husband into Canada on her skirt-tails'. The reply from a ministerial aide evinced ignorance of immigration procedures. If an aide does not know, can the Minister?

Waiting time to approval in principle varied. Once it was granted, background checks might be made. A friend in Cobourg - I call him John Smith to protect his privacy - received his permanent resident card (in 2007) eight months after he had applied. It was mailed to him, without interview, and before he applied for a health card. In my case, CIC Vegreville (in Alberta) received my application on 10 July 2006. Its website indicated nine months to approval in principle, and on cue CIC on 10 April 2007 formally advised that approval. Assuming imminent closure, I booked a flight to Ireland in May. CIC authorised me to apply for the Ontario health card. Instructed also to obtain a certificate from PSNI, I expedited it by fax link with Ballycastle police station and had it mailed direct to Vegreville. It was all in vain. When the Cobourg office of Rick Norlock MP enquired, Barbara Massey – the Member's courteously efficient assistant – was told that closure would take up to 18 months: my file had been sent to CSIS (Canadian Security and Intelligence Services). This news made sense of my treatment at visa renewal in November 2006: I had paid the fee for six-month extension but was granted extension for a year. (John Smith's payment for visa extension had been returned to him.) Finally, after waiting another 12 months, I was instructed to attend for interview at the Immigration Centre at Oshawa. Canada Post took ten days to deliver the letter – federal agencies feed off one another's inefficiencies. My card was mailed to me from the Maritimes; I received it on 29 February 2008.

John Smith's case and mine were similar: both UK citizens and pensioners, both recently married to Canadian citizens, neither of us employing an immigration lawyer. John Smith's being English is one obvious distinction: is it CIC policy to refer to CSIS applicants from Northern Ireland? If so, are there no exceptions? Why was I not profiled when I applied for residency? I had been on each of thirteen times that I entered Canada – without a visa – from November 2001 to May 2006. My financial independence was accepted, my academic research approved, my passport stamped to allow a stay of six months: it was rollover residency. I was, in effect, deemed 'Canadian Experience Class' years before that immigration stream was proposed in 2008. I was welcomed (in the Minister's words of August 2008) as being among those seeking 'to work in their fields and contribute to Canadian society'. Why, then, the change when I sought residency proper? Was my preaching in Toronto's Anglican cathedral seen as subversive? It stretches credulity, but as Canada now goes it is possible. Or was my role as Senior Presiding Officer at the UK General Election in 2005 – with police officers subject to my authority – deemed a threat to Canada's security? Reference to CSIS delayed my residency by 12 months. Which aspect of my career took a year to investigate: Army officer, headmaster, caregiver or author?

CIC's referring me to CSIS is not only offensive, but also indefensible on rational grounds. If not rational, then irrational: many English Canadians aver that Ginette attracted prejudice as a Québecoise. If that is true – and there is no rational alternative – then CIC is beyond contempt. The Harper government has formally proclaimed Québec a nation within Canada: this status is worthless unless the Québecois are accorded equal treatment throughout Canada.

My experience points up the inefficiency of CIC's administration. In June 2006, I was gratuitously issued with a visa – unnecessary in law. It labelled me 'Female' – a riot that CIC Vegreville refused to rectify at renewal. Again, I had forwarded to CIC Canon Walker's formal declaration that he had married us. It was accepted in UK for pension, in Canada for marriage certificate, purposes; but not by CIC: they demanded our delayed marriage certificate. I sent a copy. It was requested again. I sent another copy. Ordered to Oshawa later for interview, I had to bring two photographs – CIC Vegreville had 'lost' the two I supplied in 2006. It had been 'a long time', I was told. On a Monday morning I was alone – Vegreville had clearly referred me to give the Immigration Centre in Oshawa something to do.

4. 'Energy and aura of joy'

Ginette and I do without car, mobile phone, and flu jabs. We walk much, mostly for pleasure and in all weathers, safely in snow, warily on ice: the duty to clear the sidewalk is much defied in Cobourg – the worst streets during the endless snow of 2008 were within sight of the police station. After full recovery from hip surgery, I hit the ground running at 70 and acquired a 3½-pound axe. Snow-shovel and axe epitomised winter 2008. Cobourg has had no downtown grocery store since one was taken out just before my arrival. Our nearest supermarket involves a round walk of 45 minutes: a happy throwback to my childhood. In her disarmingly candid way, Ginette says that people respond to our 'energy and aura of joy'. Everybody loves

Ginette's unique winsomeness. She retired from the faculty of the Royal Conservatory of Music in 2007, and the Faculty of Music in the University of Toronto in 2008, so that Cobourg now sees more of her.

In magnificent Quebec City we stay with Ginette's brother Claude on the Rue des Remparts overlooking the St Lawrence Estuary. On Ginette's first visit to Ireland, in May 2005, we looked out on the Mournes from Jim's lovely home in Dundrum. Ginette fell in love with Ireland – the people, the scenery after rain, road-hungry 'sheeps' in the West. My rugby friends Padraig and John gave Ginette a special Inishowen welcome. Mother took us to Corrs, Peter Holmes to Howth Yacht Club. Kaye Marshall and Ginette took to each other on sight when we stayed with Kaye at Sandymount. Seán O Boyle gave us lunch, as did Ginnie Kennerley in her beautiful home in Dalkey. Ginnie, reassured, told Ginette that I had been lost before I met her. We attended the reunion organised by Bert Wilson to mark the 50th anniversary of 8th World Jamboree in Canada; out of that came friendship with Colin and Sarah Angliker of Virginia, USA. A week across the water allowed visits to A. E. Housman's Clunton, where we stayed with Eirlys Ellams and husband Richard, to Malcolm and Kath Montgomery above Conwy, and to York where, in Caroline's absence, Colin Smith gave us dinner under the Minster.

In August 2007 we arrived with John and Edith the day that summer rain ended. The highlights of Ginette's second Irish visit were a delightful weekend at The Moat with Richard and Jay Kilroy, greeting my cousin Margaret (from New Zealand) in George and Barbara's new home, and meeting Ginnie Kennerley's American husband Ed when Kaye Marshall took us all to dinner. We missed our dear Jim: he had died suddenly just after my hip surgery. Ginette met my other brothers: Mervyn when he came to a family dinner and Chris, with Noreen, when we took them to lunch. Ginette sensed how proud I was of my youngest brother, a Queen's graduate and Principal of the well-regarded Beechlawn school in Hillsborough. We finally enjoyed a week in the Loire valley, where the sun was shining after ten weekends of rain.

In 2008, May was the month that summer happened in UK!

My six grandchildren greeted me with a picnic in a Surrey park, in glorious sunshine. I was Peter Barrett's guest in east London while visiting family – Ginette would see Peter in Dublin later. After she joined me, we breakfasted outdoors in the Mournes with Paul, Janice and Daniel, and in Lurgan with John, Edith and mother. Ginette had a warm reception at a Friendly Brothers party in Castle Upton, and from former colleagues at Portora: we toured the achool with Martin Todd as our proud guide. Alas! *The 1608 Royal Schools* had sold out. On return to Canada I e-mailed the Headmaster of Cavan Royal School, Ivan Bolton (whom I did not know). He mailed me a copy, asking only that I cover postage costs. His gifting the book implied apology that as a former headmaster I had not received a complimentary copy. A glorious holiday ended in the frustration of a 19-hour delay in our return flight with Zoom – we had been impressed with the airline's efficiency in 2007. We were, however, lucky: Zoom's sudden collapse in August 2008, less than three months later, put things in perspective.

It had not been the only setback. The day after my arrival from Canada, Charles Hurst Renault brought my car to the Mallusk MOT centre. The car failed the test. The facts here are clear. Hurst's had serviced the car for three hours. It failed for two trivial reasons – disputed by Hurst's. A repeat test was not offered for fifteen days. That does not happen in England; it ought not to happen in Belfast. The car was roadworthy. By implication, it was a reputable garage, and not my car, that was under scrutiny. As in Canada, so in this case, a monopoly of power spawns pedantic, or perverse, literalism. The consequence was stark: I could not tax the car. Being forced to drive illegally is a situation not without stress: it was not life as I expected it at 70.

From Rachel's home, I left Ballycastle for Galway at 5.00am for the opening session of the General Synod in the Radisson. I enjoyed relief and refreshment in Drumcliffe church carpark at 7.30am and parked at the Radisson with time to spare. I had a further setback when two Galway hotels charged me for my first night's stay – The Western Hotel and The Skeffington Arms, the former as a no-show. The agency recommended by the RCB had allowed double booking – I had assumed that my first e-mail attempt had failed – without advising me. When I fronted up at reception, The Western Hotel did not refund its punitive charge.

General Synod passed my Motion (seconded by Major Richard Kilroy) calling on the RCB to publish in detail the costs – of stipends, maintenance of see houses, expenses of office – of the Church's episcopal ministry. The motion was the last business taken before the President of Ireland, Mary McAleese, made history by addressing the General Synod. The two Archbishops had left the platform to meet the President on her arrival. The Bishop of Meath, Richard Clarke, was in the Chair. Clearly supportive of my initiative, he in effect bade his fellow bishops vote for the Motion. It was the first time (in the course of 30 General Synod meetings) that I had seen episcopal hands lifted – in a business context!

Shuttling between Toronto and Belfast is thought provoking. Back in Ireland in October, I asked around about 'the election being held in North America'. I was told that Obama was a winner and Sarah Palin lovely; but no one had heard of Canada's federal election on 14 October. Half of Canada had not heard either: turnout was close to 50 per cent. An autumn of financial ruin and economic disaster exposed a shared political bankruptcy: Belfast's sick paralysis, vacuous ineptitude at Westminster, chronic absenteeism in Ottawa. The Canadian Parliament had not sat for five months, appeared to have no stomach for serious business, and ensured – through behaviour that shook Canadians – that it would be sent down well before Christmas. Pride in the sacrifice of soldiers, both British and Canadian, in Afghanistan outshone contempt for politicians. Canadian dead were honoured still from crowded bridges above the Highway of Heroes. In Belfast, 30,000 turned out to welcome home soldiers of the Royal Irish Regiment. Noble spirits rose to the occasion. In Toronto, the *Globe*'s Christie Blatchford, herself an Afghan veteran, wrote with compassionate understanding, notably in her 'Mourn these soldiers – do not pity them'. In Belfast, Houston McKelvey drew on Hemingway's 'Courage – grace under pressure' in appraising from his cathedral pulpit the incessant life-saving work of 204 (North Irish) Field Hospital, on completion of their tour of duty in Afghanistan. Thus 2008 ended, in Canada and Northern Ireland, on a high note of prophetic pride, as the Afghan mission waited for 2009 – and Barack Obama.

Finale

The welcome point is near, three years on, *cum mens onus deponit*. My tale has told of faith, of hope in dark days; but supremely of love. My dear mother was, naturally, my oldest love. In May 2006 I had brought mother from Lurgan to 6 Slievecoole Park for a weekend: a nostalgic farewell to her home of over 40 years, just before her house was sold. John and Edith committed to her for years in their own home, relieved by Paul and Janice at times. On 19 September 2008, the end came suddenly for mother, so sparing her, in her 94th year, suffering and indignity.

My pride in my brothers as their careers progressed and their families grew into independence, has passed now to my children. Karen in her mid-30s became Director of Human Resources with Jaeger for all of the United Kingdom. But I am more proud of her resigning that position so that she and Mark might adopt two vulnerable children. To see Karen blossom as a mother, drawing on the human resource of love, and to see her children – Sammy and Asa – respond to that love, has been as humbling as it has been joyous. Rachel, for her part, has managed caregiving, her own health condition, and the rigours of an Open University course, with courage and determination. And Phil and Beth have had, as young parents, to cope with the challenge of having two of their three sons – of very different personality – diagnosed as autistic. The support of a caring church, their own strong faith, and above all their committed love, suffice them.

If my Memoirs reveal anything worthwhile, it is, sublimely, this: that I am blessed with friends with loving hearts. I try to do my part to cultivate friendships, and in this task e-mail now has unique value. But it gets more poignant as we get older. Having been out of touch with him since leaving Dublin, I wrote (by airmail) to Dr Stanley McElhinney just before my hip surgery. His daughter Helena replied, with sensitivity, that Stanley had died

15 months before, and sent me his obituary from *The Irish Times*. Cultivating new friendships is a late-life joy. In Sydenham Street, with Greg and Linda added to our older friends, Ginette and I live among those who 'love their neighbours as themselves'. When I preached in St Peter's, the entire Street – churchgoers and unchurched alike – turned out in support.

Love for the Church of my baptism is an enduring love. Through experience in the Army, I became an Anglican of more catholic spirit, reinforced by observing the smug arrogance of a monochrome tradition in Sydney. In Ireland, personal friends of all three Anglican traditions were consecrated bishops within two years. In St Peter's, Cobourg, the three traditions unite under Canon Peter Walker's wise and gracious leadership. While my mind is with the thinking liberals, and while Catholic spirituality, both Anglican and Roman, has strong appeal, my soul is with the Evangelicals – though I sometimes wish that my soul might be saved. The Church of Ireland is enriched by the revival of its Evangelical tradition: the danger is that puritans and low churchmen will pull it away from its essentials. At General Synod in 2005, I appealed to Evangelicals fully to accept lesbians and gays and so honour our caring tradition. I had detected an intolerance allied to a Biblical literalism that I was bound to challenge. Similarly, when worshipping in Dublin at a church of Catholic tradition and magnificent choral standard, I had a sense that it was going through the motions: Fr Willie (Acheson) would not have been comfortable there. Complacency and stagnation threaten both traditions.

In my 1999 sermon in St Finbarre's, a cathedral of liberal tradition, I had urged that 'the great traditions in our Church reclaim their heritage':

> The Catholic tradition ... must be recalled to its early integrities and passions: the yearning for holiness, the passion for souls, the stress on moral conversion, and the emphasis on an ascetic, sacrificial way of living ...
>
> Evangelicals should be recalled to the essentials of their tradition – they need to learn, from its early history, a deeper loyalty to Church principles, and a fuller involvement in Anglican patterns of devotion and disci-

pline. They need, too, to develop more strongly their historic concern for the poor, the marginalised, and the outcasts of society. And they need to learn all over again how to 'preach Christ'.

The North-South divide in the Church of Ireland is another weakness. Living for long periods in Dublin has given me to see that Church people in the Republic have no understanding of, and certainly no sympathy with, the symbiosis of Church and Orange Order in rural Ulster. But then I have never met any Church members in the South who understand the significance of their own national flag. Does not its uniting of Green and Orange have a bearing on the vexed Drumcree imbroglio or, nearer home, on the freedom of Orangemen to parade in Dublin to a church service? In another context, I was privileged – as the guest of the editor, Canon Ginnie Kennerley – to attend a *Search* symposium in Dublin. I noted that, apart from one other who was there *ex officio*, I was the only Northerner present.

These reflections return me to my Preface. Like Ginette, I too 'hate religion' – we are closer than it might appear. It was very thrilling to hear Bishop James Jones of Liverpool, at a General Synod service in Dublin, speak of 'the great church of the unchurched' – a fine affirmation by this leading Evangelical of so many loving Christians. Catholicity can be taken even further. Jenny Moreton and I used to discern the 'inasmuch' Christians: those in family and among our friends who, without intention or awareness, exhibit a Christ-like spirit. Nor will they know whom they serve (or, in the gospel's simple phrase, to whom they have 'done it') until they hear, 'inherit the kingdom prepared for you'. I tell Ginette that she who loves is born of God and knows God. I am not sure that she is listening; but love never fails. To strict religious people – of whatever tradition – such thoughts are anathema. But then he who propounded them was rejected by the religious leaders of the day: even the Son of Man, the Head of the Church.

Appendix

Text of Speech by Dr Alan Acheson in the Debate on the Draft Report of Section II (Church Unity) at ACC-5, 17 September 1981

I address myself to that part of the Report that treats of the relationship of our Anglican Communion with the Roman Catholic Church – the review of the ARClC Agreements and the recommendations for future action.

We have yet to establish whether or not our several Provinces do recognise in the Agreed Statements 'the faith of Anglicans'. But whatever the answer to that important question, it seems to me that there would be a flaw in our reasoning if we were to accept that these Agreements of themselves provide a full and sufficient basis on which to proceed further. Can they do so until a more fundamental question has been examined – the essence as it was of the division in the Church at the Reformation? I mean the doctrine of Justification by Faith.

This doctrine informs both the liturgy and the creedal confession (the 39 Articles) which our Church has received and on which it has hitherto rested. So vital was it considered by our Reformers that they hailed it as *articulus vel stantis vel cadentis ecclesiae*. And it was (I think) to this doctrine that the judicious Mr Hooker referred when, in enunciating the points of difference between the Church of England and the Church of Rome, he wrote: 'We differ from them about the means whereby Christ healeth our diseases.'

And not just our doctrine, but our development as a Communion also. For it seems to me that many experiences of renewal in the history, and many examples of missionary outreach in the growth, of the Anglican Communion, have stemmed from a rediscovery or a re-emphasising of this essential doctrine.

If we fail as a Communion to address ourselves to this question, then it is probable that it will become a fundamentally divisive issue among us. It would be invidious – but not impossible

– to identify Anglican Provinces that would have difficulty in accepting any move towards closer relations with the Roman Catholic Church if this is not done. Some Provinces – some dioceses; many Anglican Christians – will be faced with the painful choice (as they would discern it) between Church and Gospel. Before we proceed further, we need as a Communion to decide whether our essential purpose is evangelical or ecumenical. For it would seem to be as doubtful now, as it was when our Church was reformed, that it can be both.

May I therefore suggest that, perhaps through the Anglican centre in Rome, founded as it has been to share our Anglican theology and history with other Christians, we commission a study of the 16th century debates on this question and an assessment of their validity for inter-Church relations today.

Index

Places, publications, organisations etc of most personal significance are given in bold; names of headmasters in capitals.